International Political Economy Series

Series Editor: **Timothy M. Shaw,** Visiting Professor, University of Massachusetts Boston, USA and Emeritus Professor, University of London, UK

The global political economy is in flux as a series of cumulative crises impacts its organization and governance. The IPE series has tracked its development in both analysis and structure over the last three decades. It has always had a concentration on the global South. Now the South increasingly challenges the North as the centre of development, also reflected in a growing number of submissions and publications on indebted Eurozone economies in Southern Europe.

An indispensable resource for scholars and researchers, the series examines a variety of capitalisms and connections by focusing on emerging economies, companies and sectors, debates and policies. It informs diverse policy communities as the established trans-Atlantic North declines and 'the rest', especially the BRICS, rise.

Titles include:

Rachel K. Brickner (*editor*)
MIGRATION, GLOBALIZATION AND THE STATE

Juanita Elias and Samanthi Gunawardana (*editors*)
THE GLOBAL POLITICAL ECONOMY OF THE HOUSEHOLD IN ASIA

Tony Heron
PATHWAYS FROM PREFERENTIAL TRADE
The Politics of Trade Adjustment in Africa, the Caribbean and Pacific

David J. Hornsby
RISK REGULATION, SCIENCE AND INTERESTS IN TRANSATLANTIC TRADE CONFLICTS

Yang Jiang
CHINA'S POLICYMAKING FOR REGIONAL ECONOMIC COOPERATION

Martin Geiger, Antoine Pécoud (*editors*)
DISCIPLINING THE TRANSNATIONAL MOBILITY OF PEOPLE

Michael Breen
THE POLITICS OF IMF LENDING

Laura Carsten Mahrenbach
THE TRADE POLICY OF EMERGING POWERS
Strategic Choices of Brazil and India

Vassilis K. Fouskas and Constantine Dimoulas
GREECE, FINANCIALIZATION AND THE EU
The Political Economy of Debt and Destruction

Hany Besada and Shannon Kindornay (*editors*)
MULTILATERAL DEVELOPMENT COOPERATION IN A CHANGING GLOBAL ORDER

Caroline Kuzemko
THE ENERGY-SECURITY CLIMATE NEXUS

Hans Löfgren and Owain David Williams (*editors*)
THE NEW POLITICAL ECONOMY OF PHARMACEUTICALS
Production, Innnovation and TRIPS in the Global South

Timothy Cadman (*editor*)
CLIMATE CHANGE AND GLOBAL POLICY REGIMES
Towards Institutional Legitimacy

Ian Hudson, Mark Hudson and Mara Fridell
FAIR TRADE, SUSTAINABILITY AND SOCIAL CHANGE

Andrés Rivarola Puntigliano and José Briceño-Ruiz (*editors*)
RESILIENCE OF REGIONALISM IN LATIN AMERICA AND THE CARIBBEAN
Development and Autonomy

Godfrey Baldacchino (*editor*)
THE POLITICAL ECONOMY OF DIVIDED ISLANDS
Unified Geographies, Multiple Polities

Mark Findlay
CONTEMPORARY CHALLENGES IN REGULATING GLOBAL CRISES

Helen Hawthorne
LEAST DEVELOPED COUNTRIES AND THE WTO
Special Treatment in Trade

Nir Kshetri
CYBERCRIME AND CYBERSECURITY IN THE GLOBAL SOUTH

Kristian Stokke and Olle Törnquist (*editors*)
DEMOCRATIZATION IN THE GLOBAL SOUTH
The Importance of Transformative Politics

Jeffrey D. Wilson
GOVERNING GLOBAL PRODUCTION
Resource Networks in the Asia-Pacific Steel Industry

International Political Economy Series
Series Standing Order ISBN 978-0-333-71708-0 hardcover
Series Standing Order ISBN 978-0-333-71110-1 paperback

You can receive future titles in this series as they are published by placing a standing order. Please contact your bookseller or, in case of difficulty, write to us at the address below with your name and address, the title of the series and one of the ISBNs quoted above.

Customer Services Department, Macmillan Distribution Ltd, Houndmills, Basingstoke, Hampshire RG21 6XS, England

Pathways from Preferential Trade

The Politics of Trade Adjustment in Africa, the Caribbean and Pacific

Tony Heron
Professor of International Politics, University of York, UK

palgrave
macmillan

First published 2013 by
PALGRAVE MACMILLAN

Palgrave Macmillan in the UK is an imprint of Macmillan Publishers Limited, registered in England, company number 785998, of Houndmills, Basingstoke, Hampshire RG21 6XS.

Palgrave Macmillan in the US is a division of St Martin's Press LLC, 175 Fifth Avenue, New York, NY 10010.

Palgrave Macmillan is the global academic imprint of the above companies and has companies and representatives throughout the world.

Palgrave® and Macmillan® are registered trademarks in the United States, the United Kingdom, Europe and other countries

ISBN: 978–1–137–30791–0

This book is printed on paper suitable for recycling and made from fully managed and sustained forest sources. Logging, pulping and manufacturing processes are expected to conform to the environmental regulations of the country of origin.

A catalogue record for this book is available from the British Library.

A catalog record for this book is available from the Library of Congress.

For Mark

Contents

List of Illustrations

Tables

Figures

Preface and Acknowledgements

This book goes to press as the Palgrave IPE Series celebrates its thirtieth anniversary. In this time, the position of the Global South in the international order appears to have been transformed out of all recognition. The most visible manifestation of this, of course, has been the stunning emergence of the so-called 'BRICs' – China especially – alongside numerous other rapidly emerging economies. These changes have prompted the current British Prime Minister David Cameron to herald, perhaps even welcome, the emergence of a new 'global race' wherein the UK and other high-waged developed countries are now involved in a life-and-death struggle to defend affluent living standards and generous welfare systems from a global onslaught from hyper-competitive, low-waged developing countries. While there is no denying that there is something rather seismic about the deep-seated structural changes that are currently underway, a point often missing from mainstream political discourse is that for the numerical majority of developing countries the story is not one of rapid emergence but of gradual decline. Indeed, for the African, Caribbean and Pacific (ACP) group countries – the focus of this book – the dominant theme is their increasingly precarious position in the global order, characterized by dwindling shares of trade, aid and investment. The backdrop to this book, then, is not globalization and integration but marginalization and disintegration. In the spirit of other work published in this series, however, the intention here is not to analyse the fate of the ACP as somehow separate from or marginal to the main trends in global politics. Rather, what we aim to show is that the fate of the ACP – shared by many other developing countries – is in fact part and parcel of David Cameron's 'global race', that is, the flipside of the reconfiguration of global power structures and the multilateral economic institutions which underpin them. In the book we chart the entwinement of globalization and marginalization though a series of thematic chapters, each of which is underpinned by empirical case studies. The approach taken is theoretically informed but in each case chapters draw on intensive fieldwork carried out over a three-year period across Africa, the Caribbean and Pacific as well as the bureaucratic capitals of Brussels, Canberra, Geneva, London, Pretoria and Washington, DC. The research was facilitated by the financial assistance of the UK Economic and Social Research Council (ESRC) First Grant Scheme (Award No. RES-061-25-0198) and the institutional support of the following organizations: the Caribbean Policy Research Institute, University of the West Indies, Jamaica; Department of International Relations, Australian National University; School of Economics, University of the South Pacific,

Fiji; and School of Development Studies, University of KwaZulu-Natal, South Africa. I would especially like to acknowledge the following friends and colleagues who have provided invaluable support, guidance and advice at various stages of researching and writing the book: Mark Bennet, Matthew Bishop, Garrett Brown, William Brown, Stephen Buzdugan, Liam Campling, Matthew Festenstein, Stewart Firth, Greg Fry, Andrew Geddes, Peter Gibbon, Paul Goodison, Jean Grugel, Colin Hay, Stephen Hurt, Damien King, Uma Kothari, Peg Murray-Evans, Vishnu Padayachee, Sheila Page, Tony Payne, Nicola Phillips, Isabelle Ramdoo, John Rapley, John Ravenhill, Ben Richardson, Chris Reus-Smit, Gabriel Siles-Brügge, Chris Stevens, Sandra Tarte, Ian Taylor, Imraan Valodia and Rorden Wilkinson. I would also like to give thanks to all those individuals who found time in their busy schedules to agree to be interviewed for the book or otherwise provided assistance during the fieldwork. Thanks also to everyone at Palgrave Macmillan, especially to Christina Brian, Amanda McGrath and, of course, Tim Shaw. As always, the biggest bunch of thanks goes to my wonderful, loving and dedicated family – my wife Clare, son Lucas and, still going strongly, my irrepressible training partner Jessie the border collie! Finally, I would like to end here on a very personal note. On the day this book was submitted for review, I received the shocking news that Mark Duncan – a research student of mine for over four years who only had his viva in January – had passed away in his sleep. Mark was 31 years-old when he died and leaves behind a wife, Nicola, and two beautiful young daughters, Holly and Annie. The book is dedicated to his memory and to the future of those he has left behind.

List of Abbreviations

ACTIF	African Cotton and Textile Industries Federation
AfT	Aid for Trade
AGOA	African Growth and Opportunity Act
ANZ	Australia and New Zealand
AoA	Agreement on Agriculture
ASEAN	Association of South East Asian Nations
ATPDEA	Andean Trade Preference and Drug Eradication Act
CAP	Common Agricultural Policy
CARIBCAN	Canadian Tariff Treatment for Commonwealth Caribbean Countries
CARICOM	Caribbean Community
CARIFORUM	Caribbean Forum of African, Caribbean and Pacific States
CBERA	Caribbean Basin Economic Recovery Act
CBTPA	Caribbean Basin Trade Partnership Act
CMO	Common Market Organisation of Sugar
COMESA	Common Market for Eastern and Southern Africa
CRIP	Caribbean Regional Indicative Programme
CRNM	Caribbean Regional Negotiating Machinery
CSME	Caribbean Single Market Economy
DFQF	Duty- and quota-free (DFQF)
DDA	Doha Development Agenda
DSM	Dispute Settlement Mechanism
DSU	Dispute Settlement Understanding
EAC	East African Community
EBA	Everything but Arms
ECOWAS	Economic Community of West African States
EDF	European Development Fund
EEC	European Economic Community
EPA	Economic Partnership Agreement
EPZ	Export Processing Zone
ESA	Eastern and Southern African
FTA	Free Trade Agreement
FTAA	Free Trade Area of the Americas
GATT	General Agreement on Tariffs and Trade
GATS	General Agreement on Services
GNI	Gross National Income
GSP	Generalized System of Preferences
IOC	Indian Ocean Commission

ISI	Import-Substitution Industrialization
ITO	International Trade Organization
LAC	Latin America and the Caribbean
LDBC	Lesser Developed Beneficiary Country
LDC	Least Developed Country
LMG	Like Minded Group
MAAS	Multi-Annual Adaptation Strategy
MAR	Market Access Regulation
MERCOSUR	Southern Common Market
MFA	Multi Fibre Arrangement
MFN	Most-Favoured nation
MMM	Mouvement Militant Mauricien
MSG	Melanesia Spearhead Group
NAFTA	North American Free Trade Agreement
NAMA	Non-Agricultural market access
NIEO	New International Economic Order
NIP	National Indicative Programme
PACER	Pacific Agreement on Closer Economic Relations
PACP	Pacific ACP
PICTA	Pacific Island Countries Trade Agreement
PIF	Pacific Islands Forum
PMSD	Parti Mauricien Social-Démocrat
PNG	Papua New Guinea
PWC	Post Washington Consensus
REC	Regional Economic Community
SACU	Southern African Customs Union
SADC	Southern African Development Community
SDT	Special and Differential Treatment
SEA	Single European Act
SIDS	Small Island Developing States
SMM	Parti Socialiste Mauricien
SP	Alliance on Strategic Products
SPATECA	South Pacific Regional Trade and Economic Cooperation Agreement
SSM	Special Safeguard Mechanism
STABEX	Stabilization of Export Earnings
SVE	Small and Vulnerable Economies
SYSMIN	System of Stabilization of Export Earnings for Mining Products
TDCA	Trade and Development Cooperation Agreement
TRQ	Tariff-Rate Quota
UNCTAD	United Nations Conference on Trade and Development
VRS	Voluntary Retirement Scheme

1
Introduction

As the 21st century dawns, relations between the EU and the ACP countries should be put on a new footing to take account not only of changed political and economic conditions for development but also of changed attitudes in Europe. The colonial and post-colonial periods are behind us and a more politically open international environment enables us to lay down the responsibilities of each partner less ambiguously.

European Commission, November 1996.

We reaffirm that provisions for special and differential treatment are an integral part of the WTO Agreements. We note the concerns expressed regarding their operation in addressing specific constraints faced by developing countries, particularly least-developed countries.... We therefore agree that all special and differential treatment provisions shall be reviewed with a view to strengthening them and making them more precise, effective and operational.

Doha Ministerial Declaration, December 2001.

The publication of this book comes hard on the heels of the tenth anniversary of two separate global initiatives, each of which offered an ambitious prospectus for redefining trade and development cooperation between rich and poor countries that has since foundered. The first of these is the WTO Doha Development Agenda (DDA). As is well known, the DDA was launched in the aftermath of the terrorists attacks of 11 September 2001 – and two years after the acrimonious failure of the 1999 Seattle ministerial, when mass civic mobilization and violent street demonstrations came to symbolize the discord between developed and developing countries regarding the content and indeed the overall desirability of a new round of trade liberalization. The unique sense of global solidarity generated by 9/11 provided the necessary impetus to kick-start global trade talks, but policy makers also used the opportunity to recalibrate the tone and objectives of the round to address

1

developing country grievances expressed during the Seattle debacle. In the ten years or so since then, however, the WTO has demonstrably failed to translate these aims into a concrete package of development measures capable of satisfying the institution's disparate membership. In July 2011, the WTO Director General Pascal Lamy declared that, 'what we are seeing today is the paralysis in the negotiating function of the WTO ... What we are facing is the inability of the WTO to adapt and adjust to emerging global trade priorities' (ICTSD 2011). What this suggested, in short, was that the WTO Secretariat was close to throwing in the towel on the Doha round – and that the attempt to redefine the relationship between rich and poor countries within the multilateral trade system had proven to be a bridge too far.

The second global initiative to have recently marked its tenth anniversary is the EU-ACP Cotonou Partnership Act of 2000. In this case, the original objective was to replace preferences hitherto granted unilaterally under the 1975 Lomé convention with a series of region-wide reciprocal Economic Partnership Agreements (EPAs), designed to comply with Article XXIV of the General Agreement on Tariffs and Trade (GATT).[1] The EPAs were not, however, limited to satisfying multilateral trade rules as Cotonou also made provision for liberalization in areas like services, investment and competition policy, not covered by Lomé and hence subject to the original GATT ruling against it. The merits of this comprehensive approach appeared to be underlined when the Caribbean became the first region among the ACP group of countries to sign a 'full' EPA in October 2008 (see Chapter 3). Yet to date this agreement remains the only one of its kind. Elsewhere, ACP countries have either chosen not to sign an EPA and rely on inferior preferences or else conclude far less ambitious 'goods only' interim agreements. The European Commission's response to this limited take-up was to, first, permit countries to conclude interim EPAs bilaterally in the absence of region-wide consensus and then, later, turn the screw on recalcitrant states by threatening to revoke preferential access granted temporarily by the EU while at the same time tightening eligibility for alternative preferences available through the Generalized System of Preferences (GSP). Whether or not this 'carrot and stick' approach will ultimately work is doubtful, but either way the final outcome of the negotiations is likely to fall a long way short of the ambitious plans laid out in 2000.

There is, then, an obvious (and as we shall see not unrelated) parallel between the negotiating impasse in the DDA and that in the EPAs. Although, clearly, these two diplomatic arenas are characterized by different policy agendas, participants and political dynamics, the theme that cuts across the five substantive chapters in this book is that they share a common institutional pathology in the ways in which they have sought to redefine the relationship between rich and poor countries, especially in relation to the principle of special and differential treatment (SDT). Although SDT is indelibly associated with the GATT, the term was not actually enshrined in the organization's legal texts until 1979. By this point, the principles underpinning it had already been operationalized de facto in the form of two sets of institutional practices that came to define the relationship between rich and poor countries in the GATT: namely, asymmetrical reciprocity and unilateral trade preferences. Asymmetrical reciprocity, on the one hand, refers to the institutional practice whereby the developed countries waived developed countries of their obligations under Article I to offer reciprocal market access. This institutional practice did not, it is important to note, amount to a legally definable obligation; rather, it was part of an ad hoc and highly informal process by which the enforcement of GATT disciplines was over time applied to the developing countries with less and less consistency.

On the other hand, unilateral trade preferences refer to the institutional practice by which the developed countries granted one-way market access to the developed countries, above and beyond that offered on a most-favoured nation (MFN) basis to all GATT members. Although such preferences were omitted from the GATT at the time of its creation, calls for their inclusion became progressively louder as the numerical balance of the organization's membership began to shift in favour of the developing countries in the late 1950s and 1960s. This culminated in the creation of the GSP in 1968, later made permanent by 1979 Enabling Clause. Yet, as in the case of asymmetrical reciprocity, GATT disciplines governing unilateral preferences were never placed on an entirely secure legal footing. First, although the Enabling Clause legally empowered the contracting parties to grant non-reciprocal trade preferences (provided that they were offered to all developing countries and did not discriminate between them) there was nothing requiring them to do so. In fact, all decisions regarding the duration of preferences, graduation, product coverage and preference margins were left entirely to the discretion of the preference-granting country (Hoekman and Özden 2005). By far the most significant anomaly with the GSP was the legal ambiguity surrounding eligibility from preferences. While providing the legal grounds for preferential treatment in favour of developing countries the logically prior task of defining a 'developing' country was never satisfactorily resolved. Although the narrower concept of 'least developed' was codified under the Enabling Clause (referring to those countries formally classified as such by the United Nations), developing country status under the GATT became a matter of self-declaration – a practice that continues to this day under the WTO. In other words, aside from the Least Developed Countries (LDCs), the concept of a 'developing' county in relation to preferential trade came to have close to no legal standing within the multilateral trading system.

The full significance of these anomalies only became fully apparent following the conclusion of the Uruguay round and the introduction of a much-strengthened Dispute Settlement Understanding (DSU) under the WTO. In the meantime, the legal ambiguity surrounding the GSP was complicated further by two additional sets of complexities that were to make the subsequent task of recasting SDT on the basis of WTO-compatible principles all the more formidable. The first of these centres on the prior co-existence of the GSP with GATT-inconsistent preference schemes like Lomé. Although Lomé is usually the first to be cited with respect to inconsistency with multilateral trade disciplines (and hence it is not surprising that it was the first to fall foul of the WTO), it was no different in kind to discriminatory preferences schemes *still* offered by the likes of Australia, Canada and the United States. The key summative point is that each of these schemes was crafted in an era in which the opaqueness of GATT legal norms, coupled with the limited reach of its dispute-settlement system, meant that there were few consequences for violating either the spirit or the letter of multilateral trade rules. But in the era of the WTO and its enhanced dispute-settlement system, this opaqueness means that where preference-granting countries have signalled that their intention is to reshape these schemes in a more WTO-consistent mould – which is the case in each of the examples cited above – there are few precedents for how this might be achieved other than in accordance with Article XXIV, which makes no provision for SDT. In short, the legal ambiguity surrounding SDT for the developing countries did not end with the creation of the WTO on 1 January 2005.

The second set of complexities concern the relationship between the continued viability of unilateral preferences and wider patterns of trade liberalization. There has, of course, always been something of an uneasy relationship between the principles of SDT, on the one hand, and MFN, on the other. But prior to the Uruguay round the tension was arguably more theoretical than real, due to the fact that relatively high MFN tariffs – coupled with the existence of quantitative restrictions such as those administered under the auspices of the Multi Fibre Arrangement (MFA) – meant that liberalization did not necessarily jeopardize trade preferences. After Uruguay, however (which led, among many other things, to average MFN tariff reductions by the developed countries of around 36 per cent alongside the phasing out of the MFA), the policy space available for granting preference was considerably diminished. The political consequences of this, in terms of the collective action dynamics of the multilateral trade system, was supposedly to remove the incentive preference-receiving countries had for supporting freer trade (see below). This explains why the WTO's Aid for Trade (AfT) scheme was initially couched in terms of a 'compensation clause' (Page 2005) rather than the longer-term goal of integrating developing and least-developed countries into the world trading system. But since such a scheme would only appeal to those developing countries adversely affected by preference erosion (as the process has become known) – and patently not those developing countries discriminated against – it is unclear how such a scheme might achieve wider traction in the WTO. In any case, although the Uruguay accords have arguably been the single biggest contributing factor to the erosion of preferences, the main thrust of liberalization since then has come from regional and bilateral sources that are to some extent outside of multilateral jurisdiction. Hence, one has to question whether or not compensating small – and already marginalized – preference-receiving countries is really central to the fate of the global trade system.

The specific purpose of this book is to explore the global politics and political economy of trade preference erosion, against the backdrop the aforementioned complexities. In particular, we are interested in the political implications – that is to say, how reforms have played out *in practice* – of the shift from traditional forms of SDT associated with asymmetrical reciprocity and unilateral trade preferences towards reciprocal free trade with a greater emphasis of 'supply-side' measures such as technical assistance, trade-related capacity building and so on. Although much of the debate concerning the diminishing space for trade preferences has concentrated on the legal obstacles created by the strengthening of multilateral trade rules, it is important to acknowledge that this process has been accompanied by an intellectual consensus that has come to see preference erosion as not only unavoidable but also desirable. The starting point for this consensus is the premise that unilateral trade preferences rarely, if ever, succeed in promoting either long-term economic growth or export diversification. The explanation provided for this is that preferences are, generally speaking, either characterized by low-utilization rates (because 'supply-side' constraints or bureaucratic obstacles such as complicated rules of origin discourage the take-up of preferences) or the bulk of the economic rents fall to importing firms rather than preference-receiving countries (Mattoo, Roy and Subramanian 2003; Brenton and Manchin 2003; Olarreaga and Özden 2005). In addition, preferential trade is said to inhibit the process of internal policy reform, distort trade and constitute an impediment to multilateral liberalization, since preference-receiving countries have a vested interest in defending the status quo in order to protect preference margins (Panagariya 2002; Francois, Hoekman and Manchin 2006; Hoekman 2006). Finally, as alluded to earlier, because multilateral liberalization is seen from this perspective as a 'global public good', the best means of supporting preference-dependent countries is through targeted financial assistance and compensatory schemes which serve to build 'supply-side' capacity in these countries but in ways that are 'non-trade distorting' for third parties. This, in essence, is the intellectual consensus that has dominated the policy debate around preference erosion, including most notably in the diplomatic settings that form the backdrop to this book: the DDA and the EPAs.

In exploring the global politics and political economy of preference erosion, we are not primarily concerned with the veracity of the above judgements regarding the economic utility of non-reciprocal preferences (although the political naivety of some of the policy recommendations associated with these judgements is soon revealed); nor do we make the case for the continuation of preferential trade and the postponement of further liberalization. Rather, the main aim is to probe a little deeper into global trade and development politics to ask why traditional forms of SDT did not meet basic policy objectives and, more to the point, why newer forms of SDT have, at least so far, achieved only modest results. Critics of the traditional unilateral trade preferences are not wrong to point to technical deficiencies such as low utilization rates and unintended distributive effects, but they are unable to provide a satisfactory explanation for why non-reciprocal preferences fared so badly in the post-war period – or why in many cases it has proven so difficult to reform them and persuade preference-receiving countries of the merits of reciprocal free trade. It is our view that, rather than focusing on technical deficiencies, we must first explore the historical and institutional correlates of SDT within the context of the GATT, since this holds the key to understanding the peculiar way that unilateral preferences were operationalized in the post-war period – and, paradoxically, why certain developing countries have proved unwilling to give them up, in spite of their patchy record in fostering economic growth and diversification. Once this is established, we can then move on to explore such questions as the political implications of the shift towards reciprocity, characterized by power asymmetry and uneven patterns of trade diplomacy (Chapter 3); the impact of differential levels of preference dependence and utilization on the political leverage of preference-granting countries in extolling the virtues of regional integration and reciprocal free trade (Chapter 4); understanding the distinctive pathways of ostensibly similar countries with respect to exposure to preference erosion and trade adjustment (Chapter 5); and, finally, the global and regional politics of preference erosion in the light of the attempt to recast SDT away from one-way preferences towards 'supply-side' forms of development cooperation (Chapter 6).

Research base

The book constitutes the main output from a three-year UK ESRC project, involving more than 100 interviews conducted between January, 2009 and September, 2011. The book is organized thematically but each chapter is underpinned by a case study approach, based on intensive fieldwork carried out in six preference-dependent countries: Belize, Fiji, Jamaica, Lesotho, Mauritius and Swaziland. This research was supplemented with a series of interviews and 'off-the-record' briefings with key policy makers in the bureaucratic capitals of Brussels, Canberra, Geneva, London, Pretoria and Washington, DC. Although the specific political and economic characteristics of each case – and its position in the global trading system – is in some senses unique, we aim for generalizability according to what they share in common. First, all six countries are classified as 'small states' according to criteria set out by the Commonwealth Secretariat (1997), that is, a

population of no more than 1.5 million people or otherwise comparable
due to reasons of history and geography. Second, all six are broadly comparable with respect to per capita income, export dependence and reliance
on preferential trade. Third, all six have figured prominently in at least one
of the three most significant non-LDC specific trade preference schemes
analysed in the book: the Lomé/Cotonou Agreement (Belize, Fiji, Jamaica,
Lesotho, Mauritius and Swaziland), African Growth and Opportunity Act
(AGOA) (Mauritius, Lesotho and Swaziland) and Caribbean Basin Economic
Recovery/Trade Partnership Act (CBERA/CBTPA) (Jamaica and Belize).
Fourth, and related to this, the six cases provide a representative sample
of export dependence in one or more of the three sectors most exposed by
tariff and quota preference erosion: bananas (Belize and Jamaica), sugar
(Belize, Fiji, Jamaica, Mauritius and Swaziland) and garments (Jamaica,
Lesotho and Mauritius). Finally, the six cases provide a representative
sample of the key regions affected by preference erosion: Southern and
Eastern Africa (Lesotho, Mauritius and Swaziland), the Caribbean (Belize,
Jamaica) and Pacific (Fiji).

In summary, a key assumption of the book is that, while the liberalization
of trade has entailed adjustment costs for both large and small developing
countries and LDCs, preference erosion is particularly onerous for small states
such as the ones identified here because: (i) even though they often enjoy
higher incomes than larger states a much higher proportion of this is derived
from international trade; (ii) small states generally depend on preferential
trade far more than larger states; and (iii) this dependence is based heavily
on commodities like bananas, sugar and garments that have been associated
historically with high preference margins but have been subject to recent or
ongoing liberalization (Armstrong and Read 1998; Alexandraki and Lankes
2004; Heron 2008). The book adopts a thematic approach while drawing
on the six case studies to reveal the extent to which preference erosion, its
attendant adjustment costs and – most crucially – strategic responses to it
cannot simply be 'read off' from objective economic circumstances. Rather
the success or otherwise of trade adjustment also depends on prevailing
institutional structures and state capacity; the degree of national consensus
over policy goals; the presence of political solidarity at a regional level; and,
crucially, the timing and sequencing of trade reforms. In an important sense,
the book picks up immediately from where previous work (see, in particularly, Heron 2012) left off: whereas the latter was concerned with the historical and institutional determinants of patterns of trade in the specific case
of the textiles and clothing sector (and the distributive consequences these
entailed for both developed and developing countries), here we focus on
the more general problem of enshrining the special and differential needs
of developing countries and LDCs in the global trade regime – against the
backdrop of the shift towards wider and deeper forms of multilateral and,
now increasingly, bilateral trade regulation.

Conceptual framework

Conceptually speaking, the book adopts an eclectic approach wherein each substantive chapter is anchored to a specific theoretical argument, ranging from questions of policy institutionalization and path dependency in Chapter 2 to theories of asymmetric trade bargaining in Chapter 3, to interregionalism in Chapter 4 to developmentalism in Chapter 5, to the operationalization of post-Washington Consensus-inspired forms of trade adjustment and development assistance in Chapter 6. Even though each chapter deals with a different set of theoretical arguments and empirical problems, the conceptual framework for the book as a whole can be said to draw on a coalescence of three different literatures. These can be summarized very briefly as follows. First, the book is very much written in the tradition of scholarship which has sought to marry insights from International Political Economy and Development Studies (Hettne, Payne and Söderbaum 1999; Phillips 2005; Payne and Phillips 2010). Reflecting the intellectual zeitgeist of the 2000s (see, for example, Berger 2004), we look to the increasing *divergence* among developing countries – and its political and economic consequences. At the same time, the book takes seriously questions of political agency; drawing inspiration from the 'new political economy' approach (Gamble 1995), we seek to eschew the economic determinism latent in much development thinking by allowing even for small states to effect change given an appropriate institutional setting (Heron 2008; Lee and Smith 2010). We nevertheless recognize the dangers of voluntarism and insist that in the final instance the global political economy is characterized by 'structured inequalities' (Payne 2005) which limit the choices available to local policy makers in the pursuit of national development goals.

Second, the book is unavoidably concerned with the question of smallness and the degree to which our cases are faced with particular economic vulnerabilities on account of their small size. Although there has been a long-standing interest among political economists in the issue of smallness (Robinson 1960; Clarke and Payne 1987), more recent literature in this vein has sought to explore this directly in relation to global economic (dis-) integration while, at the same time, paying more attention to institutional resilience, adaptability and – most recently – political agency (Streeton 1993; Briguglio 1995; Commonwealth Secretariat 1997; Payne 2004; Heron 2008; Cooper and Shaw 2009; Lee and Smith 2010). In this vein, the book seeks to chart a middle course between earlier, structuralist writings in which the source of small state vulnerability was depicted as both exogenous and largely static, and more recent work that emphasizes 'small state agency' but – if pushed too far – runs the risk of voluntarism and political naivety (Bishop 2012).

The third relevant literature is that which focuses on the theory and practice of global governance (Hughes and Wilkinson 2002; Wilkinson 2005). Although global governance is generally taken to refer to the provision of 'global public goods' by institutions like the IMF, World Bank and WTO, critical interventions in the debate have sought to reveal the tensions, biases, silences and indeed the contested nature of global governance itself (Thérien 1999; Murphy 2000). In the book, we make use of historical intuitionalism (Wilkinson 2006; Heron and Richardson 2008; Heron 2012) to reveal how far patterns of policy institutionalization and path dependency shape the dynamics of continuity and change in global trade governance. But we also make occasional use of critical and social constructivist literatures to pinpoint the causal role of ideas in shaping political outcomes. The key substantive point is that the presumed neutrality of global governance as a project cannot be taken as given. As such, the book is designed to not simply assess the impact and effectiveness of trade adjustment strategies, but to scrutinize the plausibility and political implications of the broader claims associated with the dominant policy consensus outlined earlier.

Aims and outline of the book

Now that we have established the general remit, research base and conceptual framing of the book, our next task is to set out a more specific set of research questions to guide the study and to offer a road map of how it will proceed. In essence, the book deals with five sets of analytically separate but closely related research questions:

- What are the origins of SDT in the post-war trade architecture? How were trade preferences as the main traditional form of SDT operationalized under the GATT? What were the main drivers of reform? And what have been the dominant political and economic effects of the recasting of SDT under the WTO?
- How and in what ways have preference-dependent countries responded to the erosion of preferences and the recasting of SDT? Why is it that preference-dependent countries with ostensibly similar levels of exposure to preference erosion have adopted very different strategic responses to it? What have been the political implications for preference-dependent countries of the shift towards reciprocal trade bargaining with former preference-granting countries?
- Why has regional integration figured so prominently in the discourse accompanying the recasting of SDT? And why have preference-granting countries been so keen to promote it? How successful have these attempts to promote regional integration been? And to the extent that they have not been wholly successful how do we account for this policy failure?
- What have been the individual experiences of preference-dependent countries with the politics and political economy of trade adjustment with respect to the loss of traditional preferences? What have been the main institutional determinants of 'successful' adjustment to preference

erosion? And what have been the implications of differential performance in trade adjustment between preference-dependent countries in the light of the attempt by external actors to promote regional economic integration between them?

- What have been the practical results of the attempt to recast SDT multilaterally away from unilateral preferences towards 'supply-side' forms of development assistance? How far have measures agreed in the context of the DDA served to ameliorate the effects of preference erosion? And what are the likely alternative scenarios for preference-dependent countries and regions in the light of the probable failure of the DDA?

The first of these sets of questions is addressed in Chapter 2, which charts the origins and subsequent operationalization of the concept of SDT for developing countries as part of the post-war trade architecture. In doing so, it emphasizes two important points that do not always figure prominently in the extant literature on preference erosion – the first concerning the historical patterns and institutional practices that characterized the governance of international trade prior to the establishment of the WTO and the second the degree to which the policy space for the maintenance of preferences has been shaped as much by shifting ideological contours and changing development norms as by the legal obstacles created by the strengthening of multilateral trade rules. In sum, when tracing the origins and ultimate decline of trade preferences, the chapter will suggest, we must remain sensitive to the historical and institutional correlates that have shaped the choices available to preferences-granting countries – but also to the particular ways in which actors have chosen to interpret and utilize the policy space available for pursuing development goals.

In Chapter 3, we explore the political implications for preference-dependent countries of the shift towards reciprocal trade bargaining with former preference-granting countries with a specific look at CARIFORUM – thus far the only region to conclude a comprehensive EPA in accordance with the vision set forth in the Cotonou Agreement. The chapter starts by asking why CARIFORUM felt it was necessary or desirable to sign a comprehensive agreement, containing numerous provisions not actually mandated by the WTO, when the rest of the ACP was content to sign far less ambitious 'goods only' interim agreements? To address this question, the chapter goes beyond the extant EU-ACP trade literature to build on wider scholarship, which has analysed the actions of developing countries in relation to a whole range of 'WTO-plus' North-South regional and bilateral FTAs. On this basis, we stand back from the technical details of the agreement to analyse its wider significance, especially in terms of the presumed trade-off between the immediate economic benefits of improved and more secure market access against the longer-term costs of sacrificing the regulatory autonomy, or policy space, deemed necessary to pursue the type of trade and industrial policies deployed successfully in the past by both developed and (some) developing countries. In short, the chapter seeks to ascertain why ultimately CARIFORUM signed a comprehensive agreement, what it gained from the negotiations and at what cost.

Chapter 4 seeks to ascertain why the promotion of regional integration by external actors has figured so prominently in the discourse accompanying the recasting of SDT. In the case of the EPAs – again the main focus of the chapter – the EU has arguably gone the furthest in this direction by introducing a so-called 'regional preference' clause by which the removal of intraregional trade barriers between ACP countries represented a precondition for the maintenances of trade privileges. Accordingly, the chapter seeks to understand why, how and with what consequences the EU has promoted this in the context of the EPAs. The chapter starts from the premise that neither extant interest- nor norm-based accounts provide entirely satisfactory explanations for why the external promotion of regionalism has figured so prominently in EU external relations and, more to the point, why it has produced relatively few tangible successes. We take our cue from (predominantly) liberal constructivist accounts of interregionalism (as the process has become known) but then use these as a point of departure for a critical interrogation of the model of regional governance that the EU is seeking to promote. We delineate this model via the specific empirical case of the Pacific. In so doing, the chapter identifies a series of tensions, ambiguities and contradictions that lie within it, which, it will be argued, provide important clues to why – in spite of the obvious power asymmetries involved and the ostensible commitment of the ACP to the goal of closer economic integration – the external promotion of regionalism, as an integral component of the EPAs, has met with less success than might have been expected.

In Chapter 5, we move on to examine the individual experiences of preference-dependent countries with the politics of trade adjustment with a specific look at the case of Mauritius – arguably, the most remarkable economic success story of the Lomé era. This chapter asks what lessons, if any, Mauritius offers for other small, preference-dependent countries confronted with the loss of traditional economic privileges and the prospect of reciprocal free trade. The chapter begins with a short detour via the development state literature to provide the theoretical vocabulary for understanding how and under what circumstances the post-colonial Mauritian state was able to influence and ultimately recast its terms of trade. The chapter then uses these insights to inform a discussion of Mauritius' encounter with the political economy of trade adjustment in the 2000s. After briefly outlining the origins and modalities of relevant trade reforms, we examine how Mauritius has adjusted to them and with what consequences. We then explore how these adjustments have fed into the ongoing negotiations with the EU with the aim to establish a fully reciprocal and region-wide EPA.

Finally, Chapter 6 surveys the overall results of the attempt to recast SDT, in this case by examining critically the experiences of Lesotho and Swaziland – two tiny, landlocked countries almost entirely surrounded by South Africa (entirely so in the case of Lesotho), regularly cited as among those most highly exposed to preference erosion. Whereas Chapters 3 and 4 focused on EU trade preferences, here we are primarily concerned with the United States, AGOA specifically. The chapter situates AGOA and its diminishing importance in the context of the WTO's multilateral trade disciplines, as set out in Chapter 2. We examine the AGOA trade programme before looking, in more specific detail, at the cases of Lesotho and Swaziland. Here we provide a brief outline of Lesotho's and Swaziland's main economic characteristics and explore the role of AGOA in facilitating regional trade and investment flows. Next we relate the impact of multilateral liberalization on these flows to the wider politics of the WTO and the DDA. The chapter ends by considering the regional politics of preference erosion in southern Africa in the light of the probable failure of the Doha round, by exploring options available to Lesotho and Swaziland with respect to regional integration through the Southern African Development Community (SADC) and the possibility of a region-wide EPA with the EU.

2
The Rise and Fall
of Preferential Trade

This chapter examines the creation and subsequent operationalization of the concept of SDT for developing countries as part of the post-war trade architecture. In so doing, it identifies preferential trade as the centrepiece of this and goes on to trace its growth and subsequent decline following the 1993 Uruguay round, which heralded the deepening and widening of multilateral trade disciplines – including, most notably, the introduction of the new DSU under the WTO. The creation of the WTO is without a doubt the single most important factor behind the various trade reforms detailed in this book. In what follows, however, we treat this – and even more so the knock-on effect that the establishment of the WTO had for non-reciprocal trade preferences – as part of what has to be explained rather than an independent causal variable. To do this, the chapter emphasizes two important points that do not always figure prominently in the extant literature. The first concerns the historical patterns and institutional practices that characterized the governance of international trade prior to the establishment of the WTO. The debate about trade preference erosion is, almost invariably, couched in terms of an irreconcilable tension between the principle of SDT for developing countries, on the one hand, and that of MFN, on the other. We argue, however, that this tension was far from inevitable. Simply put, we suggest that despite the various reforms to the GATT that were administered in the name of SDT at no point was the latter placed on a secure legal footing.

The full significance of this only became fully apparent following the establishment of the DSU under the WTO. In other words, with the implementation of the DSU trade preferences were much more likely to be – and indeed in the case of the EU's Lomé protocol *were* – deemed in violation of the MFN principle. Yet the story does not end there. In recasting SDT under the WTO in terms of reciprocal free trade and 'supply-side' reforms (technical assistance, trade-related capacity building and so on), the chapter will argue in the penultimate section that these legal ambiguities remain for the most part unresolved. Moreover, with the stalling of the Doha round the recasting of SDT, where it has occurred, has largely been outside of multilateral trade disciplines (something not unrelated to the above legal ambiguities) on the basis of relatively unmediated – and therefore highly asymmetric – forms of North-South trade diplomacy. This pattern is revealed most obviously in the case of the EPAs – the successor to Lomé/Cotonou – which are the subject of Chapters 3 and 4.

The second important point to emphasize is that the diminishing space for unilateral trade preferences within the international trade system does not simply rest on the legal obstacles created by the strengthening of multilateral trade disciplines. The changes are in fact part of a wider intellectual movement, according to which preference erosion is now deemed to be not only unavoidable but also perhaps desirable. The most important illustrative case of this is the EU's Lomé regime. Although the original catalyst for the reform of Lomé did indeed come from a 1994 GATT dispute-settlement ruling, what is more significant is the way in which the decision was internalized by EU policy makers and subsequently used to justify liberalization. While the trade component of the Cotonou Agreement (the successor to Lomé which paved the way for reciprocal EPAs) was supposedly driven by the necessity of 'WTO compatibility' the subsequent negotiations included liberalization commitments in a whole raft of 'trade-related' areas like services, investment, government procurement and intellectual property rights that were not covered by the Lomé protocol and thus not subject to WTO litigation. What this suggested was that these reforms were not just the product of a dispassionate reassessment of the technical and legal merits of trade preferences following the strengthening of multilateral trade rules. They also stemmed from a series of more or less independent political and commercial interests, deemed to be best served by less discriminatory forms of development assistance (see, among many others, Gibb 2000; Hurt 2003; Ravenhill 2004; Heron and Siles-Brügge 2012). In sum, when tracing the origins and ultimate decline of trade preferences, we must remain sensitive to the historical and institutional correlates that have shaped the choices available to preferences-granting countries – but also to the particular ways in which actors have chosen to interpret and utilize the policy space available for pursuing development goals.

Special and differential treatment under the GATT

The story of the post-war trade regime duly begins with the stillbirth of the 1947 Havana Charter, which would have established the International Trade Organisation (ITO) as the 'third pillar' of the Bretton Woods economic order (Wilkinson 2006; Heron 2012). The importance of this for understanding how and in what ways SDT came to be operationalized under the GATT cannot be overestimated. Although the GATT was very much defined by what John Gerard Ruggie (1982) famously described as the 'compromise of embedded liberalism', whereby the restoration of the world economy would be checked by the new domestic priorities of Keynesian demand management and post-war reconstruction, this emergent paradigm offered few antecedents or policy lessons (comparable, say, to the wider ones drawn from the disastrous beggar-thy-neighbour trade practices of the 1930s) that might have been used to guide the crafting of SDT within the emerging trade architecture. Nor, for that matter, was there in this period much in the way of a systematic demand on the part of the developing countries for preferential treatment (Hudec 1987: 9). At that time, the prevailing orthodoxy for the management of North-South trade issues in much of the world remained that of colonialism. The notable exception to this was, of course, the United States – the ascendant global hegemon in whose image the post-war economic order would be largely fashioned – which stood apart from colonialism. By the same token, the United States saw little reason to grant special treatment to developing countries in the burgeoning trade diplomacy of the New Deal era. Between 1934 and 1942, the United States concluded reciprocal trade agreements with no fewer than 16 separate developing countries (Argentina, Brazil, Colombia, Costa Rica, Cuba, Ecuador, El Salvador, Guatemala, Haiti, Honduras, Mexico, Nicaragua, Peru, Turkey, Uruguay and Venezuela), but none contained measures specific to developing country status. Indeed, as Robert Hudec (1987: 19) describes it, 'the chief distinguishing feature of the sixteen developing country agreements was that they tended to contain fewer special derogations than did the agreements with [developed] countries such as France'.

This anomaly was present in the initial draft of the ITO Charter prepared by the United States, which contained no specific provisions or exemptions for the developing countries. Over time, however, the influence of Britain and France (which saw these provisions as necessary not only to safeguard preferences granted to their respective colonies but as a means of protecting vital export markets from foreign competition, not least from the United States) and the developing countries led, at least to some degree, to the recognition of the special and differential needs of the latter in the Havana Charter. The key concession in this respect came in the provisions relating to 'infant industry protection' allowing the use of trade restrictions – either through the raising of bound tariffs, the introduction of quantitative restrictions or taking advantage of preferences granted by third countries – that were otherwise prohibited. While recognizing the legitimacy of each of these measures, the relevant clauses of the agreement nevertheless stipulated that they could only be invoked with the explicit prior approval of the ITO. This requirement was significant since other derogations pertaining to balance-of-payments, escape clauses and agricultural safeguards – that is, measures more likely to be invoked by the developed countries – contained no such stipulation. Furthermore, the demise of the Havana Charter and the resultant stillbirth of the ITO produced an even more paltry interpretation of these development provisions: although the 'infant industry' clause allowing for the raising of bound tariffs and the imposition of quantitative restrictions (albeit still subject to the prior approval of the organization) were retained within the 'temporary' legal architecture of the GATT, those relating to trade preferences were, on the insistence of the United States, omitted from the final agreement. But what was more significant from our perspective is that the emergence of the GATT set in train a process, according to which the global regulation of trade would thereafter operate on the basis of a series of informal institutional practices and *ad hoc* decisions akin to a 'Gentlemen's Club' more than a legally codified, rule-based system.

It is largely for this reason that when the numerical balance of the GATT's membership began to shift in favour of the developing countries in the late 1950s and 1960s it did not have an immediate or obvious discernable effect on their collective power or influence. In fact, the key institutional reforms designed to accommodate the developing countries within the GATT's legal disciplines were established more or less independent of, and prior to, when the main demographic changes occurred. The first series of significant amendments were born out of the 1954–5 Review Session, which was established following the realization that a resurrection of the Havana Treaty was now a distant prospect. This led, among other things, to amendments to Article XVIII pertaining to the infant-industry and balance-of-payments clauses, rendering them more flexible and easier for developing countries to invoke. The Review Session also led to the introduction of a new Article – Article XXVIII-*bis* – requiring the contracting parties to take into account the 'needs of less developed countries for a more flexible use of tariff protection to assist their economic development and the special needs of these countries to maintain tariffs for revenue purposes' (cited in Hudec 1987: 34; see Table 2.1 below). What this meant, in other words, was that the principle of reciprocity need no longer necessarily apply to trade negotiations involving the developing countries. The crucial point to note about the Review Session is that it did not require nor lead to substantive institutional reform; indeed, none of these reforms amounted to an actual change in policy or do much to alter the legal obligations of the developed countries towards their developing country counterparts. Rather, the significance of the Review Session was that it heralded the beginning of a period when SDT would be equated with a process by which the legal enforcement of GATT disciplines would be applied to the developing countries with less and less conviction.

While the changing numerical balance of the GATT's membership did not lead to an immediate or obvious change in the balance of power, the bargaining leverage of the developing countries was strengthened somewhat by the creation of a potential rival organization in the form of the United Nations Conference on Trade and Development (UNCTAD), which was established in 1964. The creation of UNCTAD revealed the increasing purchase of Keynesian-influenced ideas of developmentalism associated, most notably, with the structuralist writings of Raúl Prebisch and Hans Singer. In other words, SDT was seen as a corollary of import-substitution industrialization (ISI): whereas ISI was designed to promote the industrial capacity of indigenous manufacturing firms, SDT was expected to provide further support through preferential access to overseas markets to enable infant-industries to capture the economies of scale associated with successful industrial expansion (Hoekman and Özden 2005). More practically, the formation of UNCTAD reflected increasing developing country frustration with the seeming inability of the GATT to address their inferior export performance and declining terms of trade. But what gave it additional significance is that UNCTAD had the backing of the Soviet Union and its allies, which had been calling for the establishment of a global trade organization within the UN as an alternative to the Western-dominated GATT. In the meantime, momentum had been building inside the GATT since the Review Session for further measures to assist the developing countries. This led to the commissioning and subsequent publication of the 'Haberler Report' in 1958, the main substantive conclusion of which was that the inferior export performance of the developing countries was unsustainable in the light of the economic resources required to fuel economic development – and that this was down to the disproportionately high trade barriers faced by developing country exports alongside unfavourable price trends affecting key commodities. However, neither the Haberler Report nor the 'programme of action' that subsequently followed its publication called for or led to any major changes in GATT policy. Indeed, as Rorden Wilkinson (2006: 58) notes, a number of the trade barriers that were identified as problematic at the time, such as tariffs on tropical products, tariff escalation, quantitative restrictions and internal taxes, were still in place when the Uruguay round was launched some 30 years later.

Despite its negligible influence on GATT policy and procedure, the 'Haberler Report' was nevertheless a significant milestone, at least insofar as it marked the beginning of a shift in orientation of developing country concerns away from the issue of reciprocity towards market access. This is not to suggest that the former was now no longer important. Indeed, it was the issue of reciprocity that provided one of the major flashpoints of the preliminary negotiations leading up to the Dillon round (1960–2) when a call by the developing countries for greater flexibility in the application of reciprocity was rejected on the grounds that this had already been provided through the introduction of Article XXVIII-*bis*. The developing countries responded to this rebuttal by calling for the contracting parties to examine issues of market access 'with a view to facilitating an early expansion of the export earnings of less-developed countries' (GATT 1961: 2; see also Table 2.1 below). This hinted at the establishment of unilateral trade preferences. In the short term, however, the trajectory of the GATT appeared to moving in precisely the opposite direction. This was especially evident in the textiles and clothing sector. In November 1960, following the recommendations of a working party which had actually been established at the very same meeting as the call for greater flexibility in the application of reciprocity and a further examination of issues of market access, the GATT adopted the 'Decision on the Avoidance of Market Disruption'. This became known subsequently as the 'market disruption clause' – the precursor to the MFA, the protectionist trade regime that would govern textiles and clothing for the next 30 years and discriminate deliberately and exclusively against developing country exports. The market disruption clause was designed to halt the rapid proliferation of voluntary export restraints in the sector by strengthening the existing safeguard mechanisms contained within Article XIX and thereby provide a sounder legal basis for the introduction of quantitative restrictions in the future.

Significantly, the market disruption clause deliberately avoided reference to the underlying *causes* of import growth leading to or threatening disruption; nor was it premised on the notion that the exporting country was penetrating overseas markets on the basis of improper or illegal practice. Rather, as Kenneth Dam (1970: 299) put it, market disruption was defined solely in terms of low prices and, as such, 'it was the principle of comparative advantage that was being called into question'. The concept of market disruption constituted a noticeable departure from extant GATT practice in a number of important respects. First, market disruption departed from normal GATT rules in that it stipulated that import restrictions could be enforced even if injury had not taken place, provided that a *potential* threat could be demonstrated. In addition, it further departed from GATT rules in that quantitative restrictions could be placed on a particular country and the MFN principle not applied. Finally, the concept of market disruption also established an important precedent with regard to the price differential between imported and comparable domestic goods. In other words, because developing countries were deemed to possess an 'unfair' trade advantage over developed countries due to lower labour costs, it was reasoned that price differentials constituted sufficient grounds for quantitative import restrictions to be imposed (GATT 1984: 65).

It is fair to say that neither the developed nor the developing countries recognized the true significance of the market disruption clause until later (see Heron 2012). In the meantime, and quite separately, calls for the creation of unilateral trade preferences were growing progressively louder. In May 1962, the United States Congress passed a bill authorizing the unilateral liberalization of duties on tropical products. The following year GATT trade ministers declared their intention to do likewise on a multilateral basis (again, without the expectation of reciprocity). Yet this pledge did not form part of the Kennedy round that was launched in 1964. Instead, the main concession obtained by the developing countries during these negotiations was the introduction of further flexibilities to the reciprocity obligations with the Trade Negotiating Committee declaring that 'the contribution of the less-developed countries to the overall objective of trade liberalisation should be considered in the light of the development and trade needs of these countries' (WTO 1999: 2; see Table 2.1). This, once again, did not amount to a legally binding commitment – the precise meaning of reciprocity was to remain a matter for each contracting party to interpret in their own way – but it nonetheless signalled that by now the developed countries had all but abandoned any expectation that trade concessions would be reciprocated by developing countries.

Although the Kennedy round reaffirmed without necessarily strengthening a future commitment to introduce unilateral trade preferences, by this point the case for reform had received significant impetus from the creation of the European Economic Community (EEC) in 1957. Although the EEC itself constituted a legally permitted form of trade discrimination under Article XXIV, its formation also brought the former African colonies of France and Belgium into the GATT fold. The reason this was significant is that, prior to the Treaty of Rome, these colonies benefited from trade preferences covered by a derogation enshrined in Article I of the GATT. The formation of the Customs Union, however, meant that these preferences would now in effect be granted by all members even though only France and Belgium were legally entitled to offer them. At the time, the EEC justified this anomaly by arguing that each arrangement constituted a separate 'free trade area' and was thus authorized under Article XXIV (a somewhat ironic position in the light of the arguments that were eventually invoked to justify the abandonment these preferences – more of which later). This was a dubious defence, not least since even though these arrangements were nominally reciprocal they did not come close to satisfying GATT legal requirements for the prompt and complete liberalization of 'substantially all trade' (Hudec 1987: 49). Yet, at the time, the contracting parties chose acquiescence over confrontation and, in so doing, established an important precedent for the granting of unilateral preferences.

By the time of the formation of UNCTAD in 1964, then, the GATT legal defence against preferences had already been breached. The next significant milestone came shortly after this with the creation of 'Part IV' of the GATT in 1965. On the face of it, Part IV provided the clearest demonstration yet of the growing political cohesion of the developing county bloc and might be interpreted as the first significant attempt to enshrine systematically principles of SDT in the GATT legal texts (Whalley 1990). In practice, however, even though Part IV heralded the introduction of three new Articles to the GATT it contained 'no definable legal obligations' (Hudec 1987: 55), either on the part of the developed or developing countries; indeed, on the important matter of trade preferences – the key demand to emerge out of UNCTAD I – the new legal text did not even mention them. Instead, Part IV provided a series of what came to be known in GATT parlance as 'best endeavour' commitments prioritizing the removal of trade barriers (including the practice of tariff escalation) in areas of particular export interest to the developing countries while underscoring the importance of, among other things, improved marked access, commodity price stability and economic diversification. Part IV also committed the contracting parties to show restraint in the application of internal taxes and other fiscal measures likely to affect negatively demand for developing county exports; it also reaffirmed the principle of non-reciprocity with regard to multilateral trade negotiations. Finally, Part IV led to the creation of a permanent bureaucracy in the form of the Trade and Development Committee – perhaps the most lasting achievement of Part IV – that would thereafter be responsible for overseeing the implementation of these commitments and otherwise attending to the concerns of the developing countries.

Although language in support of trade preferences was notable by its absence from Part IV, shortly thereafter the contracting parties consented to the establishment of a generalized system of preferences at the second UNCTAD conference held in New Delhi in 1968. However, the United States – whose opposition to non-reciprocal trade preferences had been a consistent feature of its multilateral diplomacy since the 1940s – was only willing to support this provided that preferences 'be limited to tariffs, should be temporary, should be based on voluntary adherence, and should be extended by all the developed countries to all of the developing countries on an MFN basis' (cited in Whalley 1990: 1320). In other words, the United States saw the establishment of the GSP as an opportunity to placate the developing countries while at the same time putting pressure on the EEC to abandon discriminatory preferences – including the so-called 'reverse preferences' sanctioned under the 1963 Yaoundé convention – offered to former colonies. The establishment of the first Lomé protocol in 1975 did lead, among many other things, to the abandonment of 'reverse preferences'; but it was more significant because it was precipitated by Britain's accession to the Common Market, which increased the number of former colonies eligible for non-reciprocal preferences from 18 to 46 (this figure would total 71 by the time Lomé IV was terminated in 2000). All told, while Unites States advocacy of the GSP did contribute to the abandonment of 'reverse preferences' it signally failed to prevent the widening and deepening of the EEC's special relationship with the ACP. Indeed, the United States would eventually mimic Lomé with the launching of the CBERA in 1984, which proved to be the first in a series of discriminatory preference schemes wholly at odds with its diplomatic stance in the GATT.

Returning to the GSP, despite the fact that UNCTAD II committed the contracting parties to the establishment of a global system of trade preferences, this was never actually formally enshrined in the GATT. Instead, the GSP rested on two separate legal waivers (the first providing a derogation from Article I to the degree necessary for the GSP to operate and the second permitting developing countries to offer trade preferences to each other without having to offer these to the developed countries on an MFN basis) initially granted for a ten-year period but later made permanent by the 1979 Enabling Clause. What this meant, in other words, was that the legal status of the GSP under the GATT was, to use Hudec's (1987: 60) telling phrase, a 'permissive not mandatory' regime – meaning that while the contracting parties could for the first time legally offer non-reciprocal trade preferences (provided that they were offered to all developing countries and did not discriminate between them) there was nothing requiring them to do so.[1] Furthermore, all decisions regarding the duration of preferences, country eligibility, graduation, product coverage and preference margins were left entirely to the discretion of the preference-granting country (Hoekman and Özden 2005: 7).

These legal ambiguities, not surprisingly, had a significant bearing on how the GSP operated under the GATT. This was especially evident in the case of the United States, where increasing trade activism within Congress led to the introduction of progressively more prescriptive forms of 'conditionality', eventually testing the principle of non-reciprocity to the point of destruction (Sapir and Lundberg 1984; Clark and Zarrili 1992; Devault 1996; Hoekman and Özden 2005). In the EEC, meanwhile, the GSP played second fiddle to preferences offered separately to the ACP and was designed in such a way as to avoid interfering with this scheme. Here the contrast between the GSP and Lomé is of some significance. While the GSP was legally attached to the GATT, in substantive terms it amounted to not much more than a 'best endeavour' commitment on the part of the developed countries. By way of comparison, Lomé – the first protocol (1975–9) in particularly – stands in retrospect as something of a highpoint in the attempt to recast North-South relations in the light of the demand for a New International Economic Order (NIEO) (Brown 2000: 372). This was despite the fact that the Lomé regime was clearly at odds with the GATT's legal disciplines. Unlike the GSP, preferences (including highly lucrative commodity protocols for bananas, beef, rum and sugar) granted under Lomé were legally contractual and, therefore, could not be altered or withdrawn unilaterally. The Lomé regime also reflected some of the other demands emanating from the NIEO, including a substantial aid delivery mechanism in the form of the European Development Fund (EDF), plus compensatory mechanisms to assist countries suffering price fluctuations for primary commodities (STABEX) and to guarantee the production of certain minerals (SYSMIN). Finally, Lomé was governed by an elaborate set of joint EEC-ACP institutions, including a Council of Ministers, Committee of Ambassadors and Joint Parliamentary Assembly.

The Lomé regime thus constituted something of a paradox in the post-war trade architecture. Although its existence was difficult to square with the legal disciplines of the GATT it appeared to rest on precisely what the GSP lacked: namely, a set of specified legal obligations according to which trade preferences and other forms of SDT could operate. Yet Lomé and the GSP shared much in common. Both schemes were shaped by the unique institutional environment of the GATT, wherein the dominant mode of trade diplomacy often rested on a tenuous link to the legal norms and procedures on which it was supposedly based. The accommodation of the special and differential needs of the developing countries was achieved on the basis of a series of informal concessions that stopped short of actual institutional reforms or policy changes altering the legal obligations of the developed countries towards the developing countries. Although Part IV of the GATT and even more so the 1979 Enabling Clause were designed to correct this anomaly, the centrepiece of these reforms – the GSP – was arguably beset by as many, if not more, legal ambiguities as schemes like Lomé that functioned more or less outside of the GATT.

The most striking anomaly with the operation of both sets of preferences was the legal ambiguity surrounding country eligibility and, more particularly, the concept of a 'developing country'. Despite the fact that the Enabling Clause provided legal grounds for preferential treatment in favour of developing countries (provided that such treatment did not discriminate between them) the logically prior task of defining a 'developing' country was never satisfactorily resolved. The main responsibility for this lay with UNCTAD, which initially settled on the principle of 'self-declaration' in order to maintain solidarity within the developing country bloc – only to later establish a separate category for the 25 LDCs, on the basis of more or less objective economic criteria (Fialho 2012).[2] Significantly, the LDC concept was enshrined in the 1979 Enabling Clause and became the only legal basis on which the contracting parties could discriminate between developing countries; otherwise, developing country status remained a matter of self-declaration – a practice that continues to this day under the WTO. In short, aside from LDCs, the concept of a 'developing county' in relation to SDT was and continues to be afforded close to no legal standing within the multilateral trading system.

The full implications of this anomaly would only become fully apparent after the conclusion of the Uruguay round and the introduction of the DSU under the WTO. But it is not the case that the advent of the WTO put an end to the informal institutional practices and *ad hoc* decision making that we have encountered so far. Rather, as Amrita Narlikar (2005: 42) reminds us, what these changes represented was a shift towards what she calls 'extreme legalization' embodied in the WTO's commitment to rule enforcement and dispute settlement *alongside* a continued reliance on the informality and improvisation that typified trade diplomacy under the GATT. In the remainder of the chapter, we shall explore the implications of this confluence for the recasting of SDT that occurred under the WTO.

The Uruguay round and the demise of Lomé

The Uruguay round (1986–93), the eighth and, as it turned out, final round of multilateral trade negotiations to be held under the auspices the original GATT, constituted the most protracted, ambitious and, ultimately, far-reaching agreement in the history of international trade diplomacy. The Marrakesh Declaration (which marked the official conclusion of the round) signalled the supplanting of the GATT with a new umbrella organization in the form of the WTO, which would be responsible for overseeing the implementation of a substantially augmented body of international trade law, now covering not only trade in goods (including the legal texts of 'GATT 1947' sitting alongside 'GATT 1994' covering the Uruguay round accords), but also services, investment and trade-related intellectual property rights. The Uruguay settlement was underpinned by the adoption of the 'Understanding on Rules and Procedures Governing the Settlement of Disputes' (otherwise known as the Dispute Settlement Understanding or DSU). Although the DSU essentially rested upon the GATT system of dispute settlement – specifically Article XXI (stipulating the requisite for informal 'consultations' between the parties in dispute as the first stage in the process) and Article XXIII (covering 'nullification and impairment') – it introduced a greater degree of automaticity to the process, rending it more autonomous and legally robust. This was achieved in the first instance through the abandonment of the established practice of decision by 'positive consensus' under which the offending party in a trade dispute was offered multiple opportunities to block or otherwise disrupt the convening of a panel and subsequent issuing of a report. Instead, the settlement of trade disputes under the DSU would operate on the basis of decision by 'positive consensus', meaning that, in the event of the failure to resolve a trade dispute at the 'consultation' stage, a panel would now be automatically convened unless the General Council – that is, the entire membership of the WTO – decided by 'positive consensus' to overrule this. What this meant, in other words, was that trade practices that had evolved under the aegis of the GATT on the basis of ad hoc concessions rather than legally codified obligations – including, most crucially, trade preferences and most forms of SDT – were now more likely to be deemed contrary to the MFN principle.

Another distinctive feature of the Marrakesh Declaration resulted from what became known as the 'single undertaking', by which was meant that in signing the final agreement the contracting parties were now legally bound not only by the Uruguay provisions, but also those adopted in previous GATT rounds. The reason this was significant is that the notion of a 'single undertaking' was diametrically opposed to the negotiating formulae adopted during the Tokyo round (1973–9), under which a series of 'side agreements' were concluded on a plurilateral basis (Narlikar 2005; Wilkinson 2006). The more important point from our perspective is that the 'single undertaking' served – perhaps deliberately – to undercut the established principle of non-reciprocity since the developing countries were now obligated to accept the Uruguay round in its entirety or else opt out of the multilateral trade system altogether. This, again, was in marked contrast to the approach taken in the Tokyo round during which the contracting parties had adopted the most explicit declaration yet on SDT, entitled 'Differential and More Favourable Treatment, Reciprocity and Fuller Participation of Developing Countries', otherwise known as the Enabling Clause. The late 1970s and 1980s, however, witnessed the rise of a new global ideology in the form of neoliberalism that challenged many of the development assumptions upon which these traditional forms of SDT rested. One notable feature of the Tokyo round was the limited participation of the developing countries with reportedly less than one quarter of the 78 officially declared as participants actively taking part in the negotiations (Ibrahim 1978, cited in Wilkinson 2006: 79). This led to the suggestion that in retrospect the principle of non-reciprocity did more harm than good to the developing country cause since it served to neutralize any potential collective bargaining leverage that they may otherwise have possessed (Srinivasan 1998: 24). But more significantly, the rise of neoliberalism coincided with, and was in large measure responsible for, the trauma of indebtedness and structural adjustment, prompting developing countries in most cases to abandon the predominately inward-oriented growth strategies that traditional forms of SDT were in principle designed to assist.

The Uruguay round settlement embodied in the 'single undertaking' thus came to symbolize a transformation in the political economy of North-South trade relations. This was said to be premised on a 'grand bargain' (Ostry 2000), according to which the developing countries would be rewarded for more active participation in the GATT process with concrete market access gains in the key areas of textiles and clothing and agriculture, in exchange for a willingness to accept a widening and deepening of the multilateral trade agenda. This would require eschewing the traditional privileges of non-reciprocity – but, in any case, these privileges would be worth considerably less after the conclusion of the round because of the deep cuts to MFN tariffs (and hence preference margins) that had also been agreed to. The Uruguay round would instead be premised on an entirely different approach to SDT with less emphasis on the means by which the concept was operationalized under the GATT – that is, non-reciprocity, trade preferences and the temporary uses of discriminatory tariffs and quotas to promote infant industries – and more on longer transition periods, technical assistance and other supply-side measures deemed to be less 'trade distorting' for third parties.

The banana trade dispute and the demise of Lomé

The first major indication of the significance of these reforms came almost immediately following the conclusion of the round and – perhaps

Table 2.1 Chronology of Special and Differential Treatment under the GATT

Year	Provision	Summary of Key Features
1947		
1954–5	GATT 1947 Review Session	Revision of Article XXVIII pertaining to the infant-industry and balance-of-payments clauses, rendering them more flexible and easier for developing countries to invoke. Article XXVIII-*bis* requires the contracting parties take into account the 'needs of less developed countries for a more flexible use of tariff protection to assist their economic development and the special needs of these countries to maintain tariffs for revenue purposes'.
1958	Haberler Report	Identifies dependence on export of primary products and problems in access to export markets as main trade problems of developing countries. The Haberler Report does not call for or lead to any major changes in GATT trade law.
1961	Declaration on Promotion of the Trade of Less-Developed Countries	Recognizes the need for: (i) 'a rapid and sustained expansion in export earnings of less-developed countries if their development to proceed at a satisfactory pace'; (ii) 'a conscious and purposeful effort on part of all governments to promote an expansion in the export earnings of less-developed contracting parties through the adoption of concrete measures to this end'; and (iii) the diversification in structure of trade of less-developed countries, for achieving which objective governments should give special attention to ways of enlarging opportunities to less-developed countries to sell in world markets the industrial goods they can produce.
1963–7	Kennedy Round	Trade Negotiating Committee states that that 'developed countries cannot expect to receive reciprocity from less-developed countries' and 'the contribution of the less-developed countries to the over-all objective of trade liberalisation should be considered in the light of the development needs of these countries'.

Continued

Table 2.1 Continued

Year	Provision	Summary of Key Features
1964	Part IV	Article XXXVI agrees on the need for 'a rapid and sustained expansion of export earnings of less-developed contracting parties'. Article XXXVI also formally recognizes the concept of non-reciprocity as follows: 'The developed contracting parties do not expect reciprocity for commitments made by them in trade negotiations to reduce or remove tariffs and other barriers to the trade of less-developed contracting parties'. Article XXXVI commits the contracting parties 'to the fullest extent possible' to accord high priority to the removal of trade barriers (including the practice of tariff escalation) in areas of particular export interest to the developing countries while underscoring the importance of, among other things, improved marked access, commodity price stability and economic diversification. Part IV also leads to the establishment of the Trade and Development Committee thereafter responsible for overseeing the implementation of these commitments and otherwise attending to the concerns of the developing countries.
1966	Waiver for Tariff Preferences Granted by Australia	Contracting parties grant waiver from Article I permitting Australia to accord preferential treatment to the developing countries on a non-reciprocal basis. This constitutes the first official authorization for the granting of such preferences.
1966	Report of the Committee on Trade and Development Report	Declares that 'the establishment of preferences among less-developed countries, appropriately administered and subject to the necessary safeguards, can make an important contribution to the expansion of trade among these countries and to the attainment of the objectives of the General Agreement'.

Year	Title	Description
1971	Waiver for Generalised System of Preferences	Contracting parties sign a 10-year waiver from Article I permitting 'the developed countries to accord preferential tariff treatment to products originating in developing countries and territories, without extending such treatment to like products of other contracting parties'. A separate waiver allows 'each country participating in the Protocol relating to Trade Negotiations among Developing Countries to accord preferential treatment as provided in the Protocol with respect to products originating in other parties to the Protocol, without being required to extend the same treatment to like goods imported from other contracting parties'.
1979	Decision on Differential and More Favourable Treatment, Reciprocity and Fuller Participation of Developing Countries (aka Enabling Clause)	This makes permanent the above derogations from Article I as follows: 'preferential tariff treatment by developing contracting parties under the GSP; differential and more favourable treatment with respect to non-tariff measures governed by instruments multilaterally negotiated under the GATT; regional or global arrangements among developing countries for mutual reduction or elimination of tariffs and, in accordance with criteria or conditions prescribed by the CONTRACTING PARTIES for mutual reduction of non-tariff measures on products imported from one another; and special treatment of LDCs in the context of any general or specific measures in favour of developing countries'.
1993	Marrakesh Declaration	Declares that one of the objectives of the WTO will be to ensure that developing country Members, and especially least-developed countries, 'secure a share in the growth of international trade that is commensurate with their economic development needs [and] that this objective will require a number of positive efforts from all Members'.

Source: WTO (1999).

expectedly – it concerned the Lomé regime. Although much was made subsequently about the role of the DSU in precipitating the demise of Lomé – not least by the EU itself – it is important to note that the original dispute was provoked, not principally by the legality or otherwise of the regime itself, but by the creation of the single banana market in 1992 as part of the implementation of the Single European Act (SEA) (see Alter and Meunier 2006). The dispute was a highly technical and complex one. As John Ravenhill (2004: 127–8) describes it, the central thrust of the case was that the traditional means by which the banana protocol operated – whereby preferential tariff-rate quotas (TRQs) granted to traditional ACP suppliers coexisted with an entirely separate regime for 'dollar bananas' originating from Central America that were subject to a uniform 20 per cent tariff – was immediately rendered obsolete by the SEA. In response, officials in Brussels introduced a new set of procedures and regulations based on the application of Community-wide TRQs alongside additional import tariffs applied exclusively to 'dollar bananas'. The changes also led to the introduction of a complicated import licensing scheme that turned out to be even more convoluted and market distorting than the regime it had been designed to replace. The upshot of all of this was that the new banana regime was found by three separate panels – 1993, 1994, 1997 – to contravene various aspects of GATT trade law, including Article I (non-discrimination), Article III.4 (national treatment), Article XIII (non-discrimination in the application of quantitative restrictions), Article XXIV (free trade areas) as well as Article V of the General Agreement on Services (GATS) and aspects of EU competition law.

The wider significance of all of this was that, by ruling the banana protocol in contravention of Article I, the GATT was, in effect, signalling that the entire Lomé regime was now open to legal challenge – a challenge, moreover, made far more likely to succeed in the light of the impending introduction of the DSU. The 1994 panel not only found that the protocol contravened the MFN principle, it was also unconvinced by the EU's defence that Lomé fell under the rubric of Article XXIV. The reason for this was that the absence of reciprocity meant that these trade arrangements could not possibly satisfy the GATT legal requirements for the prompt and complete liberalization of 'substantially all trade'. The panel also concluded that since Part IV did not mention Article XXIV there was no recourse to SDT provisions as the basis for exemption from the MFN requirement. Finally, because the Enabling Clause operated on the principle of self-declaration the only other basis on which to offer non-reciprocal preferences – that is, short of a legal waiver – was to extend these to all developing countries or limit them to LDCs.

In the event, the EU's immediate response was to seek and subsequently obtain a five-year waiver for Lomé (although this did not prevent further legal challenges to the banana protocol) in what was one of the very last acts of the Uruguay round. At this point, the EU possessed the option to seek a further waiver – for which there are numerous other precedents under both the GATT and WTO – it intimated that its intention would be to recast the entire Lomé system in a way which would render it compatible with Article XXIV. The reason given for this dramatic volte-face was that the tightening of rules covering the granting of legal waivers under the WTO (requiring a 75 per cent as opposed to a 66 per cent majority for approval) meant that such a request was unlikely to succeed. Yet, this argument was not entirely persuasive. First, it is worth noting that throughout the tortuous dispute settlement process (which was not fully resolved until December 2009), at no point did any of the complainants oppose the granting of a waiver from Article I for the Lomé convention (Barfield 2003). It is important to recall in this respect that the main grievance did not even relate to the granting of special trade preferences for ACP banana producers – which, in any case, only accounted for around 16 per cent of the EU market – but the way in which the TRQs and import licences discriminated against 'dollar banana' producers and in favour of European commercial interests respectively (Ravenhill 2004: 129). And, of course, Lomé was no different in principle to other non-reciprocal trade programmes like the CBERA, Canadian Tariff Treatment for Commonwealth Caribbean Countries (CARIBCAN) and AGOA established before and after the DSU came into operation.

What all this suggested was that the fate of Lomé did not rest simply on a dispassionate reassessment of its technical and legal merits following the creation of the EU internal market and the strengthening of multilateral trade rules. Rather, as William Brown (2000) has pointed out, the deeper point was that these matters were themselves being shaped by a fundamental shift in the ideological underpinnings of global economic governance in general and the EU's external relations with the developing countries in particular. According to Brown (2000: 368–74), Lomé was originally premised on the notion of 'ideological neutrality', wherein the effectiveness of alternative programmes and policies was deemed to be measurable against objective development criteria; over time, however, this sentiment was replaced by faith in the universalism of neoliberal doctrine and the policy conditionality with which it became associated. By the time that Lomé was renewed for the fourth time in 1990, language had already been introduced supportive of the wider structural adjustment efforts of the international financial institutions, while the 1995 mid-term revision went even further by attaching explicit political conditions to development aid for the first time. These changes provided an ideological snapshot of what EU policy makers had in mind with the Cotonou Partnership Act of 2000, which would ultimately replace the Lomé convention as the basis for governing EU-ACP trade relations.

It was not long after the mid-term revision of Lomé IV that the European Commission published its landmark *Green Paper on Relations between the European Union and the ACP Countries*, which made the startling admission that Lomé had been an almost unqualified failure in meeting more or less all of its principal objectives. No matter what economic benefits had been bestowed on individual farmers and commodity producers, the EU focused on the fact that, despite 25 years of trade preferences and generous aid provision, Lomé had signally failed to promote export growth or diversification. In fact, quite the reverse had occurred: between 1976 and 1994 ACP exports to the EU as a proportion of the total shrank from 6.7 per cent to 3.4 per cent, while the ACP's overall share of world trade fell from 3 per cent to 1 per cent (Gibb 2000: 463). What served to harden European attitudes towards Lomé was the further enlargement of the EU to include Spain, Portugal and, to differing degrees, the Nordic countries, which generally saw little logic in a pro-development policy based on targeting aid at countries with strong colonial links to certain member states and excluding other, equally or even poorer, countries without this historical connection. Crucially, both the Maastricht Treaty of 1992 and the Amsterdam Treaty of 1997 made references to the need to integrate 'developing countries into the world economy', with particular emphasis on *'the most disadvantaged among them'*.

Although the *Green Paper* set out a number of alternative options (including the standard application of GSP, a single agreement based on the principle of uniform reciprocity as well as a series of 'differentiated' FTAs involving individual regions and countries), the trade component of Cotonou would eventually lead to the formulae of replacing Lomé with separate EPAs based on six ACP 'regions' identified by the Commission (see, especially, Chapter 4). In order to make this possible, the EU would seek an extension to the WTO waiver (which was subsequently granted during the 2001 Doha Ministerial in Qatar) in order to allow the ACP sufficient breathing space to prepare for the EPA negotiations, scheduled to begin in September 2002 and end no later than 31 December 2007. The Cotonou Agreement, however, made special provisions for LDCs, which would be granted Lomé-equivalent duty- and quota-free (DFQF) preferences under what became the 'Everything but Arms' (EBA) agreement of 2001. By replacing Lomé with reciprocal EPAs for non-LDCs while offering DFQF treatment to eligible LDCs, the EU would therefore resolve the problem of WTO incompatibility since the regime would now be legally consistent with both the Enabling Clause and – via Article XXIV – the MFN principle. In sum, the Cotonou Agreement appeared to offer a prospectus for how SDT might be operationalized under the new global trade architecture, heralded by the arrival of the WTO.

The recasting of 'special and differential treatment' under the WTO

It was not long after the Cotonou Agreement that, following several false starts, the successor to the Uruguay round, the DDA, was launched, in Qatar in December 2001. The launching of the DDA, of course, occurred in the immediate aftermath of the terrorist attacks of 11 September 2001. An arguably more important backdrop to the round, however, was the acrimonious failure of the 1999 Seattle ministerial, when mass civic mobilization and violent demonstrations on the streets mirrored deep divisions between developed and developing countries inside the conference hall regarding the content and indeed the overall desirability of a further round of trade liberalization. The key to understanding this impasse was the belief among the majority of developing county delegations that the developed countries had failed to live up to their side of the aforementioned 'grand bargain' of the Uruguay round – what had become known as the 'implementation issues' – but were now seeking to open up negotiations in new trade areas such as competition policy, investment, trade facilitation and government procurement – what had become known as the 'Singapore issues' – without first addressing these grievances. Following the collapse of the Cancún ministerial in September 2003 (after which competition policy, investment and government procurement were dropped from the negotiating agenda) there was a considerable lowering of expectations for what could be achieved by the round. It was within this setting that the Hong Kong ministerial meeting – the first since Doha not to end in abject failure – took place in November 2005, at which point the contracting parties fleshed out a series of policy proposals which, alongside the gains expected to come from the liberalization of agriculture (in particular), it was hoped, would serve to re-embed SDT in the multilateral trade architecture.

Aid for Trade

The most notable part of the Hong Kong Declaration was the call by ministers to create a 'task force' to provide recommendations on how to operationalize an AfT programme capable of contributing to the 'development' dimension of DDA. The Task Force duly reported its findings in July 2006 and these were subsequently endorsed by the WTO General Council (WTO 2006). Among other things, the Task Force reaffirmed the principles of the Paris Declaration on Aid Effectiveness (see OECD 2005) but noted that these needed to be tailored to the specific requirements of individual countries. In particular, the Task Force recommended strengthening the 'demand side', 'donor response' and closing the gap between 'demand' and 'response' at the country, regional and global levels. In addition, the Task Force recommended that the precise activities to be funded through AfT should rest largely with recipient governments in terms of those activities identified as trade-related development priorities in national development plans. The Task Force suggested that the WTO should play a key role in monitoring and evaluating AfT, assessing progress in trade-related capacity building and devising incentives to improve its effectiveness.

Significantly, the Hong Kong pledge did not mandate the WTO Task Force to deal in detail either with the quantity or the nature of financing, leaving this to the WTO Director General. The Task Force nevertheless did reiterate the principle of 'additionality', that is, increased funding for AfT should be *in addition* to planned increases in general aid budgets. This obviously left the most relevant question – that is, the amount of money available for AfT in the event of a successful conclusion to the round leading to a further dramatic cut to MFN tariffs – unresolved. In 2009, the OECD claimed that total multilateral and bilateral AfT disbursements amounted to US$28.4 billion, claiming in a separate report co-authored with the WTO Secretariat (2009: 13) that the bulk of this constituted additional spending rather than the reallocation of existing aid flows. However, developing countries claim that, because the reporting of AfT spending is primarily the responsibility of aid donors, there is nothing to prevent the relabeling of existing funds – suspicions fuelled by the difficulties aid recipients reportedly have in obtaining independent scrutiny of the OECD's Creditors Reporting System used to collate aid statistics (Heron 2012). Similarly, critics point to the fact that the trade needs of countries in receipt of AfT appears to be a poor indicator of resource allocation, with the lion's share of disbursements going to war-torn states like Afghanistan and Iraq alongside emerging economies including China, India, Turkey and Vietnam (Cali 2008; Langan and Scott 2011).

Duty-free, quota-free

Alongside AfT, the Hong Kong Declaration was notable for the ostensible decision to grant DFQF preferences to all LDCs. The impetus for this commitment came from the EU (although all WTO members had agreed to this in principle in 1999), which had by this point granted DFQF access to LDCs unilaterally through its 2001 EBA initiative. In practice, however, neither the EBA initiative nor the Hong Kong pledge was as generous as first appearances suggested. On the one hand, despite offering DFQF treatment to all products from LDCs (apart from bananas, sugar and rice where full market access was delayed until 2009), the EBA stuck with the notoriously complex rules of origin that had discouraged eligible developing countries from taking advantage of free market access available previously through the GSP (Heron 2012). On the other hand, the Hong Kong pledge stopped short of offering DFQF treatment to LDCs for all products, with Japan, Canada and the United States agreeing to extend market access to only 97 per cent of tariff lines. As James Scott and Rorden Wilkinson (2011: 623) note, this meant that in the case of the United States, for instance, something in the order of 300 tariff lines would be excluded under the proposal. To make matters worse, even this paltry offer appeared conditional on significant progress in the rest of the talks with the US rejecting calls to offer DFQF unilaterally as part of a so-called 'early harvest' before the rest of the DDA was completed.

Relating this to the issues explored in the first part of the chapter, the Hong Kong pledge was significant for another reason in that (despite its imperfections) it would appear to legally bind preference-granting countries to the agreement (we can recall that similar measures under the GSP were offered previously on a voluntary basis and at the discretion of the importing country), but based on the principle that preferential trade should only be maintained in the case of those countries formally classified as LDCs. To underscore the significance on this, it is important to highlight that approximately two-thirds of the WTO's 152 members are classified as 'developing' countries but only 32 as LDCs. But what is most striking about the Hong Kong Ministerial Declaration is that it did not, in fact, deviate that much from the historical pattern we have traced throughout this chapter. That is to say, neither AfT nor DFQF appear to be based on a great deal more than 'best endeavour' commitments similar to those offered under the GATT. And while the DFQF initiative did at least attempt to place the provision of trade preferences for the LDCs on a more secure legal footing it is still unclear how far, if at all, this departed from the 'permissive' character of its predecessor, the GSP. Finally, the proposal did little to clear up the legal ambiguities concerning preferences for non-LDCs, or cases where preferential market access is offered to both LDCs *and* non-LDCs.

Conclusion

The purpose of this chapter has been to examine the origins and subsequent operation of the concept of SDT as a necessary first step to analysing the wider political economy of trade preference erosion. In so doing, we have underscored two key points that do not always figure prominently in the extant literature. First, we drew attention to the specific historical patterns and institutional practices that characterized the governance of international trade prior to the establishment of the WTO. This helped to shed light on the difficulties that the contracting parties encountered in seeking to operationalize SDT – both before and after the introduction of the DSU under the WTO. Second, we have underscored the degree to which the policy space for the maintenance of preferences has been shaped as much by shifting ideological contours and changing development norms as by the technical/legal obstacles created by the strengthening of multilateral trade rules. Although at first glance the insights gleaned from this finding would appear to go against our first point, the aim has been to show that both institutions *and* ideas have played a role in delimiting the policy space and choice sets available to trade actors in the pursuit of development goals.

In concrete terms, the light shone on the informal institutional practices and *ad hoc* decision making procedures that evolved under the aegis of the GATT helps us to appreciate the influence of path dependency on efforts to recast SDT in terms of reciprocity and supply-side reforms. Hence despite the best of intentions, coupled with the favourable political circumstances generated in the immediate aftermath of the terrorist attacks of 11 September

2001, the evidence suggests that participants in the DDA have largely failed to break the traditional mould of SDT associated with technically ambiguous principles and (for the most part) legally unenforceable concessions. At the current juncture, it now seems very unlikely that the DDA will ever come to pass. The potential consequences of this – measured against the backdrop of a notable acceleration in the proliferation of bilateral activism on the part of key trade powers – is that the further recasting of SDT is now most likely to be seen outside multilateral trade disciplines on the basis of even more asymmetric forms of North-South trade diplomacy. This pattern is revealed most obviously in the case of the EPAs, to which we turn in the next two chapters.

3
Understanding the EU-ACP Economic Partnership Agreements: The Case of CARIFORUM

On 15 October 2008, the Caribbean Forum of African, Caribbean and Pacific states (CARIFORUM) became the first and, at the time of writing, only region to sign a comprehensive EPA with the EU.[1] The agreement came less than a year after the expiry of the WTO waiver and thus provided early symbolic affirmation of the merits of the EU's post-Lomé trade vision. The timing of the CARIFORUM agreement was also significant in that it appeared to underscore the importance that European Commission officials placed on a swift conclusion to the EPA negotiations in order to safeguard preferences from further WTO litigation. As a general explanation for why CARIFORUM chose to sign a comprehensive agreement, however, the necessity of WTO compliance has become progressively less plausible over time. Indeed, the central thrust of the academic literature accompanying the EPAs has been to question the importance of this – especially when weighed against the independent, political and commercial interests of the EU (see *inter alia* Gibb 2000; Hurt 2003; Ravenhill 2004; Goodison 2007; Faber and Orbie 2009; Heron and Siles-Brügge 2012). But in dismissing the importance of WTO compatibility such accounts have generally failed to offer a satisfactory alternative explanation for the behaviour of ACP countries (as opposed to the EU) in the EPA negotiations. The CARIFORUM agreement is particularly noteworthy in this respect because, in signing a full EPA, the region effectively broke ranks with the rest of the ACP, which has so far resisted much of the EU's post-Cotonou trade agenda.

The purpose of this chapter is to examine more closely the political economy of EU-ACP trade diplomacy in the post-Cotonou era – and to do so with specific reference to the case of CARIFORUM. In so doing, the chapter asks why CARIFORUM felt it necessary or desirable to sign a 'full' EPA, containing numerous provisions not actually mandated by the WTO, when the rest of the ACP was content to sign far less ambitious 'goods only' interim agreements? The chapter starts from the premise that, even though the EPA process has obviously been shaped in a decisive way by the actions of the EU, the small and vulnerable developing countries that make up the bulk of the membership of the ACP still retain the ultimate decision to sign, or not sign, an agreement. Hence the fact that CARIFORUM chose to sign a relatively far-reaching agreement tells us something important about the strategic calculations of the governing elite within the region. The straightforward explanation for why CARIFORUM decided to go further than the rest of the ACP in concluding a comprehensive agreement draws attention to key differences in terms of regional institutions and negotiating structures between the Caribbean and the rest of the ACP.[2] That is to say, the Caribbean Regional Negotiating Machinery (CRNM), the quasi-autonomous body that led the negotiations on behalf of CARIFORUM, provided the region with the type of bureaucratic capacity and supranational authority deemed necessary to negotiate region-wide reciprocal trade agreements but generally absent in the ACP. The other often-cited explanation focuses on differences in the perceived urgency of the EPA negotiations and the limited choice set available to CARIFORUM. Because CARIFORUM is unique among the ACP in the sense that it is almost entirely made up of non-LDCs – the sole exception being Haiti – it was ineligible for Cotonou-equivalent preferences available through the EU's EBA initiative. Hence the region had little alternative but to conclude an EPA in order to lessen the effects of preference erosion, especially in relation to key tropical commodities like bananas and sugar. At the same time, by the late 2000s more than half of CARIFORUM export revenue was derived from non-traditional service industries, especially tourism, not covered by the Cotonou agreement. Caribbean heads of governments and CRNM officials therefore perceived the EPA not only as an opportunity to arrest the progressive erosion of the value of traditional preferences but also to improve access to the EU market in areas like services and investment.

While none of this can be dismissed, this chapter offers a deeper reading of the CARIFORUM-EU EPA. In order to do so, it goes beyond the extant EU-ACP trade literature to build on wider IPE scholarship, which has analysed the actions of developing countries in relation to a whole range of 'WTO-plus' North-South regional and bilateral FTAs. The significance of this wider body of research is that, not only does it point to the unequal power dynamics inherent in North-South trade bargaining, but to the specific developmental consequences of the proliferation of reciprocal FTAs concluded outside of the multilateral trade system. In contrast to the power-balancing effects of multilateral trade regulation, FTAs are said to take place in the context of asymmetric bargaining, the consequence of which is that developing countries often sign agreements that go beyond what they have been willing to agree to in the WTO – especially in terms of restricting their subsequent ability to pursue relatively autonomous trade and industrial policies. Yet, while power asymmetries may account for the lopsided nature of North-South FTAs, they do not necessarily explain why developing countries choose to sign such agreements in the first place. To this quandary, analysts have advanced a range of explanations, including the role of ideology, the strength and influence of export-oriented interests, the demonstration effect and fear of marginalization, plus the benefits of signing agreements based on less than full liberalization that serve to exclude the most politically-sensitive sectors from trade reform (Gruber 2001; Ravenhill 2003; Phillips 2005; Shadlen 2008; Gallagher 2008).

Building on these insights, this chapter argues that the CARIFORUM agreement was a product of the unequal bargaining dynamics associated with North-South FTAs. Although the bureaucratic autonomy and technical competence of the CRNM provided CARIFORUM with the means to negotiate an EPA, neither this nor differences in economic interests is sufficient to explain the comprehensive nature of the agreement. Rather, the chapter suggests, the agreement is understood best as a 'political bargain' forged in a highly asymmetrical context. Although cognizant of the effects of power asymmetry, CARIFORUM elites nevertheless made the strategic calculation that a willingness to conclude a WTO-plus agreement would maximize the bargaining position of the CRNM vis-à-vis the EU in order to craft a deal best suited to the region's particular development needs. This strategic calculation was informed by two sets of considerations. First, an overriding concern for the very small, preference-dependent islands of the Caribbean was the fiscal rather than the trade implications of import liberalization, because of the heavy dependence on tariff revenue to fund government spending. This meant that, at least in the short term, securing a 'goods only' agreement involving the removal of tariffs was far more politically contentious than commitments made to the EU in the area of regulatory harmonization. From this perspective, a WTO-plus agreement represented an acceptable quid pro quo for EU concessions that – it was assumed – would help to offset the costs of import liberalization. Second, the thinking of CARIFORUM was also influenced by the internal distributive politics of the ACP – especially in relation to access to trade-adjustment and capacity-building resources provided by the EDF and the EU's AfT budget. In this case, the strategic calculation was that a willingness to sign a comprehensive agreement – and to do so first – was key to extracting further commitments from the EU, the most important of which was preferential access to the financial component of the EPAs. In sum, the CARIFORUM agreement was a product, not simply of unique institutional structures or economic interests, but a set of asymmetries associated with the EU's market and financial power, amplified by the vulnerabilities, competitive dynamics and interregional rivalries inside the ACP.

The rest of the chapter is organized as follows. The first section surveys the relevant IPE literature on North-South FTAs in order to establish an analytical template for the rest of the chapter. The second section sketches out the background to the CARIFORUM EPA by detailing, albeit rather briefly since this story is relayed elsewhere in the book, the various factors which led to the rise and fall of the Lomé protocol and to the establishment of the Cotonou Partnership Agreement in 2000. A key task for this section will be to identify the sources of preference erosion that were most relevant to the Caribbean, particularly since these are argued to have persuaded regional elites to the merits of a reciprocal FTA with the EU. The third section then looks specifically at the EPA, summarizing its main provisions as well as offering an initial assessment of its likely development impact. The fourth and final substantive section attempts to gauge the wider significance of the agreement by relating the specifics of the EPA to the broader debate regarding the trade-off between the immediate economic benefits of improved and more secure market access against the longer-term costs of sacrificing development policy space. Put simply, this section seeks to ascertain what ultimately the Caribbean gained from the EPA negotiations and at what price. The final, concluding section briefly summarizes the main findings of the chapter and speculates on the wider implications of these in furthering our understanding of the development consequences of the shift towards reciprocal free trade.

The political economy of North-South FTAs: Market access versus development policy space?

In the last 10 to 15 years, the governance of international trade has undergone a significant transformation as a result of the proliferation of regional and bilateral FTAs, mainly though not exclusively concluded between developed and developing countries. The WTO estimates that close to 400 FTAs had been implemented by 2010, close to three-quarters of which were negotiated after 1995.[3] From a development perspective, free-market economists typically balk at FTAs and other forms of preferential trade on the grounds that they (allegedly) deliver smaller benefits to developing countries than global free trade, are potentially trade distorting and reduce pressure for further liberalization in preference-receiving countries, thereby undermining the process of internal policy reform (Panagariya 2002). The trade agreements that have dominated recent North-South bilateral diplomacy, however, present a challenge to this traditional liberal viewpoint, in both normative and analytical terms. The reason for this is that these agreements are typically geared more to the harmonization of domestic regulatory standards in areas like foreign direct investment and intellectual property protection, than to liberalization in the traditional sense of removing tariff and non-tariff barriers to trade – or, more accurately, the current crop of FTAs are based on a 'political bargain' whereby developing countries receive greater market access but only in exchange for deeper commitments in regulatory harmonization (Shadlen 2005: 751). Finally, it hardly needs to be added that the degree of regulatory harmonization evident in FTAs has now gone way beyond what remains under discussion in the WTO Doha round, thus rendering the conventional 'regionalism/bilateralism-versus-multilateralism' calculus somewhat misplaced.

The prominence of regulatory issues within the current set of FTAs has led an increasing number of scholars to focus on the international political economy of North-South trade diplomacy (Phillips 2005; Shadlen 2005, 2008; Gallagher 2008). The key point of departure for these theorists is the emphasis they place on the political dynamics of FTAs, and in particularly how the asymmetrical bargaining context changes developing countries' perception of the relative costs and benefits of signing an agreement. It is important to emphasize that these costs and benefits are understood here, not principally as market efficiencies or immediate welfare effects, but rather as an essential trade-off between the economic benefits of 'shallow' integration against the political constraints associated with 'deeper' forms of integration (Shadlen 2005: 751). In other words, whether trade integration is pursued via the bilateral, regional or multilateral route, the economic benefits to developing countries through better market access are only available at the cost of sacrificing the regulatory autonomy, or policy space, deemed necessary to pursue the type of trade and industrial policies deployed successfully in the past by both developed and (some) developing countries (Chang 2002).

Although the concept of policy space is not always defined in the literature, the UNCTAD has described it, as part of the so-called 'Sao Pāulo consensus', in the following terms: 'the scope for domestic policies, especially in the area of trade, investment and industrial development', which might be otherwise constrained by 'international disciplines, commitments and global market considerations' (UNCTAD 2004: 3). Up until recently, most discussion of development policy space has taken place mainly with reference to the WTO and multilateral trade disciplines (Amsden and Hikino 2000; Wade 2003; Weiss 2005; Rodrik 2007; Page 2007; Gallagher 2008a). The key point of reference in this debate is the 1993 Uruguay round allegedly premised on a 'grand bargain' (Ostry 2000), whereby developing countries received improved market access for textiles and clothing and agriculture in exchange for regulatory harmonization with respect to intellectual property, investment, services and so on. The intellectual consensus is that the Uruguay round bargain reduced but did not eliminate altogether development policy space, but the fear now is that FTAs are now removing what little scope there remains for developing countries to pursue relatively autonomous trade and industrial policies (Shadlen 2005: 752; Gallagher 2008: 46). The main reason for this is that, despite the procedural inequities of the current system of multilateral trade regulation – and they are considerable – the WTO does at least offer developing countries opportunities to balance against power politics through, for example, issue linkage and the formation of international coalitions (Narlikar 2003). In contrast, FTAs are said to take place in the context of unmediated forms of asymmetric bargaining, the consequence of which is that developing countries often sign agreements that go way beyond what they have been willing to agree to in the WTO.

Although FTAs have now been established in almost all parts of the developing world, including Asia-Pacific, Africa and the Middle East, no other region has been subject to quite so much diplomatic activity as Latin America and the Caribbean (LAC). The LAC region also best illustrates the contrasting negotiating dynamics between multilateral and regional/bilateral trade integration. On the multilateral front, LAC was within the vanguard of developing countries that fought successfully to prevent the further erosion of policy space through resistance to the inclusion of the three most controversial Singapore Issues (competition policy, transparency in government procurement and investment – the other being trade facilitation) within the Doha round negotiations. This involved, among other things, active membership in South-South coalitions, including the Core Group of developing countries, the Like Minded Group (LMG), the Small and Vulnerable Economies (SVE), the Alliance on Strategic Products (SP) and the Special Safeguard Mechanism (SSM), and the G20 (Narlikar and Tussie 2004).[4] By way of contrast, in regional and bilateral negotiations some, but by no means all, LAC governments were apparently willing to surrender more policy autonomy in exchange for better access to the markets of the United States and, to a far lesser though increasing extent, the EU. Kenneth Shadlen (2005) has convincingly shown that, in specific relation to the North American Free Trade Agreement (NAFTA), the relevant chapters on trade, investment and intellectual property protection are all considerably more exacting than WTO rules in restricting the ability of member states to follow independently determined economic policies.

A similar pattern has been detected in relation to other FTAs modelled on NAFTA, such as the agreements concluded between the United States and the five Central America republics (Costa Rica, El Salvador, Guatemala, Honduras and Nicaragua) and the Dominican Republic, Chile, Colombia and Peru. The important point to register here is that the contrasting position of certain LAC states in multilateral and regional/bilateral settings does not simply reveal an inconsistent trade strategy. It also shows that, in the absence of power-balancing institutions, asymmetries in negotiating power are more likely to lead to asymmetries in negotiating outcome. As Nicola Phillips (2005: 9) has argued in relation to the launching of the original Free Trade Area of the Americas (FTAA) process in the mid-1990s, the initial preference of LAC was for a trading regime that, with the sole exception of market access, was based on the principle of 'WTO compatibility'. By late 2003, however, the FTAA process had given way to an accelerating proliferation of bilateral agreements along the lines of the traditional 'hub-and-spoke' model. Crucially, the shift from a hemispheric to a bilateral approach enabled the United States to use its bargaining leverage more effectively to shape the ideological parameters of the negotiations in a manner reflective of its primary interests and preferences: that is, to secure a series of commitments on regulatory harmonization that were fundamentally WTO-plus in nature (Phillips 2005: 1, 3).

Although such power asymmetries account for the typically lopsided nature of North-South FTAs, this does not explain why developing country elites choose to sign such agreements in the first place. To this quandary, analysts have advanced a range of explanations, a number of which are especially worth highlighting. Some analysts have approached this question from the perspective of instrumental rationality. As Kevin Gallagher notes (2008: 42), citing the econometric work of Carsten Kowalczyk and Ronald Wonnacott (2002), even under neo-classical assumptions it is theoretically possible for small developing countries to increase the volume of trade and see their terms of trade improve through signing an FTA with a larger and richer neighbour. Such improvements would, however, be short lived if comparable developing countries follow the same course of action; and, should these rivals establish an FTA first, then the original developing country would likely see its terms of trade worsen. Hence, from this perspective, not only is it economically rational for the governments of developing countries to seek a bilateral FTA with a larger and richer neighbour, it is also rational for them to do this before rival states beat them to it. Lloyd Gruber (2001) has described this competitive logic in terms of the concept 'bandwagoning', by which is meant the fear of marginalization compels states to seek membership of FTAs even though they may actually prefer the status quo. Drawing on the example of NAFTA, Gruber asserts that the 1989 United States-Canada FTA precipitated a u-turn on the part of the Mexican elite, which calculated that, even though its preferred option was the restoration of the original (more protectionist) status quo, reaching a new (freer trade) accommodation with the United States and Canada was preferable to possible exclusion from the new trade reality.

In an extension of Gruber's argument, Shadlen (2008) has introduced the concept of 'political trade dependence' to account for the favourable response that certain LAC governments have shown to the United States' regional and bilateral agenda. Whereas Gruber focuses on the precipitative effect of changes to the status quo, Shadlen highlights the degree to which the response of developing countries to such changes is determined by the level of trade dependence. One of the most puzzling aspects of the current enthusiasm among developing country elites for FTAs is that the amount of additional market access available through these agreements is, typically, fairly modest because of the prior existence of unilateral trade preferences (see Chapter 2). According to Shadlen, however, the problem with these schemes is that they are unilateral in nature and hence subject to arbitrary change and political manipulation by the preference-granting country. Crucially, also, preference-receiving countries cannot under multi-lateral trade disciplines challenge a preference-granting country through the DSU in response to changes to or the removal of unilateral trade concessions (Shadlen 2008: 6). It is the degree to which preference-receiving countries are sensitive to this type of political interference which, according to Shadlen, constitutes political trade dependence. Importantly, political trade dependence differs from ordinary trade dependence in the sense that, not only are preference-receiving countries subject to the normal vagaries of fluctuating demand and changing patterns of production, they often end up on the receiving end of interest group conflict and distributional struggles from within the preference-granting country.[5] The importance of this insight, with respect to Shadlen's overall argument, is that the governments of countries experiencing high levels of political trade dependence or more likely to wish to place their trading relations on a more stable and secure footing by signing up to a fully reciprocal FTA (Shadlen 2008: 3–8). The prior existence of unilateral trade preferences, moreover, renders this outcome even more likely, since such schemes tend over time to build powerful coalitions among export-oriented interests within preference-receiving countries with a strong vested interest in the maintenance and deepening of these trade relationships (Shadlen 2008: 14).

In summary, then, the foregoing analysis of the relevant political economy literature on regional and bilateral FTAs offers a number of potentially crucial insights into the CARIFORUM-EU EPA. Three points are especially worth underlining. First, the conventional liberal preoccupation with market access largely misses the point about the current crop of FTAs which tend to revolve around regulatory issues like national treatment for foreign investors and intellectual property regimes. Because of this, these agreements are best understood in terms of an assessment of the immediate economic benefits of enhanced market access against the longer-term costs associated with reduced regulatory policy autonomy. Second, in the absence of power-balancing institutions North-South FTAs are generally characterized by an asymmetrical bargaining context. This has the effect of altering the perceptions that elites within developing countries hold about the costs and benefits of signing an agreement with a richer and more powerful trading partner. Third, despite these costs there are a variety of reasons why elites in a developing country may still prefer to sign rather than not sign an agreement, including the bandwagoning effect and the desire to place current trade preferences on a more stable and secure footing. Of course, these dilemmas are not unique to FTAs. But the heightened power asymmetries involved in these agreements do serve to intensify the market access/development space trade-offs which characterize the limited choice set available to small developing countries in all trade bargaining scenarios. In the rest of the chapter we explore how these dilemmas played out in the CARIFORUM-EU EPA.

From Lomé to Cotonou to the EPAs: EU-ACP trade relations, 1975–2000

As was discovered in the previous chapter, the Lomé convention (which preceded the Cotonou Agreement and hence the EPAs) was established in 1975 following the United Kingdom's accession to the Common Market in 1973, which required extending the geographical focus of the Yaoundé convention – which had offered reciprocal trade preferences to former African colonies of France and Belgium since 1963 – to include the Caribbean and Pacific Commonwealth states. Unlike the Yaoundé convention, preferences under Lomé were granted on a non-reciprocal basis while commodity protocols for bananas, beef, rum and sugar offered eligible ACP states guaranteed prices in excess of those available on the world market. All told, the Lomé convention was renewed on three separate occasions – 1981, 1985 and 1989 – but was ultimately deemed to have failed in its principal objectives of promoting economic growth and diversification (European Commission 1996b; Gibb 2000).

Important as these policies' failings were, as we have seen, the key catalyst for the demise of Lomé was a series of adverse legal rulings against the EU's banana protocol under both the GATT and the WTO. In 1994 the GATT ruled that Lomé was inconsistent with the MFN clause because it did not constitute a 'free trade area' or 'customs union' (due to the lack of reciprocity) but nor was it consistent with the 1979 Enabling Clause (because it discriminated between developing countries). In response, the EU immediately sought and received a five-year waiver for Lomé in advance of the introduction of the much-strengthened dispute-settlement mechanism in 1995 (Ravenhill 2004; Heron 2011). Although the EU possessed the option to seek a further waiver – for which there are numerous other precedents under both the GATT and WTO – it soon intimated that its intention would be to recast the entire ACP trade relationship in such a way as to make it 'WTO compatible'. Accordingly, the Cotonou Partnership Act of 2000 settled on the formula of replacing Lomé with separate EPAs based on six 'regions' – the Caribbean; the Pacific; West; Central; Eastern and Southern; and Southern Africa (SADC-minus) – as identified by the Commission.[6] In order to make this possible, the EU would seek an extension to the WTO waiver (which was subsequently granted during the 2001 Doha Ministerial in Qatar) in order to allow the ACP sufficient breathing space to prepare for the EPA negotiations, scheduled to begin in September 2002 and end no later than 31 December 2007.

To ensure compatibility with WTO rules the Cotonou Agreement made special provisions for LDCs, which were granted Lomé-equivalent DFQF preferences under the EBA agreement of 2001 (the significance of this decision is explored further in Chapter 4).[7] This meant that, by including the handful of UN-designated LDCs that had been excluded from Lomé, the

EBA effectively got around the issue of GATT inconsistency since the regime was now legally consistent with the 1979 Enabling Clause. Dealing with the non-LDCs was, however, more problematic for the realization of the trade arrangement envisaged by Cotonou due to the fact that preference-receiving states were effectively being asked to sign up to fully reciprocal agreements in exchange for benefits they already received. Further, Article 37.6 of the Cotonou Agreement made reference to offering countries which failed to sign an EPA a trade framework at least 'equivalent to their existing situation'. Yet, since Cotonou had introduced the deadline of December 2007 and the only other option available was the substantially inferior GSP programme (which offered preferences on approximately 54 per cent of tariff lines in contrast to approximately 95 per cent under Lomé), the non-LDCs were confronted with an unpalatable choice: either negotiate a fully reciprocal EPA or run the theoretical risk of being downgraded to GSP. Finally, not only did Cotonou require the establishment of WTO-compatible EPAs, Articles 41–52 of the agreement also made provision, albeit vaguely, for reciprocal liberalization in trade-related areas not covered by the original Lomé protocol and hence not subject to WTO litigation. Therefore, the issue to be determined was, if the non-LDCs did sign an EPA, would the subsequent agreement merely be 'WTO compatible' or would it come to resemble the WTO-plus North-South FTAs which by now had become widespread in other parts of the developing world?

The CARIFORUM-EU Economic Partnership Agreement

Even since the 1996 *Green Paper* there has been a general expectancy among scholars, policy makers and non-governmental organizations alike that the negotiation of a post-Lomé trade regime would be more straightforward in the Caribbean than elsewhere in the ACP. The main reason for this is that, although the negotiating groups identified for the purpose of the EPAs did in some other cases correspond to existing regional institutions (see Chapter 4), very few of these are characterized by the type of bureaucratic capacity and supranational authority deemed necessary to negotiate region-wide reciprocal trade agreements (Stevens 2008: 212). The CRNM arguably provided the Caribbean with the regional coherence, technical competence and negotiating capacity generally missing in the rest of the ACP. Although the CRNM was – before its demise[8] – often superficially likened to the European Commission with respect to the latter's delegated role in leading negotiations with third parties on behalf of the Council of Ministers, the former's role was more limited and its origins more idiosyncratic than implied by this comparison. These differences are worth describing briefly since they do have quite an important bearing on how the CARIFORUM-EU negotiations actually unfolded.

As Cedric Grant (2000) describes it, the CRNM was created in 1997 following a series of ad hoc steps designed to help Caribbean governments cope with the multiple demands of liberalization pressures on both regional and multi-lateral fronts. As originally envisaged, the CRNM was supposedly intended to operate inside CARICOM and exist only so long as was necessary to assist Caribbean governments in the FTAA and WTO negotiations. In practice, however, the subsequent institutional trajectory of CRNM came to reflect the forceful personality of its first Chief Negotiator – Shridath Ramphal – leading to a series of important and controversial organizational changes, the most important of which was the decision to upgrade the ambassadorial rank of the Chief Negotiator to that of minister, reporting directly to Caribbean heads of government rather than to the CARICOM Secretariat. Ramphal also used his forceful personality to shape, perhaps decisively, the intellectual character of the CRNM in a pro-liberalization direction by identifying the need to respond in a pro-active manner to the 'imperative' of reciprocity as the central reason d'être of the new collective negotiating framework (Grant 2000: 473).

For its part, the European Commission approached the EPA negotiations on the insistence that it had no underlying motive in securing a reciprocal agreement other than promoting sustainable development through the gradual regional and global integration of CARIFORUM countries into the world economy in a manner consistent with WTO rules (EU 2006: 3). Although critics were quick to question, if not ridicule, the suggestion that the EU had no offensive interests at stake in promoting the EPAs (Stoneman and Thompson 2007; Oxfam 2008; Brewster, Girvan and Lewis 2008), the claim nevertheless rested on an important half-truth: beginning with Lomé IV (1990–2000) the European Commission increasingly used the policy leverage afforded by the Lomé and Cotonou agreements as a means to steer ACP countries in a broadly neoliberal direction but for ideological rather than straightforward commercial reasons (Brown 2000; Holland 2002; Hurt 2003). Yet the importance of the EU's wider economic interests cannot be ignored. Crucially, the 1996 *Green Paper* that presaged the demise of Lomé coincided, more or directly, with a recalibration of EU wider trade strategy built on a more aggressive approach towards penetrating overseas markets (Faber and Orbie 2009).

Later, following the debacle at Cancún in 2003, the EU found itself having to respond to the United States' pre-emptive shift towards 'competitive liberalization' (Zoellick 2003). This it duly did, albeit somewhat belatedly, when the Commission launched its *Global Europe* trade strategy document in October 2006. The essential thrust of *Global Europe* was that the aim of promoting internal competitiveness and job creation through further liberalization and marketization under the auspice of the Lisbon Agenda needed to run in tandem with a more offensive external trade strategy built on a new generation of bilateral trade deals, trade defence instruments, vigilant protection of intellectual property and so on (Hay 2007; Heron and Siles-Brügge 2012). Revealingly, the strategy document identified a whole range of emerging markets in Asia, Latin America and elsewhere deemed ripe for commercial exploitation, but at no point did it mention the ACP other than to suggest that these countries were peripheral to Europe's main commercial interests and that the EPAs were thus designed to meet development rather than trade objectives (EU 2006a: 10–11). As Gerrit Faber and Jan Orbie (2009) argue, however, the very fact that Lomé preferences were in the past considered such a major diplomatic impediment to closer trading relations between Europe and the more dynamic countries of Latin America and Asia suggests that the EPAs were not unrelated to the EU's wider economic interests. Finally, parallels with the United States' strategy of 'competitive liberalization' – which also embraced developing countries peripheral to its main commercial interests – reveals that the new bilateralism was not driven exclusively, nor in many cases predominantly, by market access considerations. It is also related to an attempt to establish what Craig VanGrasstek (2000: 169–7, cited in Phillips 2005: 9) calls a 'spiral of precedents' intended to influence the trade agenda of subsequent bilateral, regional and multilateral negotiations.

Returning specifically to the CARIFORUM EPA, the preamble to the agreement set out a series of lofty aims and objectives wherein the notion of 'development cooperation' figured prominently ('development cooperation' and 'cooperation' appeared in the text 13 times and 135 times respectively). More substantively, the agreement liberalizes approximately 92 per cent of bilateral CARIFORUM-EU trade over a 25-year period, although most of the liberalization occurs in the first 10 years. Further, the agreement is based on the principle of 'asymmetrical reciprocity' which means that, whereas the EU is committed to offering DFQF treatment to 100 per cent of the value of its imports from CARIFORUM from 1 January 2008 (with the exception of the transitional arrangements for sugar and rice), CARIFORUM will liberalize 82.7 per cent of the value of its imports from the EU within the first 15 years and 86.9 per cent within 25 years. The agreement also extends the principle of asymmetrical reciprocity to the liberalization of services, where the EU sectoral commitment provides 94 per cent coverage compared to 65 per cent for CARIFORUM 'lesser-developed countries', 75 per cent for 'more-developed countries' and 86 per cent in the case of the Dominican Republic. It is important to remember at this stage that, insofar as the goods agreement is concerned, the principle of asymmetrical reciprocity was largely nominal because approximately 95 per cent of CARIFORUM exports to the EU have benefited from preferential trade since 1975. It should also be noted that the value of goods that the EU exports to CARIFORUM is an estimated four-fifths greater that the value of goods that CARIFORUM exports to the EU. Hence the adjustment costs associated with the shift to reciprocity will be borne more or less exclusively by CARIFORUM (ECLAC 2008: 27). The presence of lengthy transition periods, along with product exclusions for the most sensitive items, make it difficult at this stage to predict what the precise costs associated with liberalization will actually entail. Yet initial studies suggest that the shift towards reciprocity will involve significant challenges, especially in the area of fiscal adjustment in a region containing seven of the ten most heavily indebted countries in the world and where import duties as a per cent of total tax revenue range from between 7.6 per cent and 50.2 per cent (World Bank 2005; Milner 2005).

The CARIFORUM agreement contains a number of more specific market access provisions that have attracted controversy because of their potentially adverse development implications. One area of complaint has centred on the presence of a 'standstill clause' within the CARIFORUM text, under which signatories will be obligated to respect fixed tariff ceilings even before they are reduced or eliminated altogether. This principle is controversial because it goes against current practice within the WTO, which merely requires tariff liberalization over a reasonable length of time without any stipulation that duties are maintained at a predetermined rate prior to their eventual reduction or elimination (South Centre 2008: 3). Another widely discussed provision is the so-called 'MFN clause' mandating CARIFORUM to extend to the EU any more favourable treatment granted to a 'major trading country' in a subsequent FTA. This has led some to argue that the MFN clause will diminish any future bargaining leverage that CARIFORUM would have in signing an FTA with a major developing county like Brazil, India or China, since the region would be unable to offer preference margins vis-à-vis the EU to any country or group of countries or would otherwise have to extend these trade benefits to the EU (Tidiane and Hanson 2008).[9] The presence of the MFN clause also raised the possibility that this, along with other aspects of the CARIFORUM agreement, may come to jeopardize the unilateral trade concessions offered to the Caribbean by the United States and Canada under the CBERA and CARIBCAN respectively (Lande 2008). Furthermore, if as seems likely these preferences eventually give way to reciprocal FTAs, the precedents set in the EPA would make it extremely difficult for the Caribbean to resist the pressure to grant similar concessions to the United States and Canada.

Beyond market access, the CARIFORUM agreement includes a number of other commitments that are neither mandated by the WTO nor under discussion in the current Doha round. According to the South Centre (2008: 3–4), the CARIFORUM agreement contains provisions in five main areas – the elimination of customs duties; rules governing trade-defence instruments; prohibition on export taxes; removal of technical barriers to trade; and regulatory harmonization with respect to customs administration and trade facilitation – but only the first is actually required by WTO rules. Furthermore, the CARIFORUM text also contains a whole raft of other measures relating to the harmonization of domestic regulations, ranging from transparency in government procurement to investment, from competition policy to intellectual property protection to rules on data protection. The rationale that is offered for inclusion of these measures is that, while they may not be required by the WTO nor be under discussion in the Doha round, they never-theless pertain to regulatory 'best practice' and will facilitate key develop-ment objectives of the EPA in the sense of enhancing the general economic competitiveness of the Caribbean (European Commission 2008: 2).

It is also suggested that, because the CARIFORUM agreement is informed by development rather than trade objectives, these provisions are not directly comparable to those contained within the more comprehensive regional and bilateral FTAs established by the United States. The investment provisions contained within the EPA, for example, do not seek to guarantee investors protection against expropriation of their property without fair compensa-tion; nor do these provisions include a dispute-settlement process granting investors recourse to legal arbitration as in the case of Chapter 11 of NAFTA (European Commission 2008a; Westcott 2008). Similarly, it is argued that the trade disciplines relating to government procurement in the CARIFORUM Agreement are based largely on 'best endeavour' language designed to promote transparency in the awarding of government contracts. As such, these provisions are considerably weaker than those contained within the WTO plurilateral Agreement on Government Procurement, to which the EU is a key signatory (Dawar 2008). Nevertheless, the presence of so many behind-the-border provisions within the EPA text – irrespective of whether or not they are based on weaker trade disciplines than those contained within other agreements – remains contentious for the simple reason that they are not strictly necessary to satisfy WTO compatibility. The inclusion of these provisions is also difficult to square with the stance adopted by the Caribbean in other diplomatic settings, where its stated position has been to resist trade issues that might prejudice the outcome of the Doha round. Finally, it needs to be recalled that CARIFORUM remains the only region belonging to the ACP which has so far signed a 'full' EPA containing these WTO-plus measures.

Understanding the CARIFORUM-EU EPA as a 'political bargain': power asymmetry, development trade-offs and the erosion of policy space

The purpose of this, penultimate section of the chapter is to gauge the deeper motives behind the CARIFORUM EPA. We do this by relating the specifics of the agreement to the broader debate outlined earlier regarding the trade-off between the immediate economic benefits of improved and more secure market access against the longer-term costs of sacrificing devel-opment policy space. To recall, because regional and bilateral FTAs are said to take place in the absence of power-balancing institutions, asymmetries in negotiating power are more likely to lead to asymmetries in negotiating outcome. In the case of the EPA, the precise bargaining dynamics were obvi-ously shaped by an enormous disparity between the two parties in terms of technical, bureaucratic and negotiating capacity. In more substantive terms, however, the defining characteristic of the EPA was the extent to which EU-CARIFORUM trade relations are based on a high degree of what Shadlen (2008) calls political trade dependence – at least in the sense that the overwhelming majority of CARIFORUM's exports to the EU were up until this point dependent on unilateral trade concessions. This provided EU negotiators with a degree of political leverage that would not have existed in the absence of such political trade dependence. Conversely, because the EU had little to gain from the EPA in strict commercial terms, CARIFORUM lacked an equivalent source of political leverage with which it could counterbalance the negotiations. In fact, to the extent that CARIFORUM possessed any meaningful influence over the course of the negotiations, it was more likely to be derived from its apparent eagerness to sign an agreement, thus providing symbolic affirmation of the merits of the EU's post-Cotonou trade vision.[10]

In 2008, the CRNM published a policy briefing identifying at least six separate justifications for why it was deemed necessary to not only sign an EPA, but to do so on the basis of an agreement that went beyond what was strictly necessary to meet the legal requirements of the WTO.[11] Although limited space precludes a thorough analysis of each of these justifications, the remainder of this chapter considers a few of the more pertinent issues in order to provide a snapshot of how and in what ways power asymmetry shaped the political bargain of the CARIFORUM-EU EPA. First of all, the CRNM cited the objective of binding the current level of EU preferences available through the Cotonou Agreement and safeguarding these preferences from further WTO litigation. To once again invoke Shadlen's terminology, this objective seems to correspond to political trade dependence in the sense that the CRNM was motivated by the need to defend existing preferences rather than secure additional market access. Yet if the motive was to lessen the region's political trade dependence it would have made far more sense for the Caribbean to have prioritized an FTA with the United States, which absorbs approximately 55 per cent the region's total exports – almost all facilitated by unilateral trade preferences – compared to just 11 per cent in the case of the EU. In any case, it is far from certain that the CARIFORUM agreement actually succeeded in making EU trade preferences more secure. This is almost certainly not true with respect to key agricultural commodities like bananas and sugar where the EU had already independently signalled its intention to extend the process of internal and external liberalization to the point where sectoral preferences to the Caribbean will be practically worthless.[12] The concept of political trade dependence also has difficulty explaining why Caribbean heads of government and the CRNM found it necessary to eschew the option made available by the EU and favoured by the majority of the ACP of signing a 'goods only' interim agreement – which would have been sufficient to immunize Lomé preferences from further

WTO litigation – with the contentious WTO-plus issues dealt with over a longer schedule after 1 January 2008. Finally, and related to this, even though as a region the Caribbean historically made more use of traditional Lomé preferences than the rest of the ACP, this still does not explain why it would be willing to sign up to a WTO-plus agreement, when the rest of the ACP resisted these issues without apparently jeopardizing a market access agreement.

A second justification offered by the CRNM for the necessity of the EPA rested on improving access to the EU market for non-traditional Caribbean exports as a means of fostering economic diversification and lessening the region's long-standing dependence on agricultural commodities blighted by preference erosion and declining terms of trade. This objective is particularly important for understanding why the CRNM chose to forgo the option of a 'goods only' interim agreement. According to CRNM officials, concerns regarding the fiscal implications of import liberalization for those islands heavily dependent on tariff revenue meant that securing a 'goods only' agreement was far more politically contentious than securing agreement on the WTO-plus provisions. Hence the CRNM saw little merit in an interim agreement limited to trade in goods.[13] Moreover, as Ambassador Richard Bernal (2008: 22), the CRNM Chief Negotiator during the EPA negotiations, has put it, a 'goods only' EPA 'would have entailed the adjustment costs of liberalization without garnering the gains from the inclusion of services, investment and development-boosting measures'. Echoing Gruber's concept of 'bandwagoning', CRNM officials have also suggested that their willingness to engage in serious talks prior to the expiry of the Cotonou waiver, before other ACP regions got their act together, persuaded EU negotiators to cede considerable ground to CARIFORUM in order to secure a more comprehensive agreement.[14] In support of this, the CRNM point to a number of aspects of the CARIFORUM agreement which appear to grant significant concessions to the region while providing favourable access to the EU market. The most notable provisions in this respect include EU commitments regarding the temporary movement of natural persons (Mode IV), granting Caribbean professionals market access for the supply of cross-border services in 29 different industries, lengthy transition periods for the removal of tariffs to enable revenue-dependent economies to undertake tax reform, plus the exclusion of approximately 75 per cent of agriculture for any import liberalization and the exemption of sensitive sectors like public services and utilities from commitments under the investment chapter.[15]

While the significance of these concessions should not be underplayed, the extent to which the CARIFORUM text as a whole will be sufficient to spur the kind of economic diversification envisaged by the CRNM remains debatable. Indeed, some critics have argued that the EPA is more likely to achieve the precise opposite (Brewster, Girvan and Lewis 2008; South Centre 2008). The main reason for this, they suggest, is that the CARIFORUM agreement mainly consists of improving market access, even if only marginally, for traditional commodities like rum, beef and dairy products while exposing the region to a greater level of import competition for higher-value added industrial and other processed goods. Hence, the EPA will reinforce rather than lessen the Caribbean's existing terms of trade. Furthermore, it is argued that the level of tariff and regulatory harmonization required by EPA risks robbing the region of the very policy tools that might be used to effect a successful diversifications strategy. Although tariffs constitutes only one of a number of WTO-compatible policy tools potentially available to assist developing countries, discretion over this area is seen as particularly important for small states which lack the resources required to implement larger-scale industrial policies (South Centre 2008: 18).

As we have seen, the EPA requires CARIFORUM to eventually remove close to 90 per cent of the tariffs currently levied on imports from the EU. The lengthy transitions periods and product exclusions secured for sensitive imports do potentially offer a means – albeit mostly temporary – to mitigate the loss of tariff policy space. Yet even here the CRNM has taken less-than-full advantage of the available flexibilities since even the EU's conservative interpretation of Article XXIV would permit the exclusion of a much higher proportion of trade than actually granted under EPA.[16] Furthermore, to the extent that the CRNM did take advantage of available flexibilities with respect to transition periods and product exclusions, its negotiating position seems to have been largely informed by static considerations related to the need to protect fiscal revenue and agricultural interests rather than dynamic considerations related to longer-term industrial policy objectives (South Centre 2008: 8). Where specific industrial policy objectives are cited explicitly in the EPA text, the relevant provisions are generally characterized by attendant restrictions and limitations that render such mechanisms difficult to invoke. In the case of the EPA Safeguard Clause which offers protection for infant industries, for example, the provision restricts action to the first ten years of the agreement and defines 'infant industries' in such a way so as to exclude cases where imports may be hindering the start up of an industry that does not yet exist. The Safeguard Clause also limits action to a rise in import duty only to the level of the *current* bound rate under the WTO, meaning that the safeguard would be rendered immediately obsolete following a successful outcome to the Doha round (South Centre 2008: 13).

A third justification offered by the CRNM to account for the relatively far-reaching nature of the CARIFORUM agreement relates to the aim of strengthening and reinvigorating the Caribbean regional integration process. This objective has been advanced by the EU in support of the EPAs elsewhere (see Chapter 4) – but it has added resonance in the Caribbean due to the relatively advanced stage of the regional integration process. Even so, it is not altogether clear how and in what specific ways EPAs actually serve to strengthen or invigorate the regional integration process, either in the

Caribbean or elsewhere in the ACP. One the key challenges presented by the CARIFORUM agreement resides in those areas where the level of trade liberalization and regulatory harmonization goes beyond what has been agreed to at the regional level. In spite of the launching of the Caribbean Single Market Economy (CSME) in 2006, one estimate suggests that close to one-half of the measures required for the Single Market are yet to be implemented – including a number of areas such as government procurement, e-commerce and the free circulation goods which are contained in the EPA (Girvan 2008: 6). Another problem relates to the 'regional preference' clause (see Chapter 4) which obliges CARIFORUM signatories to extend to each other the same treatment they extend to the EU. This clause is seen as controversial even within the English-speaking Caribbean due to a divergence in base rates and individual liberalization schedules, but it is potentially far more problematical in the case of the Dominican Republic whose market access offer includes no less than 125 tariff lines excluded by CARICOM (South Centre 2008: 23). Although an FTA between CARICOM and the Dominican Republic was signed in 1998 and entered into force in 2001, the agreement is yet to extend the liberalization in goods to services while the level of regulatory harmonization eventually envisaged is not comparable to the EPA. Finally, concern has been expressed about the different approaches of CARICOM and EPA towards the question of SDT for the region's lesser-developed countries. Although the CARIFORUM agreement does contain a number of references to SDT, their precise meaning remains ambiguous which has provoked some of the smaller economies like Belize to complain that they are being robbed of important derogations and flexibilities permitted under both the CSME and the CARICOM-Dominican Republic FTA.[17]

A fourth and final justification offered by the CRNM for the EPA relates to development assistance and, more particularly, the belief that a willingness to sign a comprehensive agreement would place CARIFORUM in an advantageous position vis-à-vis the rest of the ACP with respect to the financial component of the EPAs. The European Commission committed funds from the 10th EDF Caribbean Regional and National Indicative Programmes (CRIP/NIP), worth approximately €454 million and €39 million respectively, to support EPA implementation. The Commission has also pledged to commit approximately half of its annual €2 billion Aid for Trade contribution to support ACP countries, largely though not exclusively through EPA implementation projects.[18] Yet, despite numerous references to 'development cooperation' in the text the financial component of the CARIFORUM agreement remains almost entirely unbound. In this sense, the political bargain behind the EPA can be said to resemble the lopsided deal struck in the Uruguay round wherein developing countries agreed to take on 'bound commitments to implement in exchange for unbound commitments of assistance to implement' (Finger and Schuler 2000: 514). What makes this comparison particularly apposite is that the EPA itself does not

contain a funding facility but simply reaffirms that development cooperation will be facilitated by existing aid mechanisms linked to the Cotonou
Agreement and the EDF. This being case, historical precedent would suggest
that funds earmarked to support the implementation of the EPA are likely
to be characterized by a significant, if not an indefinite, time lag between
the announcement and disbursement of financial aid (Grynberg and Clarke
2006). Even if this proves not to be the case, the actual resources that the EU
has pledged to support EPA are likely to be dwarfed by the actual adjustment
and implementation costs which one study has placed close to €1 billion
(Milner 2005). Finally, because these financial commitments have been
conceived within the context of asymmetrical bargaining, it seems plausible
to expect that, to the extent that development finance is available to support
the EPA, it is likely to reflect the EU's priority of targeting narrowly-defined
trade adjustment and implementation needs rather than addressing wider
capacity issues which might enable Caribbean countries to come to terms
with reciprocal free trade.

Conclusion

In this chapter we have sought to resolve the puzzle of why CARIFORUM
chose to break ranks with the ACP in order to sign a 'full' EPA, even though
the option remained of signing a less onerous 'goods only' agreement. The
straightforward solution to this puzzle draws attention to key differences in
terms of regional institutions, economic interests and available policy choices.
But these differences cannot explain the nature of the CARIFORUM agreement. On the one hand, even though the bureaucratic autonomy and technical competence of the CRNM provided CARIFORUM with the 'capacity' to
negotiate a comprehensive EPA, the agreement itself was neither a necessary
nor sufficient condition for safeguarding preferences. On the other hand, to
the extent that a willingness to sign a comprehensive EPA enabled the CRNM
to extract important concessions from the EU, it appears that CARIFORUM
has surrendered significant amounts of policy space (among numerous other
things) in exchange for trade benefits that in many cases may very well turn
out to be illusory. Given that the EPA is based on lengthy transition periods
designed to cushion the effects of liberalization, it is likely to be some time
before the long-term development consequences of the agreement become
clear. Even so, the precedents set in the CARIFORUM text are likely to impact
well beyond the region's bilateral relationship with the EU by redefining the
ideological and policy parameters of the Caribbean's wider trade and development options for some time to come.

Since EPAs constitute a subset of a much wider pattern of trade governance, the significance of this chapter goes beyond the specifics of the
CARIFORUM agreement. Not only does this case provide further confir-
mation of the skewed developmental consequences of North-South trade

bargaining, it adds more weight to VanGrasstek's (2000: 169–7) claim that the wider motive behind such agreements is to create a 'spiral of precedents' intended to influence the trade agenda of subsequent bilateral, regional and multilateral negotiations. Theoretically speaking, the chapter has served to substantiate what is already known about the limited choice set available to developing countries in bilateral trade negotiations; it has also provided further evidence of how the absence of power-mitigating institutions serves to intensify the development trade-offs that are invariably necessary in these scenarios. On the question of motives, however, the nuances of the CARIFORUM case call into question some of the theoretical assumptions underpinning the existing literature. Gruber's concept of 'bandwagoning', for example, provides important clues as to why changes to the status quo would alter the strategic calculations of preference-dependent countries, but it does not explain why this is precipitative in some cases but not others even though they may share similar economic interests. Likewise, Shadlen's notion of 'political trade dependence' is only useful if we can establish a causal link between the degree of dependence and the willingness to sign a reciprocal FTA. Not only are there reasons to doubt that this was the case with CARIFORUM, we have also shown that the EPA largely failed to place preferences – especially for key commodities like bananas and sugar which have been disproportionately and adversely affected by preference erosion – on a more stable or secure footing.

Applied specifically to our case, the shortcomings of existing theories suggest that the EPAs are at least to some degree defined by features that are more particular to the ACP. In this respect, there are two points that are especially worth reiterating. First, an important but often-unremarked fact is that the ACP is dominated numerically by very small, trade- and aid-dependent states, with over half the ACP possessing populations of less than two million people. The importance of this, with respect to the issues explored in this chapter, is that the immediate concern for the smaller countries of the ACP was the fiscal rather than the trade implications of import liberalization, due to a heavy dependence on tariff revenue to fund government spending. As we have shown in the case of the Caribbean, the preoccupation with the loss of import duties proved to be far more politically contentious than a WTO-plus agreement. This calculation was not just down to the immediacy of import liberalization, but also to the widespread perception in the region that the islands possessed neither the resources nor the capacity to effect a state-led development strategy. This does not mean, however, that the 'smallness' of the Caribbean simply determined its EPA preferences; rather, the loss of regulatory policy autonomy came with fewer short-term distributive effects and thus constituted a politically-acceptable quid pro quo for EU concessions in areas where the costs were far more tangible. In these circumstances, it is not entirely surprising that CARIFORUM was willing to sacrifice development policy tools even for relatively modest gains in market access. Second, the

EPA process was shaped by the wider distributive politics of the ACP. In the case of CARIFORUM, the belief was that a willingness to sign a comprehensive agreement – and to do so first – was key to extracting important concessions from the EU in areas such as Mode IV, delayed liberalization schedules and product exemptions, and – most importantly – preferential access to development finance. In sum, the CARIFORUM agreement was not simply a product of a unique set of institutional structures or economic interests. It also constituted a political bargain forged in a highly asymmetrical context, wherein the EU's market and financial power was amplified by the vulnerabilities, competitive dynamics and interregional rivalries inside the ACP.

4
European Policy Diffusion and the Politics of Regional Integration in the Pacific

One of the major criticisms levelled at unilateral preference schemes is that they discourage 'South-South' trade by inhibiting local integration through encouraging preference-receiving firms to target exports at preference-granting countries rather than regional trading partners (see Chapter 2). Accordingly, the promotion of regionalism and the furthering of 'South-South' trade are seen as vital components in cushioning the loss of preferences and smoothing the transition to reciprocal free trade. In the case of the EPAs – again the main focus of the chapter – the EU has arguably gone the furthest in this direction by introducing a so-called 'regional preference' clause by which the removal of intraregional trade barriers between ACP countries represented a *precondition* for the maintenances of trade privileges (albeit now on the basis of reciprocity). This mechanism can be traced back to the Cotonou Agreement, which linked the successful conclusion of WTO-compatible EPAs to creating and consolidating regional institutions in accordance with the regional configurations identified later by the European Commission. The general vagueness of Cotonou meant that, at the time, the precise means by which these two processes would be causally linked remained underspecified. But even at an early stage it was easy to detect a tension between the need to conclude the EPAs before the expiry of the WTO waiver on 31 December 2007 and the logically prior necessity of creating viable regional institutions on which to base the agreements. On the one hand, the impending expiry of the waiver, coupled with the EU's implied threat to downgrade ACP countries to the (vastly inferior) GSP, provided the former with an obvious source of political leverage over the latter in its aim of securing reciprocal free trade. On the other hand, the desire to conclude these agreements on an interregional basis meant that in practice this political leverage was immediately dissipated because of the vastly differing levels of preference-dependence – and hence sensitivity to the effects of liberalization – within each ACP region. In sum, from the outset the two principal objectives of the trade component of the Cotonou Agreement – WTO consistency and the promotion of regional integration – appeared to be pulling in different directions.

In this chapter, we seek to understand and explain why, how and with what consequences the EU has attempted to promote regional economic integration in the context of its post-Lomé trade vision. Although the EU model of regionalism is often regarded as the quintessential case of successful integration, and has traditionally served as a beacon for region-building processes in other parts of the world, it is only within the last few years that external support for this has been promoted as an explicit policy objective (Aggarwal and Fogarty 2004; Söderbaum and Van Langenhove 2006; Telò 2007; Lombaerde and Shultz 2009). In theoretical terms, the external promotion of regionalism chimes with social constructivist notions of the EU as a 'civilian' or 'normative' power (Manners 2002; Orbie 2008). In other words, interregionalism, as the process has become known, provides a vehicle for the advancement of a distinctively 'European' norm-based model of international relations. At the same time, it is said to be driven by the desire to uphold the EU as a 'model for regional integration between countries in other regions of the world' (European Commission 2004: 3), thus serving to underscore and legitimize the EU as a global 'actor' and regionalism as the exemplar for post-Westphalian governance (Söderbaum, Stålgren and Van Langenhove 2005; Aggarwal and Fogarty 2004). Finally, these norm-based accounts do not dismiss questions of material interests; on the contrary, the promotion of regionalism is inextricably bound up with the furthering of the EU's economic and commercial interests – particularly within the context of the Lisbon Agenda designed to promote the EU as 'the most competitive and dynamic knowledge-based economy in the world'. In official public discourse, the EU has sought to promote the idea that strengthening regional trade links through liberalization and the furthering of its own international competitiveness represent two sides of the same coin – a process, moreover, that is deemed by EU policy makers to be of particular benefit to the developing countries (Siles-Brügge 2012).

In exploring the political dynamics of the external promotion of regionalism, then, this chapter engages critically with wider debates concerning the EU's purported civilian or normative power. The main empirical reference point for the chapter is the case of the Pacific. The Pacific ACP (PACP) is, arguably, the most problematic of the seven groupings that currently make up the EPA regional configuration: the 'region' consists of some 14 island states belonging to one of three distinct subgroups of countries – Melanesia, Micronesia and Polynesia – scattered across a huge archipelago covering an oceanic area some 20 million km², six of which are classified as LDCs while only four are actually full members of the WTO (Primack 2007: 4). The PACP is characterized by low levels of inter- *and* intraregional trade, with the EU accounting for just 11 per cent of the region's exports and 4 per cent of its imports in the mid-2000s; meanwhile, intra-PACP trade stood at a paltry 0.2 per cent (South Centre 2007: 4, 15). All told, the objective conditions in the PACP appear to go a long way to explaining why, in this particular case, the external promotion of regional economic integration has stuttered. Yet despite the apparent 'outlier' status of the PACP within the context of the EPAs, a closer inspection of the overall pattern suggests it is a good deal closer to the norm than the case of CARIFORUM examined in the previous chapter: indeed, it is only in the latter case and that of the East African Community (EAC) that all countries belonging to the relevant 'region' have actually got to the point of signing a full or even interim EPA. In all other cases, the interim EPAs rest on bilateral or subregional configurations out of step with the local integration projects on which they are supposedly based.

The question that we are concerned with in this chapter is why the EU insisted – via the regional preference clause – on regionalism as a precondition for the maintenance of trade preferences and why this strategy has seemingly foundered? The extant ACP trade literature provides us with some clues to where we might find answers to these two questions. Chris Stevens (2006), for example, expresses the problem in terms of the disruptive effects of externally driven liberalization as an 'unintended consequence' of policy leverage, as individual countries within each region adopt different (in many cases mutually incompatible) liberalization schedules under EU pressure to satisfy WTO trade rules. There is no doubt that this is the case. But the emphasis on 'unintended consequences' does not get to grips with the fundamental issue of why the EU adopted this approach in the first place or why its officials failed to notice (or chose to ignore) these problems. One possible explanation for this is found in the more overtly 'critical' literature that has interpreted the external promotion of regional integration through the lenses of the independent, economic and commercial interests of the EU (Goodison 2007; Stoneman and Thompson 2007; Brewster, Girvan and Lewis 2008; Hurt 2012; Buzdugan 2013). This motive cannot be discounted but it does rather beg the question of why the EU persisted with the insistence on regionalism as the organizing principle behind the EPAs, since it hardly made the task of securing reciprocal free trade – if indeed this is the ultimate commercial imperative – with the ACP any easier.

In this chapter, we aim to provide a more nuanced understanding of the EU's promotion of regionalism. In the next (second) section, we explore the extant literature on the EU's global role in promoting interregionalism in greater critical depth to provide a conceptual frame for what then follows. The third and fourth sections of the chapter are more substantive and deal specifically with the promotion of regional integration within the context of the EPAs. In the third section, we trace the origins and subsequent development of the EU regional integration agenda for the ACP through Lomé to Cotonou to the EPAs. The fourth section draws primarily (but not exclusively) on the Pacific case and ties this to three distinctive features of the

EPAs – the legal ambiguity concerning eligibility for preferential treatment, the limited and uneven nature of the EU's policy leverage, and the blurring of the boundaries between the EU's developmental and commercial priorities – that, it will be argued, provide the key to understanding why the external promotion of regionalism has been met with less success than might have been expected. The final, concluding section briefly summarizes the main findings and implications (both theoretical and substantive) of the chapter.

Theorizing interregionalism

Accounts of the EU's role in international affairs often begin by citing François Duchêne's concept of Europe as a 'civilian power' (Orbie 2008; Telò 2007). The most frequently cited variant of Duchêne's original concept is the closely-related idea of 'normative power' pioneered by Ian Manners. The central insight provided by Manners was to show a close affinity between the normative underpinnings of the EU as a set of institutions and the types of external policies it tends to pursue. Manners (2002) argued that a mixture of historical context, the existence of a hybrid polity and legal constitution meant that the EU was uniquely committed to putting internal norms at the centre of its external relations. Specifically, Manners (2002: 242–3) highlighted five 'core' norms (peace, liberty, democracy, the rule of law and human rights) and four 'minor' norms (social solidarity, anti-discrimination, sustainable development and good governance) that supposedly lay at the heart of the EU's international relations. In short, the values that were integral to the formation and subsequent consolidation of the European project represent the cornerstone of the external projection of its power.

The key insight provided by Manners was not so much to draw attention to the normative character of the EU's external relations in substantive policy terms – although this was presumably important to the overall argument – but rather to make a connection between the EU as a distinct institutional form and political entity, and its presence in global politics. In this sense, 'the most important factor shaping the international role of the EU is not what it does or what it says, *but what it is*' (Manners 2002: 252, emphasis added). Applying this logic to our case, it is possible to identify a close affinity between the EU's institutional and normative character and its support for regional integration elsewhere. Bjorn Hettne (2005), for example, describes the EU's commitment to spreading regionalism as the by-product of a 'regionalist ideology', informing both intra-EU affairs and the support for region-building processes in other parts of the world. The European project is premised on the belief that economic integration offers the best means of preventing conflict (Kühnhardt 2003); it therefore follows that the external promotion of regionalism holds the key to securing peace, democratic consolidation and good governance. Similarly, the promotion of interregionalism as the basis for world order is closely associated with the EU's particular emphasis on economic growth and sustainable development. During the late 1990s and 2000s, the idea that openness to trade and economic integration approximated economic growth and hence poverty reduction came to dominate EU policy discourse (Doidge 2011). The key summative point is that the normative underpinnings of the European project – with an emphasis on liberal internationalism and the promotion of peace, prosperity and social justice – are said to form the basis for the EU's external economic policy and that interregionalism constitutes the ultimate expression of this vision.

The emphasis placed by the extant literature on the EU's external relations as a 'spillover' effect from its internal organization and value system helps us to understand why European policy makers would seek to lend support to regional integration in other parts of the world. But this does not necessarily explain why the promotion of regionalism emerged as an explicit policy objective – or why it did at a relatively late stage in the EU's gestation. It is at this point that we encounter an additional set of arguments concerning the EU's place in the world. According to these arguments, the EU's external relations stem not just from internal norms and identity but are also increasingly part of a conscious effort to promote and legitimize its 'presence' and 'actorness' to the rest of the world. As Fredrik Söderbaum and his colleagues explain:

> During the last decade it seems to have become evident in the Commission and in leading policy circles that the EU's increasing economic weight and geographical size are linked to an imperative to become a global actor by playing a more important political and security role in the world. Thus, in order to play such a global role in the world, it is necessary that the EU increases its 'actorness' and attain the qualities of an actor that is capable of making more autonomous foreign policy decisions. (Söderbaum, Stålgren and Van Langenhove 2005: 371)

In other words, to the extent that there is a common theme underpinning the EU's external relations, it can be summed up as establishing it as an effective and legitimate global actor. Jean Grugel (2004: 621) argues, in this vein, that the EU's export of regionalism is part of a project to set itself up as a normative power acting as 'an identity marker of what it perceives as a more humane governance model in its relations with the developing world'. This normative power, moreover, is contrasted favourably with the supposedly 'interest-based' hegemonic power of the United States, with the latter portrayed as a promoter of '(bad material) interests, while the EU exports (good moral) values' (Börzel and Risse 2009: 22). Expressed in these terms, the external promotion of regional integration not only constitutes the EU as a global actor but serves to underscore its internal legitimacy – both by juxtaposing European identity with regional 'others' (Rüland 2010: 1278) and by promoting regionalism as a universally effective and legitimate mode of global governance (Söderbaum and Van Langenhove 2006: 251).

At this point, it is important to take note of an observed shortcoming of the normative power Europe conceptual framework: namely, a reliance on a characterization of the EU that comes very close to the way in which it has sought to define itself (Robles 2008; Sjursen 2006). As Tanja Börzel and Thomas Risse (2009: 22) explain, to accept the juxtaposition between 'normative' Europe and 'self-interested' others is to reify the EU's own identity construction and take it at face value. Hence, a key point that needs to be taken from the extant literature is that interregionalism must be understood as part of a discursive strategy to construct a normative international (and domestic) identity and foreign policy agenda. As such, it is a project that should be looked upon with circumspection. The problematic nature of this juxtapositioning between norms and interests is relevant not just for how the EU is understood in relation to other global actors. It also impacts on how we intepret the presence of material interests – especially those of an economic and commerical nature – in what we might otherwise consider to be a norm-based policy agenda.

The most obvious point of reference here is the Lisbon Agenda designed to promote the EU as 'the most competitive and dynamic knowledge-based economy in the world' (George, Iwanow and Kirkpatrick 2009; Söderbaum, Stålgren and Van Langenhove 2005). In the area of external relations, Lisbon is associated most closely with the European Commission's 2006 trade strategy document, *Global Europe*. The essential thrust of this was that promoting internal competitiveness and job creation through further internal liberalization and marketization needed to run in tandem with a more offensive external trade strategy (Hay 2007; Heron and Siles-Brügge 2012). More particularly, *Global Europe* signalled the end of the EU's self-imposed 'moratorium' on commercially oriented regional and bilateral free-trade agreements introduced by Trade Commissioner Pascal Lamy in 1999 as part of a policy of 'multilateralism first', designed to advance what later became the WTO Doha round. While *Global Europe* reaffirmed the EU's continued support for the WTO, it nevertheless argued the case for FTAs going 'further and faster in promoting openness and integration' by extending coverage to issue areas like services, investment, public procurement and competition policy 'which are not ready for multilateral discussions' (European Commission 2006: 10).

The importance of all of this, with respect to the specific issues dealt with here, lies in the fact that many of the trade priorities identified in *Global Europe* found their way subsequently into the EPAs, even though these were neither mandated by the WTO nor necessarily specified in the Cotonou Agreement. This obviously complicates the argument concerning the promotion of regional integration as a norm-driven policy agenda. One way around this is to think about interregionalism as a vehicle for exporting the 'regulatory norms' that govern economic relations inside the EU to other regions of the world (Farrell 2009: 1180). In many cases, however, the evidence suggests that the EU has been equally motivated by classic power-balancing concerns. This has been noted, for instance, in the case of Latin American regionalism vis-á-vis the United States (Bajo 1999; Hardacre and Smith 2009; Roloff 2006). In other regions, such as our own case, the EU's export of its model of economic governance has been interpreted as a means of exercising control in order to exploit commercial opportunities (Farrell 2005; Söderbaum, Stålgren and Van Langenhove 2005).

How, then, do we square the circle between norm- and interest-based accounts of interregionalism? In official public discourse, the EU has sought to promote the idea that strengthening regional trade links through liberalization and the furthering of its own international competitiveness represent two sides of the same coin – a process, moreover, that is deemed by the EU to be of particular benefit to developing countries (European Commission 2004; Söderbaum, Stålgren and Van Langenhove 2005; Siles-Brügge 2012). It is tempting to dismiss this 'win-win' account of liberal economic goverance as essentially false rhetoric designed to disguise the commercial imperatives behind interregionalism. But, as was pointed out earlier, in our case the insistence on interregionalism has hardly made the task of securing recip-rocal free trade with the ACP any easier. In what follows, we start from the premise that the presence of commercial interests – which are intricately bound up with interregionalism – does not in itself invalidate the idea that this is a norm-based policy agenda. Hence, we reject the argument promoted by some that the promotion of regional integration in the context of the EPAs can be boiled down to straightforward questions of economic self-in-terest. Instead, we trace the origins and subsequent crystallization of the EU's promotion of regionalism in the ACP as a norm-based policy agenda associ-ated with neoliberal conceptions of development. In so doing, we take our cue from the (predominantly) liberal constructivist literature summarized above but then use this as a point of departure for a critical interrogation of this regional model of economic governance and the means by which the EU has sought to promote it.

Charting the EU's regional agenda for the ACP

As chronicled in Chapter 2, the Lomé convention was established in 1975 and renewed on three separate occasions – 1981, 1985, 1989 – but was ultimately deemed incompatible with multilateral trade rules and, in any case, judged to have failed in its principal objectives of promoting economic growth and diversification (European Commission 1996; Gibb 2000). Although the EU originally depicted Lomé as a series of 'free trade areas' in accordance with Article XXIV of the GATT, there is little evidence (apart from a small proportion of EDF aid allocated to regional projects) that the promotion of regional integration was given much priority – certainly in comparison with the status it was accorded under the Cotonou Agreement and the EPAs. This is not to suggest that regionalism itself did not flourish under Lomé; indeed, it was during the 'second wave' (Hurrell 1995; Breslin and Higgott 2000) of regionalism in the late 1960s and 1970s that many of the blocs that would eventually form the basis of the EPAs were first conceived. However, the prevailing orthodoxy of 'ideological neutrality' held by EU policy makers at this point in time ruled out 'the possibility of the Community living by doctrines' (European Commission, cited in Brown 2000: 368). As such, the promotion of regional integration was, like other things, largely a matter for the ACP to decide upon.

In 1996, the European Commission published its landmark *Green Paper on Relations between the European Union and the ACP Countries,* which marked the point at which the commitment to 'ideological neutrality' gave way to a creeping faith in the universalism of neoliberalism and the policy condition- ality with which it became associated. In line with these ideological trends, the policy diagnosis of Lomé offered by the *Green Paper* placed heavy emphasis on the role of 'supply-side' blockages, declaring that the 'state of institu- tions and economic policy in the recipient country have often been major constraints' on the effectiveness of trade preferences (European Commission 1996: iv). In other words, the absence of reciprocity was problematic not only because it was now incompatible with strengthened multilateral trade rules, but also because it served to inhibit the types of policy reform that were by this point deemed essential for economic development.

Although the *Green Paper* set out a number of alternative options (including the standard application of GSP, a single agreement based on the principle of uniform reciprocity and the establishment of several 'differentiated' FTAs involving individual regions and countries), the trade component of the Cotonou Agreement would eventually lead to the formulae of replacing Lomé with separate EPAs based on six regional configurations: namely, the Caribbean; the Pacific; West; Central; Eastern and Southern; and Southern Africa (SADC-minus). Yet Cotonou provided few clues how these agreements might operate in practice. In essence, the agreement rested on three separate principles: reciprocity, regionalism and differentiation. First, the principles of reciprocity and regionalism found expression in Articles 34–37, which set out the terms for replacing Lomé with reciprocal trade and cooperation agreements to the degree necessary to comply with Article XXIV. There were certainly practical reasons behind the Commission's decision to opt for regionally-based EPAs, given the heterogeneity and complexity of the ACP group that, by this point, numbered more than 70 countries.[1] However, it is difficult to ignore the fact that this blueprint coincided with a growing enthusiasm among EU policy makers for the external promotion of region- alism – an enthusiasm that rested on the belief that the EU's own unique experience meant that it had an obvious comparative advantage in offering this type of development assistance. The EU thus promised to 'add value' to the efforts of other donors (European Commission 1996: xii), in cementing the idea that South-South regionalism would foster integration into the global economy, produce economies of scale, stimulate investment and lock in trade reforms (European Commission 1995, 2002).

Second, the principle of differentiation found expression in Article 37.9, which stated that the EU would provide DFQF access to 'essentially all' LDC products by 2005, at the latest. Here the EU was seeking to reaffirm the demarcation established multilaterally under the GATT and the WTO, where the LDC concept is, to all intents and purposes, now deemed to be the only legal basis on which non-reciprocal preferences should be offered (see Chapter 2). When the EBA was launched – a mere three months after the signing of Cotonou and only six months from when Trade Commissioner Pascal Lamy first picked up on the idea – it appeared to have been designed with only the most cursory attention to how it might impact on the realization of the remainder of the post-Lomé settlement.[2] In fact, this initiative was primarily conceived in WTO circles as an early component of what became the DDA (Young 2007), as opposed to an integral component of the Cotonou Agreement. There is also evidence that its primary purpose was not, in actual fact, meeting the trade needs of the LDCs but to undercut the EU's highly restrictive sugar import regime, which had stubbornly resisted all previous reform efforts (Richardson 2009; see also Chapter 5). Either way, the EBA exposed a latent tension that existed in the Cotonou Agreement between the principles of regionalism and reciprocity, on the one hand, and that of differentiation, on the other. That is to say, even though by including the handful of UN-designated LDCs that had been excluded from Lomé the EBA effectively got around the issue of WTO incompatibility (meaning the regime was now legally consistent with the 1979 Enabling Clause – see, again, Chapter 2), this came at the cost of removing the main incentive the LDCs had for signing reciprocal EPAs or liberalizing trade bilaterally with regional trade partners, whether they be other LDCs or non-LDCs.

Although the EPA negotiations were scheduled to take place in two separate phases (the first between the EU and the ACP group as a whole and the second between the EU and the subregions that would form the basis of the final agreements) the first phase lasted little more than a year and achieved little of substance. The main reason for this is that the European Commission was anxious to proceed to the second phase of the negotiations – to the extent that it reportedly invited the subregions to begin 'informal' discussions more or less as soon as the all-ACP phase of the talks got underway (Bilal 2006: 17). At this stage, however, the precise configuration of the subregions was still to be determined. Although the Cotonou Agreement stipulated that this would be matter for the ACP, the evidence suggests that by this point the EU already had a firm idea of the final configuration it had in mind. In 2001, for example, the European Commission released a communication stating that

EPA Regional Configurations, 2004

CARIFORUM	West Africa	Central Africa	ESA	Pacific
Antigua and Barbuda	Benin	Cameroon	Burundi	Cook Islands
Bahamas	Burkina Faso	Central African Republic	Comoros	East Timor
Barbados	Cape Verde	Chad	Djibouti	Fiji
Belize	Ivory Coast	Congo	Eritrea	Kiribati
Dominica	Gambia	DR Congo	Ethiopia	Marshall Islands
Dominican Republic	Ghana	Equatorial Guinea	Kenya	Micronesia
Grenada	Guinea	Gabon	Madagascar	Nauru
Guyana	Guinea-Bissau	Sao Tome and Principe	Malawi	Niue
Haiti	Liberia		Mauritius	Palau
Jamaica	Mali	**SADC-Minus**	Rwanda	Papua New Guinea
Saint Lucia	Mauritania	Angola	Seychelles	Samoa
Saint Vincent and the Grenadines	Niger	Botswana	Somalia	Solomon Islands
Saint Kitts and Nevis	Nigeria	Lesotho	Sudan	Tonga
Surinam	Senegal	Mozambique	Uganda	Tuvalu
Trinidad and Tobago	Sierra Leone	Namibia	Zambia	Vanuatu
	Togo	Tanzania	Zimbabwe	
		Swaziland		

EPA Regional Configurations, 2013

CARIFORUM	West Africa	Central Africa	ESA	Pacific
Antigua and Barbuda	Benin	Cameroon	Comoros	Cook Islands
Bahamas	Burkina Faso	Central African Republic	Djibouti	East Timor
Barbados	Cape Verde	Chad	Eritrea	Fiji
Belize	Ivory Coast	Congo	Ethiopia	Kiribati
Dominica	Gambia	DR Congo	Madagascar	Marshall Islands
Dominican Republic	Ghana	Equatorial Guinea	Malawi	Micronesia
Grenada	Guinea	Gabon	Mauritius	Nauru
Guyana	Guinea-Bissau	Sao Tome and Principe	Seychelles	Niue
Haiti	Liberia		Somalia	Palau
Jamaica	Mali	**SADC-Minus**	Sudan	Papua New Guinea
Saint Lucia	Mauritania	Angola	Zambia	Samoa
Saint Kitts and Nevis	Niger	Botswana	Zimbabwe	Solomon Islands
Saint Vincent and the Grenadines	Nigeria	Lesotho	**EAC**	Tonga
Surinam	Senegal	Mozambique	Burundi	Tuvalu
Trinidad and Tobago	Sierra Leone	Namibia	Kenya	Vanuatu
	Togo	Swaziland	Rwanda	
			Tanzania	
			Uganda	

Figure 4.1   The EPA regional configurations

the configurations were 'not entirely at the discretion of the ACP' (European Commission 2001: 3). In setting out the criteria by which groups would qualify to take part in the negotiations, the document went on to declare, among other things, that each region must be 'effectively engaged in an economic integration process', that negotiations must take place in a single setting, lead to a single agreement and that participating countries would be prohibited from belonging to more than one subregion.

Although these criteria seemed to present few problems for the Caribbean and Pacific countries given their geographical separation from the rest of the ACP (which is not to say that these cases were unproblematic – see below), the situation was obviously more complicated in the case of sub-Saharan Africa,

Table 4.1 The EPAs – who has signed?

	CARIFORUM	Central Africa	EAC	ESA	Pacific	SADC-Minus	West Africa
Signed Full EPA	Antigua & Barbuda Bahamas Barbados Belize Dominica Dominican Republic Grenada Guyana Haiti* Jamaica Saint Lucia Saint Kitts & Nevis Saint Vincent & Grenadines Surinam Trinidad & Tobago						
Signed Interim EPA		Cameroon	Burundi* Kenya Rwanda* Tanzania* Uganda*	Madagascar* Mauritius Seychelles Zimbabwe	Fiji Papua New Guinea	Botswana Lesotho* Mozambique* Namibia† Swaziland	Ghana† Ivory Coast

| No EPA | | | | |
Signed				
Central African Republic*	Comoros*	Cook Islands	Angola*	Benin*
Chad*	Djibouti*	East Timor	South Africa	Burkina Faso*
Congo	Eritrea*	Kiribati*		Cape Verde
DR Congo*	Ethiopia*	Marshall Islands		Gambia*
Equatorial Guinea*	Malawi*	Micronesia		Guinea*
Gabon	Somalia*	Nauru		Guinea-Bissau*
Sao Tome & Principe*	Sudan*	Niue		Liberia*
	Zambia*	Palau		Mali*
		Samoa*		Mauritania*
		Solomon Islands*		Niger*
		Tonga*		Nigeria
		Tuvalu*		Senegal*
		Vanuatu*		Sierra Leone*
				Togo*

* LDCs.

† Country has initialled but not signed interim EPA.

given the plethora of overlapping regional organizations with conflicting mandates. In fact these (and other) problems affected all the subregions to some degree. For one, in no case other than the EAC – whose membership originally straddled the Eastern and Southern and SADC-minus configurations before it broke away in 2007 to form a seventh subregion – did the EPA configuration match the contours of an existing regional institution. In the case of the Caribbean, for example, the Dominican Republic's inclusion was complicated by the fact that it did not belong to CARICOM (although a limited FTA was signed between the two parties in 1998) – an anomaly that helps to explain why the former would include no less than 125 tariff lines excluded by the latter in its market access offer to the EU (South Centre 2008: 23; see also Chapter 3). In other cases, the negotiations were complicated by the presence of non-ACP countries – Australia and New Zealand (ANZ) in the case of the Pacific Islands Forum (PIF), Egypt and Libya in the case of COMESA, and, at least initially, South Africa in the case of SADC – which were excluded from the negotiations despite membership of the regional organizations charged with handling the talks.

Another problem that arose – which was especially widespread in sub-Saharan Africa – because existing regional economic obligations meant that some countries were entitled to membership of as many as three different EPA groups. In the case of SADC, for example, the 'SADC-minus' group included only seven of the fourteen members of the corresponding Regional Economic Community (REC) (Murray-Evans 2012). The incongruity between the EPA negotiating configurations and existing regional integration schemes thus raised questions about the practical implications of signing region-wide EPAs, not least of which was the possibility that the imperfect nature of the latter might serve to raise rather than lower regional trade barriers. By the same token, the Commission's insistence on region-wide reciprocal EPAs presupposed the existence of regional institutions with the bureaucratic capacity, technical competence and, perhaps most important of all, the supranational authority required to negotiate these agreements (Stevens 2008: 212). To once again cite the SADC case, this led to multiple problems within the organization's secretariat due to the fact that more than one-half of its members chose to negotiate as part of other EPA configurations. The proposed solution to this was the establishment of a small 'EPA unit' within SADC separate from the Secretariat, with very few staff, limited resources and a remit restricted to facilitating negotiations and providing technical assistance to the SADC-minus member states (Murray-Evans 2012).

On the eve of the expiry of the waiver the Europe Commission – which continued to insist that this WTO deadline was an immovable and external constraint (see, for example, European Commission 2008) – decided to permit individual countries and subregions to initial 'goods only' interim EPAs committing the signatories to the negotiation of 'full' region-wide EPAs at a later date. In order to facilitate this, a new trade regime – Market

Access Regulation (MAR) 1528 – was introduced providing temporary Lomé-equivalent treatment to ensure continuity of market access once the waiver expired. In the case of non-LDCs failing to initial an agreement, however, the expiry of the waiver would entail an automatic downgrade to the GSP. All told, the enforced rush to sign agreements by the 31 December 2007 deadline proved to be highly divisive and did little to support the EU's stated objective of promoting regional economic integration in the ACP. The one notable exception to this pattern was CARIFORUM (see Chapter 3; and also Heron 2011; Bishop, Heron and Payne 2013). The only other subregion to sign as a group was the EAC, whose defection (reportedly with the active encouragement of officials in DG Trade) from the Eastern and Southern Africa (ESA) and SADC-minus groups respectively came with a heavy price. In all other cases, the pattern reflected the skewed incentive structures generated by the conflicting principles of the Cotonou Agreement. The Pacific region offers the most vivid illustration of this, where the only countries to sign – Fiji and Papua New Guinea (PNG) – did so at the last minute and for no other reason than to protect vital sugar and tuna preferences respectively (see below; and also Primack 2007). Meanwhile, in sub-Saharan Africa, Bilal and Stevens (2009: 22) report that, apart from South Africa (which continued to trade under the 2004 Trade and Development Cooperation Agreement [TDCA]), Namibia and the oil-based economies of Congo, Gabon and Nigeria, all the continent's non-LDCs signed interim EPAs by the end of 2009. Whereas the only LDCs to do so were the four belonging to the EAC alongside the tiny mountain kingdom of Lesotho (largely due to fears about rules of origins changes affecting garment exports to the EU – see Chapter 6). But in each case the countries that signed did so according to entirely different liberalization schedules and exclusion lists (Stevens 2006, 2008). Hence while the decision to allow ACP countries to conclude interim EPAs bilaterally with the EU no doubt speeded up the process, it made the task of translating these different agreement into a regional template a Herculean task.

Explaining the limits to interregionalism

In 2011, the European Commission reported that only 36 out of 79 ACP states had signed interim EPAs, while only 18 (only four outside of CARIFORUM) were deemed to have taken sufficient steps to ratify and implement these agreements (Bilal and Ramdoo 2011). This fact, together with the accompanying failure to make much headway in promoting regional integration in the ACP, raises several important theoretical and substantive policy questions concerning the appropriateness of interregionalism as a basis for, among other things, North-South trade diplomacy. In this specific case, the question that we are most concerned with is why, in spite of the obvious power asymmetries involved and the ostensible commitment of the ACP to the goal of closer integration, the EU's promotion of regionalism has been met with so little success? In what follows, we answer this question with reference to the (predominantly) liberal constructivist literature outlined earlier but use this as a point of departure for a critical interrogation of the model of regional governance that the EU is seeking to advance and the means by which it has chosen do so. We begin by outlining the specifics of the Pacific case (which will serve as the main but not exclusive empirical reference point) before delineating the aforementioned model according to three distinctive characteristics – the legal ambiguity concerning eligibility for preferential treatment, issues of conditionality and the limited and uneven nature of the EU's policy leverage, and the blurring of the boundaries between development and commercial objectives – that, it will be argued, provide the key to understanding why the promotion of regionalism in the context of the EPAs has met with less success than might have otherwise been expected.

The case of the Pacific

The PACP region consists of 14 island countries belonging to one of three distinct subgroups of countries – Melanesia, Micronesia and Polynesia – scattered across a huge archipelago covering an oceanic area some 20 million km^2 (Primack 2007: 4). At the time of writing (late 2012), only two PACP states – Fiji and PNG – have signed an interim EPA. The remainder of the regional configuration is made of seven non-LDCs (Cook Islands, Tonga, Marshall Islands, Micronesia, Nauru, Niue and Palau), which have nominally traded under the GSP since 1 January 2008 – the only non-LDCs in the ACP apart from Namibia and the oil-based trio of Congo, Gabon and Nigeria to do so – and five LDCs (Kiribati, Samoa, Solomon Islands, Tuvalu and Vanuatu) that are eligible for EBA. Although 10 PACP states submitted market access offers to the EU in the autumn of 2007 and reportedly came very close to initialling an agreement[3], progress since then has been slow, to say the least. When the PACP trade ministers met in January 2011 to discuss a way forward and new regional EPA strategy, it was the first such meeting in 18 months, with the participants apparently still unable to agree upon the appropriate negotiating forum for handling the negotiations (Julian, Dalleau and de Roquefeuil 2011).

The prospects for a region-wide agreement in the Pacific hinge on two forms of tension that are, to greater or lesser degree, visible in the other six configurations. First, the above pattern reflects the limited and uneven nature of the EU's trade relations with the PACP and hence its ability to effect outcomes at the regional level. Although the decision of Fiji and PNG (which together account for 85 per cent of the region's total population and 78 per cent of its GDP) to initial (and later sign) interim EPAs in 2007 provided early impetus to the negotiations it did so at the cost of rendering the conclusion of a region-wide agreement more difficult to achieve. This is not least because the interim EPAs were based on very different agreements, both in terms of liberalization schedules and exclusions lists (Stevens, Kennan and Meyn

2008: 14–18). Whereas Fiji (whose overriding motive for signing was to avoid the introduction of prohibitive tariffs on its sugar exports to the EU equivalent to more than two-thirds of the total value of those exports) is committed to liberalizing approximately 81.6 per cent of its imports from the EU over a 15-year period, PNG (whose decision was based on the need to protect duty-free access to the EU market for processed tuna) liberalized close to 88 per cent of tariff lines (almost all of which was already subject to a zero rate of duty on a MFN basis, meaning that in practice this commitment involved very little in the way of actual liberalization) with immediate effect.[4]

What all this means, in effect, is that the Pacific EPA, such that it exists, is made up of two quite different trade agreements negotiated bilaterally with the EU. And even though the absence of land borders, coupled with the relatively small amount of trade with the EU, means that this is unlikely to disrupt interregional trade or lead to problems with transhipment (as is expected to be the case in much of sub-Saharan Africa), it has served to establish a series of 'soft' precedents for what the EPAs are expected to entail while, at the same time, potentially erecting barriers to the establishment of a regional-wide agreement. The main issue here is that, although the 'goods only' interim EPAs signed by Fiji and PNG contain rendezvous clauses committing the parties to conclude comprehensive agreements in the future, the region has so far steadfastly refused to move further with the negotiation of services and other forms of regulatory harmonization until these issues have been dealt with at the regional level (Bilal and Ramdoo 2010: 12). The problem with this – that is, with respect to the conclusion of a region-wide agreement – is that, if the negotiations do not succeed in moving beyond the current 'goods only' arrangements, there is little incentive for the remaining, largely serviced-based economies of the PACP to sign up, other than for reasons of regional solidarity.[5]

The second set of tensions centre on the aforementioned ambiguity concerning the appropriate negotiating forum for handling region-wide negotiations and, perhaps more crucially, the not entirely separate issue of the knock-on effect these negotiations are expected to have for trade relations with the region's immediate neighbours: namely, ANZ. When the EPA negotiations began in 2002, the PACP was not engaged in a fully fledged process of regional integration other than through the PIF and Pacific Agreement on Closer Economic Relations (PACER), both of which include ANZ. In essence, PACER constitutes the hemispheric equivalent of the Cotonou Agreement in the sense that it is designed as a mechanism for transforming trade preferences traditionally granted unilaterally by ANZ to the Pacific islands under the South Pacific Regional Trade and Economic Cooperation Agreement (SPATECA) into a fully reciprocal regional free trade agreement under the auspice of the so-called 'PACER-plus' initiative.[6]

The complication is that the timeframe for negotiations leading to this outcome, which were not scheduled to begin until 2011 (Kelsey 2005: 45), was disrupted by the decision of Fiji and PNG to initial interim EPAs, which ANZ officials deemed to be sufficient to trigger an MFN clause in the PACER agreement requiring 'consultations as soon as practical with Australia and New Zealand, whether individually or jointly, with a view to commencement of negotiations of free trade agreements' (PACER Article 6 (3) (a), as cited in Pacific Institute of Public Policy 2008: 2). The Pacific islands states were thus confronted with the prospect of negotiating separate reciprocal FTAs with the EU and ANZ at the same time, guided by the fear that any agreement signed with the former had the potential to set important precedents for negotiations with the latter, with whom the economic implications of freer trade would likely be far more significant (South Centre 2007; Nathan Associates 2007; Pacific Institute of Public Policy 2009). Meanwhile, to complicate matters even further, the PACP states belatedly launched their own regional integration process exclusive of ANZ in the form of the Pacific Island Countries Trade Agreement (PICTA), which was established in 2003. Although PICTA has made only modest progress toward promoting regional economic integration beyond the Melanesia Spearhead Group (MSG) – Fiji, PNG, Solomon Islands and Vanuatu – its significance as a potential alternative to the PIF for handling the EPAs heightened significantly following the decision to suspend Fiji from the latter (despite the fact that the regional Secretariat is housed in the country's capital of Suva) in 2009 because of its failure to abide by an ultimatum to hold democratic elections by March of that year.[7]

The legal ambiguity concerning eligibility for preferential treatment

The numerous complexities outlined above no doubt lend credence to the interpretation of the Pacific as an 'outlier' case with respect to the wider prospects for regionally-based EPAs. However, as we have hinted already, even though the objective conditions in the PACP go some way to explaining why the EU's commitment to interregionalism failed to resonate in this particular case, the underlying political dynamics share much in common with the experience elsewhere in the ACP. In search of a more general explanation, we therefore take a closer look at the (more or less) generic model of regional integration that the EU has promoted. In this subsection, we focus on the first of three distinctive features of the EPAs – the confusion surrounding eligibility for preferential treatment – and reveal the extent to which this stems not so much from the external constraints imposed by multilateral trade disciplines (although clearly this cannot be ignored), but from the specific ways that EU policy makers chose to link the *necessity* of reciprocity for the purpose of satisfying WTO trade rules with its *desirability* as a means of fostering neoliberal policy reform.

The first point to note is that it has become something of a truism to attribute the general failure of the EU's regional integration agenda for the ACP to Trade Commissioner Pascal Lamy's fateful decision in 2001 to grant

DFQF treatment to the LDCs unilaterally under the EBA (see, among the many possible examples of this, Ravenhill 2004; Stevens 2008). To do so, however, begs an obvious question: in designing a successor to Lomé why did the EU seek to differentiate between LDCs and non-LDCs with respect to eligibility for preferential treatment in the first place and how is it that it has been unable to reconcile this objective with the promotion of regional integration? A common answer to these questions centres on the issue of policy incoherence brought about by the competing bureaucratic interests and overlapping competences of DG Trade, on the one hand, and DG Development, on the other (Carbone 2007; van den Hoven 2007). While this interpretation in not entirely wide of the mark, it does rather neglect the fact that the 1996 *Green Paper* – which established the differentiation between LDCs and non-LDCs – was authored entirely by officials in DG Development and before DG Trade had responsibility for the ACP (Siles-Brügge 2012: 172).

Other explanations, instead, focus on the sheer diversity and complexity of the ACP as a source of the difficulties. John Ravenhill (2004: 135), in this vein, refers to the general absence in the ACP of 'a coincidence between geography and level of development', meaning that the two categories of countries – LDCs and non-LDCS – are scattered across each region (the Caribbean being the only partial exception to this rule), which in turn makes it almost impossible to construct a regional order that at the same time corresponds with the legal requirements of multilateral trade rules. This characterization is almost certainly true. If pushed too far, however, it serves to reify the distinction between these categories and thus confirm the Commission's version of events, regarding the necessity of WTO compliance and appropriateness of Article XXIV as the means to achieve this. Although the 1996 *Green Paper* was prompted by adverse GATT rulings against the banana protocol, the normative thrust of the document was the belief that Lomé failed to achieve basic development objectives because the lack of reciprocity served to inhibit the types of policy reform that were by this point deemed essential for economic development. The corollary to this logic was that the introduction of reciprocity would not only produce a more legally robust trade regime but – and this is the crucial point – would expose the economies of the ACP to the exigencies of the global trade system, thus creating an environment conducive to market-oriented policy reform.

In order to achieve this objective the EU found it necessary to discursively present WTO compliance as an immovable and external constraint, setting the policy parameters inside of which post-Lomé trade arrangements would, by necessity, have to be conceived. The problem with this is that it oversold the robustness of GATT norms and rendered them unproblematic in a way that reduced the EU's room for manoeuvre, arguably making the goal of reciprocal free trade harder rather than easier to achieve. To put the point another way, the difficulties that the EU encountered in prosecuting its post-

Lomé trade vision do not stem, at least not primarily, from the diversity and complexity of the ACP but from the fact that eligibility for trade preferences in accordance multilateral trade disciplines is something that was never adequately addressed, either under the GATT or WTO. The reason for this, as shown in Chapter 2, is that the development provisions that evolved under the aegis of the GATT rested for the most part on ad hoc concessions rather than legally codified obligations. Despite the widespread recognition of the special and differential needs of the developing countries, eligibility for such treatment (apart from for LDCs afforded special treatment under the 1979 Enabling Clause) rested on the principle of self-declaration – a principle with close to no legal standing under international trade law (see, again, Chapter 2).

The significance of all this, with respect to the specific aims of this section of the chapter, is to show that the legal norms that the EU placed at the heart of its post-Lomé trade vision were a good deal more opaque than it was willing to acknowledge. This is not to deny that the introduction of the DSU under the WTO constituted a genuine challenge to traditional unilateral preferences – not least because of the highly informal and ad hoc basis on which these schemes typically operated. But the important point to take note of is that, the more the EU's case for reform rested on the pretext of WTO compatibility, the more it needed to rely on the GATT's idiosyncratic approach to SDT – an approach informed by a curious mix of informality and extreme legalism (Narlikar 2005; and Chapter 2 here). Applying these insights to our specific case, we begin to get a sense of the scale of the problem that the EU faced seeking to promote regional integration in a WTO-consistent way. Although – as in other cases – the passage of the EBA served to drive a wedge between the LDCs and non-LDCs, this was less of a problem in the Pacific than elsewhere in the ACP because in this case the levels of trade involved were negligible. Hence the EBA did little to lessen (or increase) the EU's bargaining leverage.

What was arguably more decisive was the absence of a clear organizing principle around which a region-wide agreement could be constructed. This absence, to be clear, was not due to the disparate nature of the PACP region. Indeed, despite the enormous geographical distances separating many of the Pacific islands their shared status as Small Island Developing States (SIDS) – a formal UN classification that has existed since 1992 – appeared to offer an obvious alternative basis on which to recast special and differential treatment for the region. The problem, of course, was that because the EU's regional agenda for the ACP was prosecuted more or else exclusively in accordance with WTO compliance and the legal requirements for satisfying Article XXIV, the only basis on which SDT provisions could be enshrined in a regional EPA was if they applied solely to LDCs. The argument, then, is that the failure of interregionalism to resonate in the Pacific should not be attributed the region's 'outlier' status. Rather, this specific case exposes the central contradiction evident in the EU's wider post-Lomé strategy between the need to satisfy the WTO rules following the expiry of the waiver on 31 December 2007 and the logically prior necessity of creating viable regional institutions on which to base the agreements.

The limited and uneven nature of the EU's policy leverage

As we have noted, the Cotonou Agreement tied the establishment of WTO-compatible EPAs to the promotion of regional integration in the ACP without identifying the precise mechanisms by which these two processes would be linked. It is worth noting in this respect that the original rationale behind the promotion of regional integration expressed in the 1996 *Green Paper* rested primarily on the *practicality* of having all ACP states coalesce around a single plan – that is, uniform reciprocity – as opposed to an explicit policy objective in and of itself (Siles-Brügge 2012: 173). Although elements of policy conditionality begun creeping into EU-ACP development cooperation from the mid-1980s this was mainly in relation to EDF resources while the centrepiece of Lomé – non-reciprocal market access – was to intents and purposes immune from these pressures. Indeed, it was precisely for this reason that EU policy makers sought to introduce reciprocity in the belief that greater exposure to global market pressures would help to promote the types of policy reform that, it was believed, would spur economic growth and diversification. The introduction of reciprocity, in other words, turned the traditional logic behind Lomé of its head by rendering preferential market access *conditional* on import liberalization. Hence the Cotonou Agreement and, even more so, the EPAs rested on the ability of the EU to exercise the policy leverage afforded by the ACP's dependence on preferences to impose domestic and regional reforms. By invoking WTO compliance as an unavoidable external constraint the beneficiaries of Lomé would be left with little alternative but sign reciprocal EPAs or else incur the loss of preferential access to a primary export market.

The flaw in this strategy, which became apparent more less as soon as the EPA negotiations began in earnest in 2002, was twofold. On the one hand, the policy leverage afforded by the ACP's dependence on preferences only extended as far as each beneficiary was equally dependent on preferences and hence similarly exposed by liberalization. On the other hand, even if this was the case – which it patently was not – there would still be an incongruence between the desire to secure reciprocity at a regional level and the fact that the policy levers used to achieve this could only be deployed at a national level. This incongruence, furthermore, was accentuated by the principle of differentiation enshrined in the Cotonou Agreement and later implemented through EBA, which ensured that there would be zero costs for LDCs because preferential access was guaranteed whether they signed an EPA or not. Looking at all of this in relation to the specifics of the Pacific, it is demonstrably the case that the EU did not actually possess the policy leverage required to persuade PACP states either to liberalize trade with their neighbours or, indeed, in most cases, sign a bilateral agreement with the EU. In actual fact, it can be argued that in this case the EU's policy leverage was not only limited and uneven, but also counterproductive. The reason for this is that, as we discussed earlier, by permitting those states actually sensitive to effects of the withdrawal of preferences – Fiji and PNG – to conclude separate reciprocal agreements bilaterally it raised rather than lowered the costs of establishing a regional-wide agreement in the future.

The limited and uneven nature of the EU's policy leverage helps to explain why, in public at least, the European Commission was keen to downplay any coercive element to the agreements and to, instead, emphasize the desirability of the EPAs based on their 'comprehensive' nature above and beyond ensuring continuity of preferential market access. Yet this discursive tactic ran into two immediate problems. The first was that, as EU policy makers were all too aware, although the ACP as a whole viewed pro-market economic reforms as necessary for development (with greater or lesser degrees of enthusiasm) the group had been sceptical from the outset about the prospect of reciprocal free trade with the EU (McQueen 1998: 422). In the absence of coercion it therefore seemed unlikely that many would be persuaded by the case for enshrining these commitments in a new contractual arrangement with the EU – a case, moreover, not helped by the latter's insistence on the inclusion of a raft of WTO-plus provisions that served to confirm the suspicion among many that the desired reforms were ultimately driven by commercial self-interest (Murray-Evans 2012). The second, closely related, point is that by emphasizing the 'non-coercive' and 'development-friendly' nature of the EPAs the EU's norm-based argument was open to contestation by critics of the negotiations (ACP governments, sceptical member states, NGOs and activists) which portrayed the agreements in a far more negative light (Tradecraft 2003; Action Aid 2005; Oxfam 2008). This is an issue we shall return to shortly, after first considering the consequences of the entanglement of the EU's development and commercial trade objectives.

The blurring of the boundaries between the EU's 'development' and 'commercial' priorities

As can be recalled from our earlier discussion, theoretical accounts of interregionalism – as well as the extant literature focusing specifically on the EPAs – can be divided between interest- and norm-based explanations. In this chapter, we have taken our cue from the former but used this as a point of departure for a critical interrogation of the model of regional governance that the EU is seeking to promote. In this subsection of the chapter, we turn to what has arguably been the most contentious and politically divisive aspect of the entire EPA process – the inclusion of the so-called 'Singapore issues' (see, especially, Chapter 3) – with the aim of showing that this, too, is best understood as part of the normative framework that EU has promoted in respect of the ACP. There is no doubt that the inclusion of the Singapore issues has added grist to the mill of those critical voices which have questioned, if not ridiculed, the EU's often-repeated assertion that it has no 'offensive' economic interests at stake in promoting the EPAs (Goodison 2007; Stoneman and Thompson 2007; Brewster, Girvan and Lewis 2008; Hurt 2012). If pushed too far, however, this critique leads to a crude form of economism that is difficult to square with the relatively negligible importance of the ACP to the EU's objective economic interests (see Faber and Orbie 2009).

Instead, we argue that the European Commission's usage of the policy leverage afforded by the Lomé and Cotonou agreements to steer ACP countries in a neoliberal direction has been driven by normative – or ideological – rather than straightforward economic reasons. This does not mean the EU's wider economic interests can be ignored. Indeed, it is noteworthy that the 1996 *Green Paper* that presaged the demise of Lomé coincided, more or less directly, with a recalibration of EU wider trade strategy built on a new '*emphasis on the objective of third country market opening* in the Community's commercial policy' (European Commission 1996: 4, emphasis in the original; see also Faber and Orbie 2009; Heron and Siles-Brügge 2012). This recalibration was not simply an unreflexive response to external economic pressures; rather, it resulted from the internalization and subsequent strategic deployment of a discourse of 'global competitiveness' as a pretext for neoliberal policy reform (Tsoukalis 1997; Rosamond 2002). These discourses, moreover, did not just appeal to the EU's economic and commercial interests; in time, they would form the prism through which the recasting of the EU's trade and development cooperation would occur. In other words, under this rubric 'development' and 'competitiveness' would represent two sides of the same coin – and what was good for the EU would be good for the ACP also.

We can recall from our earlier discussion that, although the abandonment of Lomé hinged on the necessity of WTO compliance, the decision was informed by a more or less independent set of normative convictions concerning the desirability of reciprocity and market-oriented policy reform. Even so, it is important to note that the Cotonou Agreement made only fleeting references to the Singapore issues and offered few grounds for thinking that they would form an integral component of the EPAs. Indeed, the importance of regional integration itself at this point appeared to rest on the grounds of overcoming the practical difficulties associated with 'uniform reciprocity' given the heterogeneous nature of the ACP (Siles-Brügge 2012: 191; see also Meyn 2008). It is worth noting in this respect that, of the four Singapore issues (investment, services, competition policy and government procurement), only services was mentioned explicitly in the Cotonou Agreement as a potential negotiating issue and, even in this case, only after the ACP had first 'acquired some experience in applying the Most Favoured (MFN) treatment under the GATS' (Cotonou Agreement

2000: 41.1).[8] Although each of these four issues would eventually find way into the EPA negotiations, it is significant that they did not figure as negotiating issues until 2004 – a full two years after the talks got under way and almost five years from when responsibility for the ACP was moved from DG Development to DG Trade at the insistence of Trade Commissioner Pascal Lamy (Heron and Siles-Brügge 2012: 8).[9]

The increasing prominence of the Singapore issues in the EPA negotiations appeared to coincide with the arrival of Peter Mandleson at DG Trade, which took place against the backdrop of the acrimonious failure of the Cancún ministerial in September 2003, prompting WTO trade ministers to abandon the three most contentious Singapore issues (services, investment and government procurement) and to scale back ambitious for what the DDA could achieve. The EU's eventual response to the Cancún debacle was to launch its *Global Europe* trade strategy, the essential thrust was that the internal dimension of the Lisbon Agenda needed to run in tandem with a more offensive external trade strategy (Hay 2007). In making the case for a new generation of FTAs *Global Europe* identified a whole range of emerging markets in Asia, Latin America and elsewhere deemed ripe for commercial exploitation. In contrast, at no point did it mention the ACP other than to suggest that these countries, along with Central America and the Andean Community, were peripheral to Europe's main commercial interests and that the EPAs and other similar agreements were designed to meet development rather than trade objectives.

In sum, *Global Europe* appeared to offer a clear demarcation between the EU's 'main trade interests' in which 'economic factors must play a primary role' (European Commission 2006: 10–11) and its trade agreements with peripheral countries in which the primary motive was promoting sustainable development through the gradual regional and global integration of these countries into the world economy in a manner consistent with WTO rules (European Commission 2006: 3). Accordingly, the first of these agreements, the CARIFORUM EPA, was described as follows:

> By explicitly taking into account the development objectives, needs and interests of the CARIFORUM region the EPA is very different from every other trade agreement negotiated up to now between developed and developing countries. This comprehensive approach is what constitutes the development dimension of the EPA and all the provisions of the EPA are designed to support it. (EU 2008: 1)

Although, as detailed in the previous chapter, the objective of 'development through cooperation' figured prominently in the preamble to the CARIFORUM agreement (recalling that 'development cooperation' is mentioned 13 times and 'cooperation' 135 times in the text), the most striking aspect of the agreement is that, in substantive terms, it is virtually indistinguishable from the 'commercial' FTA concluded with South Korea under the auspice of *Global Europe* more or less at the same time (see, again, Heron and Siles-Brügge 2012). It is clear, moreover, that the expectation on the part of the European Commission was that the CARIFORUM agreement would serve as a benchmark EPA in its coverage of the Singapore issues. Here the PACP would be an exception (see below) to the general pattern, according to which the interim 'goods only' agreements initialled in 2007 and signed (in some cases) in 2009 by the other regional configurations contained rendezvous clauses committing the parties to the conclusion of comprehensive agreements, including chapters on services and investment, government procurement and competition policy.

Even so, the convergence of the EU's 'development' and 'commercial' agendas after 2004 should be interpreted neither as a direct response to Cancún nor necessarily as a straightforward attempt to further its commercial interests in the ACP. In this respect, it is worth noting another important parallel between the EPAs and supposedly more commercially oriented agreements pursued under the auspices of *Global Europe*. As Gabriel Siles-Brügge (2012) has noted, despite the fact that *Global Europe* was ostensibly aimed at securing preferential access to emerging markets for the EU's export-oriented firms it also dovetailed with the 'internal' dimension of the Lisbon Agenda designed to weed out the few remaining 'pockets of protectionism' (excluding agriculture which was still deemed to be a special case) that had hitherto managed to escaped liberalization relatively unscathed. In the same way that the abandonment Lomé was deemed to be not only necessary but also desirable on the grounds that reciprocal liberalization would support market-oriented policy reform in the ACP, trading away these pockets of protectionism in exchange for market access gains for export-oriented firms would, in effect, 'kill two birds with one stone' (Siles-Brügge 2012: 189).

Returning to the specific concerns of the chapter, then, from the mid-2000s onwards the external promotion of regionalism would become inextricably bound up with the entwinement of the EU's commercial and development agendas associated with the advancement of Lisbon Agenda. This led to three problems. The first was that the more that the EU emphasized the Singapore issues, the less traction was to gained from continuing to invoke the necessity of WTO compliance, since this obviously went beyond what was strictly required to satisfy multilateral trade rules. In the case of the Pacific – where, as have just seen, the EU's policy leverage was already tenuous and uneven – the entwinement of the two imperatives acted to drive a wedge between the larger, preference-dependent economies of Fiji and PNG and the smaller, largely service-based economies that made up the rest of the PACP region, which had little to gain from a 'goods only' agreement but might conceivably benefit from a more comprehensive agreement, especially so had the EU been willing or able to give more ground in the crucial area of Mode IV (South Centre 2007; Pacific Institute of Public Policy

2008). By permitting – and even encouraging – Fiji and PNG to break ranks to sign interim 'goods only' agreements, EU policy makers thus conceded the little policy leverage it had over the rest of the region while undermining whatever (admittedly slim) prospects that might otherwise have existed for the conclusion of a region-wide agreement.[10]

The second problem caused by the entwinement of commercial and development agendas is that it served to raise the political costs associated with concluding an EPA, either bilaterally or regionally. This was most in evidence in respect of the MFN clause. The EU's principle justification for the insistence on the MFN clause – namely, that it did not want to be put at a competitive disadvantage as a result of having signed EPAs[11] – is difficult to square with the often-cited claim by its officials that there were no 'offensive interests' at stake in the negotiations. But what is more crucial is that this clause raised the stakes in the EPA negotiations, especially so in cases where the EU was not the dominant trade partner. In the case of CARIFORUM, as we saw in the last chapter, the willingness of the CRNM to countenance the MFN clause rested on a strategic calculation (albeit perhaps a somewhat short-sighted one) that this move would not unduly worry the United States while dismissing the prospects of signing a future agreement with an emerging power, such as China or India (see, again, Chapter 3). By contrast, in the Pacific, the initiation of the EPA negotiations in 2002 had already been deemed significant enough to trigger the equivalent clause in the PACER agreement. The PACP states were therefore justified in their concerns that the presence of an MFA clause in a reciprocal agreement with the EU would be unpalatable because of the likely knock-on effects that any such agreement would have on trade relations with ANZ (Kelsey 2005; Nathan Associates 2007).

The third, and final, complication created by the entwinement of commercial and development agendas is that it exposed the EU to a discursive onslaught from the various critics of the EPAs – ACP governments, sceptical member states, NGOs and activists – which mobilized effectively to rebut the European Commission's depiction of the EPAs as 'non-coercive' and 'development-friendly' and to, instead, portray them as coercive, driven by commercial self-interest and potentially deeply damaging to the ACP. Although opposition to the EPAs from elements of global civil society began almost as soon as the talks got underway in September 2002 (Tradecraft 2003; Action Aid 2005), there is no doubt that the increasing prominence of the Singapore issues in the negotiations after Cancún meant that the Commission officials could no longer hide behind the pretext of 'WTO compatibility' but now had to rely more and more on moral suasion to convince the ACP of the merits of the 'comprehensive' EPAs. In this context, opposition groups were able draw on what Frank Schimmelfennig (2001) calls 'rhetorical action' – the strategic use of norm-based arguments – to, first, question and, ultimately, undermine the EU's case. In promoting the complementarily of 'development' and 'competitiveness' discourses in order to downplay the coercive element and emphasize the positive-sum nature of the EPAs, EU policy makers were, in short, hoisted by their own petard.

Conclusion

In this chapter we have examined the puzzle of why the EU's support for regionalism in the ACP has achieved only modest results. To this end, the chapter engaged critically with wider debates concerning the EU's purported civilian or normative power. Although the extant EU-ACP literature focusing, among other things, the EU's economic interests and the unintended effects of policy leverage provide some initial insight, the wider literature was found to be more apposite – especially given the emphasis placed on the link between the EU's distinct institutional form and the attempt to legitimize itself as a global actor and promote regionalism as a model for global governance. This helps to account for why EU policy makers continued to insist on regional integration as an integral component of the EPAs, long after it became clear that this prerequisite made the task of securing reciprocal free trade with the ACP more difficult rather than easier to achieve. It also helps to explain why the insistence on regional integration was pursued even in cases, such as the Pacific, where the presence of independent political or economic interests was difficult to discern.

This literature does not, however, provide a ready-made explanation of why the EU's promotion of regionalism within the context of the EPAs foundered – despite the obvious power asymmetries involved and the ostensible commitment of the ACP to the goal of closer economic integration. At this point, it was necessary to examine more closely the model of regional economic governance that the EU is seeking to promote and the means by which it chose to promote it. Accordingly, were able to highlight a series tensions, ambiguities and contradictions associated with the attempt by EU policy makers – deliberate or otherwise – to conflate the *necessity* of reciprocity for the purpose of satisfying multilateral trade rules with its *desirability* as a means of fostering neoliberal policy reform. Applied specifically (but not exclusively) to the case of the Pacific, the incongruence of this approach was revealed in, among other things, the extent to which WTO compliance served to limit the timeframe and negotiating options for both EU and ACP policy actors while shining a light on the limited and uneven nature of the political leverage of the former.

But perhaps the most crucial dimension of the EPA story is the entanglement of the EU's development and commercial trade objectives. On the surface, the presence of the Singapore issues in the negotiations lends credence to those accounts that interpret the EPAs through the prism of the EU's independent, political and commercial interests. What we have shown, however, is that the presence of these issues are understood best as part of a norm-based policy agenda associated with the internalization and subsequent promotion of neoliberal conceptions of development. In fact, it precisely because EU policy makers informed by this doctrine sought to collapse the distinction between 'development' and 'competitiveness' (and hence the distinction between the EU's economic interests and its normative preferences for dealing with the ACP) that actors opposed to the EPA were able to contest and, in no small measure, ultimately resist the EU's attempt to promote reciprocal free trade with the ACP on the basis of interregionalism.

5
Developmentalism and the Political Economy of Trade Adjustment in Mauritius

By any measure, Mauritius must be regarded as one of the most remarkable – and improbable – economic success stories of the post-war period. Mauritius inherited a legacy common to many post-colonial societies of monocrop agriculture, extreme racial inequality, population pressures, unemployment and poverty. At the time of independence from Great Britain in 1968, sugar was responsible for practically all economic activity on the island, accounting for no less than 93 per cent of exports and 94 per cent of all cultivated land (Bowman 1991: 104). By the 1990s, however, Mauritius had undergone a remarkable transformation: while sugar remained an important mainstay of the economy, the island had successfully diversified into manufacturing, luxury tourism, offshore financial services and, most recently, information and communications technology. In the process, it recorded one of the highest sustained rates of economic growth in the world – GDP has grown at 6 per cent per annum more or less uninterrupted since the early 1980s – witnessing a tripling of real income in the process. What is more, this growth record was underpinned by an impressive performance according to a range of broader human development indicators including life expectancy, adult literacy, education and income equality (Kothari and Wilkinson 2013).

Although the precise reasons behind Mauritius's remarkable economic performance are still a matter of debate, few dispute the central importance of unilateral trade preferences (Subramanian and Roy 2001). Following independence, Mauritius became the first 'associate member' of the EEC and thereafter a principal beneficiary of the Lomé convention, including (more crucially) the Sugar Protocol attached to it. Under this, Mauritius received an annual quota of approximately 500,000 tons of sugar – which amounted to 38.5 per cent of a total quota of 1.3 million tons shared between the 19 countries belonging to the agreement – at a guaranteed price roughly three to five times higher than typically available on the world market. Likewise, quota- and duty-free market access under Lomé, coupled with an elaborate system of quantitative restrictions administered under the auspice of the MFA, provided the conditions for the creation of a dynamic export-processing zone (EPZ) sector specializing in garment manufacture, which replaced sugar as the country's largest source of foreign exchange in the 1980s (Meisenhelder 1997). The key summative point is that the economic rents associated with these preferences generated a large pool of domestic savings and played a crucial role in sustaining the high levels of investment that were the key to the success of Mauritius's export-oriented growth model (Subramanian and Roy 2001: 22).

As we now know, by the mid-2000s the value of traditional preferences diminished to such an extent that they no longer provided a reliable competitive advantage for preference-receiving countries. In the case of Mauritius, the costs of preference erosion were especially significant because not only was the island exposed to the effects of liberalization in its two most important sectors – garments and sugar – it was also confronted with the prospect (albeit from its point of view perhaps less significant) of further economic fallout, following the signing of a fully reciprocal interim EPA with the EU in August 2009. Yet Mauritius appears to have taken these challenges in its stride. Although the Mauritian economy experienced a significant downturn in the early 2000s in the immediate aftermath of the abolition of the MFA, by the end of the decade the island's rate of economic growth had returned to its post-1970s average. Similarly, even though as the principal beneficiary of the Sugar Protocol Mauritius was exposed more than most to the effects of sectoral liberalization, by the time that the 36 per cent price reduction had been administered in full, the island's reform programme had been deemed reasonably successful.[1] Similarly, in contrast to much of the rest of sub-Saharan Africa, Mauritius appeared to welcome the prospect of a fully reciprocal EPA, with trade officials declaring (in a mirror image of the EU's frequently-invoked refrain that we have already encountered) that there were 'no defensive interests' standing in the way of the conclusion of a comprehensive agreement.[2]

This chapter looks more closely at these trends. In particular, we are concerned with establishing what lessons – if any – the case of Mauritius offers for other small, preference-dependent countries confronted with the loss of traditional economic privileges and the prospect of reciprocal free trade. We begin (in the next section) by tracing the origins of Mauritius's economic model; here, we are especially interested in identifying the institutional correlates of export dynamism that enabled the island to make more effective use of trade preferences than was apparently the case elsewhere in the ACP. This task necessarily requires a short detour via the development state literature to provide the theoretical vocabulary to understand how and under what circumstances the post-colonial Mauritian state was able to influence and ultimately recast its terms of trade. In the third section of the chapter, we use these insights to inform our discussion of Mauritius's encounter with the political economy of trade adjustment in the 2000s – in the aftermath of the abolition of the MFA and the denunciation of the Sugar Protocol. After briefly outlining the origins and modalities of these trade reforms, we examine how Mauritius has adjusted to them and with what consequences. In the fourth section, we explore how these reforms have fed into the ongoing EPA negotiations and ask how far the institutional tools that are said to have enabled Mauritius to cope with the loss of preferences – that is, issues of domestic 'capacity' – will be sufficient to enable it to overcome the numerous problems with the EPA process on which we have commented in previous chapters. A brief concluding section summarizes the main findings of the chapter.

The origins of the 'democratic development state' in Mauritius

Mauritius is one of a very select group of countries outside of East Asia to which the label 'development state' appears apposite (Kearney 1990; Meisenhelder 1997; Goldsmith 1999; Lange 2003; Sandbrook 2005). In the East Asian context, accounts of the development state duly begin by referencing Charmers Johnston's path-breaking 1982 book, *MITI and the Japanese Miracle* (Leftwich 2000; Payne and Phillips 2010). The central insight provided by Johnson was to draw attention to the importance to economic development (understood here in terms of growth, production and competitiveness rather than welfare) of a small but capable and politically insulated bureaucratic elite with the means and capacity to promote 'market conforming' methods of state intervention. Although this insight initially went against the grain of the neoliberal orthodoxy of the 1980s – which initially proclaimed the spectacular economic successes of East Asia as testimony of the merits of laissez-faire and market-led industrialization – subsequent work in the same vein served to substantiate and refine the development state concept (Hamilton 1986; White 1987; Amsden 1989; Wade 1990). The work of Robert Wade, for instance, sought to infuse what he saw as Johnston's overly descriptive thesis with what he called a 'comparative-analytic' dimension, capable of identifying the causal link between specific policies and industrial performance. In particular, Wade (1990) argued that the key to the industrial transformation in East Asia lay not with the role of the state per se, but with early and specific forms of intervention – especially heavy investment in human capital and infrastructure, which subsequently propelled export-oriented industrialization. As Tony Payne and Nicola Phillips (2010: 106) explain, the logic underpinning Wade's argument (and hence the development state concept more generally) was to turn the orthodox neoliberal interpretation on its head: the adoption of 'market-friendly' policies and the promotion of exports were, in short, a consequence rather than a cause of East Asia's industrial transformation.

Another aspect of the development state concept subject to critical refinement – which has particular relevance for our case – is the presumed affinity between developmentalism and authoritarianism. In Johnston's original formulation, and in much of the literature that subsequently followed, the development state necessitated an unavoidable trade-off between state autonomy (understood here as autonomous bureaucratic decision making resting on the monopolization of political power) and democratic accountability. But as Richard Sandbrook (2005: 551–3) has argued, Johnston's model provided no means to actually test this proposition. Further, Sandbrook refutes the underlying assumption that authoritarian regimes are necessarily more stable or predictable than democracies. Nor in his view are there compelling theoretical reasons for thinking that bureaucratic elites will eschew predatory behaviour in the absence of mechanisms of democratic accountability. Sandbrook draws on the work of Gordon White to argue that democracy is in fact reconcilable with the development state. On the one hand, he suggests that not only may democratic politics motivate elites to act developmentally but such a tactic – if successful – will help consolidate democratic institutions. On the other hand, he continues, democracy has the potential to strengthen state capacity by generating legitimacy and improving administrative efficiency and fiscal rectitude through mechanism of accountability. Finally, democracy can paradoxically enhance the autonomy of political and bureaucratic elites. The reason for this, argues Sandbrook, is that the democratic process is capable of engendering an 'inclusive autonomy' (c.f. White 1998) sufficient to bind rulers to class compromise while providing the state with leverage necessary to override the veto power of interest groups and external powers. Sandbrook concludes, however, by suggesting that such inclusive autonomy can only succeed in pluralistic societies – and this is the reason why democratic development states are relatively rare – if all ethnic and communal groups are represented fairly and political and bureaucratic elites are embedded in society.

With this caveat in mind, the obvious starting point for our investigation is the question why did the democratic developmental state – if indeed the characterization is accurate – take root in Mauritius but not elsewhere in Africa, the Caribbean or Pacific?[3] According to Richard Kearney (1990: 198), the main likeness between Mauritius and the development states of East Asia was the conjunction of an initial set of favourable circumstances with social and political stability anchored to a (not unrelated) consensus among elites on the appropriateness of an export-oriented development strategy. At the time of independence, however, few would have interpreted Mauritius's colonial inheritance as anything other than highly unfavourable; indeed, the Nobel Prize-winning economist James Meade famously dismissed the island's economic prospects in the following way:

Heavy population pressures must inevitably reduce real income per head below what might otherwise be. That surely is bad enough in a community that is full of political conflict. But if in addition, in the absence of other remedies, it must lead either to unemployment (exacerbating the scramble for jobs between Indians and Creoles) or to greater inequalities (stoking up still more the envy felt by the Indian and Creole underdog for the Franco-Mauritian top dog), the outlook for peaceful development is poor. (Meade 1961, cited in Subramanian and Roy 2001: 4)

As Arvind Subramanian and Devesh Roy (2001: 9–10) make clear, Meade's gloomy assessment of Mauritius's development prospects was far from wide of the mark at the time, given population pressures, ethnic tensions, commodity dependence and the island's remoteness from major export markets. But what was overlooked was the extent to which Mauritius was bequeathed a colonial inheritance more or less unique among plantation-based economies. This had a crucial bearing on the island's subsequent development. First of all, because Mauritius was uninhabited until the arrival of Dutch settlers at the end of the sixteenth century, the country constituted a capitalist social formation from the very beginning. The importance of this was that, as Sandbrook (2005: 570) explains, Mauritius largely avoided the reactionary politics of neopatrimonial rule and clientelism associated with peasant-based colonial societies. Instead, Mauritius 'developed a powerful mercantile and agrarian bourgeoisie, a large class of landowners and merchants, and a rural and urban proletariat'. This, Sandbrook suggests, ultimately formed the basis of 'a disciplined capitalist state', paving the way for an eventual 'social-democratic class compromise'.

The main distinctive feature of Mauritius's colonial inheritance is the highly unusual extent to which mutual rivalry between the island's two colonial masters – France (1715–1810) and Great Britain (1810–1968) – imbued not only capitalist state formation but also bureaucratic capacity and, ultimately, participative democracy. There are several different aspects to this. For one, unlike other African societies in which colonial rule generally operated on the basis of arm's length control via local strongmen, Mauritius's experience with imperialism was more direct, extensive and of a longer duration. According to Matthew Lange (2003: 404), during the period of British colonial rule Mauritius possessed, on a per capita basis, four times the state revenue, three times the number of police officers and ten times the number of magistrate court cases compared to other African colonies. In this respect, the colonial experience of Mauritius is said to resemble that of Singapore more than other parts of Africa. Further, in contrast to its other colonies in Africa, the British relied much more heavily on the local population to administer the colony, with approximately 93 per cent of government positions filled by native Mauritians by the beginning of the twentieth century.

Although British officers occupied most of the high-level government positions in this period, by the 1930s approximately 65 per cent of all officer-level posts were held by Mauritians – a figure that reached 85 per cent before independence (Lange 2003: 404).

Another key aspect of Mauritius is the way in which the complex interplay of different colonial structures and associated racial and economic cleavages led to the de facto separation of economic from political power (Sandbrook 2005: 571). Although Great Britain abolished slavery in 1835 against the wishes of the Franco-Mauritian sugar elite, the colonial authorities nonetheless continued to promote the plantation economy through the reduction of tariffs, construction of roads and, most crucially of all, the importation of some 300,000 indentured labourers from India and China. It is important to understand, also, that despite the abolition of slavery the British left the economic power of the Franco-Mauritian planter class largely intact. By the same token, the mutual antagonism between the British colonial authorities and the Franco-Mauritian elite prompted the former to extend civil and political rights to plantation workers after 1860 to shore up political support among the Indo-Mauritian majority. This decision more or less coincided with a process by which the sugar estates responded to declining profitability in the midst of the long recession of the late nineteenth century by 'parcelling out' (Meisenhelder 1997) the least productive assets, sparking something of a frenzy of land acquisition among newly liberated Indo-Mauritian plantation workers. By the 1920s, an estimated 72,000 fewer plantation workers were employed on the large sugar estates with the amount of sugarcane controlled by Indo-Mauritian smallholders reaching 46,000 arpents (roughly equivalent to an acre) prior to the outbreak of the First World War, peaking at 82,000 in 1921 (Lange 2003: 407).

The parcelling out of smallholdings had two important consequences that were crucial to the success of Mauritius's subsequent development trajectory. On the one hand, the redistribution of land acted to empower the Indo-Mauritian population by undoing the ties that had hitherto bound agricultural labourers to the sugar estates. On the other hand, the population disbursal associated with this process fed the creation of scores of independent rural villages characterized by 'dense associational networks' (Lange 2003: 409) that became the breeding ground for a nascent civil society and – in time – a political movement that would propel the Mauritian Labour Party (MLP) and the independence movement with which it became synonymous. Although the roots of the labour movement lay in urban areas among Afro-Creoles challenging the privileges of the Franco-Mauritian elite, it only gained serious traction following a series of agricultural disturbances and national strikes – 1937, 1938, 1943 – coordinated by predominantly rural-based, Indo-Mauritian agricultural workers that forced the colonial administration into political reform. But while these societal demands proved to be the catalyst for reform, we need to remain cognizant of the fact that political and economic transformation in Mauritius was also a by-product of the coordinative and bureaucratic capacity of the colonial administration – and of its readiness to countenance reform (Lange 2003: 410). All told, the labour disturbances of the 1930s and early 1940s fuelled by the exclusion of the rural population from political life led directly to democratic reforms – including the creation of village and district councils, the removal of property and income suffrage requirements from the legislative assembly, the strengthening of worker rights and the expansion of social welfare programmes – that formed the basis of the democratic development state in Mauritius following the granting of independence in 1968.

After independence, the government of Mauritius was headed by prime minister Seewoosagur Ramgoolam, whose MLP, in alliance with two smaller parties, the *Comité d'action Musulman* and the Independent Forward Bloc, won 55 per cent of the vote and 39 of the 62 elected seats in the 1967 general election; the *Parti Mauricien Social-démocrat* (PMSD), which represented the Franco-Mauritian sugar elite that had campaigned against independence, gained 43 per cent of the vote and 23 seats. The first coalition government headed by Ramgoolam sought to govern on a largely Fabian socialist platform but was immediately confronted with the aforementioned economic problems: the economy was highly dependent on sugar, population growth was running at four per cent per annum, unemployment high and economic growth suffered a precipitous decline due to a collapse in export earnings (Bräutigam 1997: 49). What is more, newly independent Mauritius was also faced with political problems: the 1967 elections were marred by inter-communal violence, mainly between Afro-Creoles and Muslims, while the MLP-led coalition proved to be very short lived, prompting the MLP to form a new coalition with the Franco-Mauritian PMSD. The country then witnessed the emergence of a new electoral force with the formation of the *Mouvement Militant Mauricien* (MMM), a class-based coalition of radical intellectuals and trade unionists advocating a leftist agenda of land reform and income redistribution. The government responded to the political threat posed by the MMM by declaring a state of emergency, postponing the 1972 election, detaining party leaders and banning its newspaper. In 1982, the MMM would go on to form a government in a coalition with the *Parti Socialiste Mauricien* (SMM), another new party created by disaffected left-wing members of the MLP, but by this point it was forced to moderate its demands due to the constraints imposed by the exigencies of structural adjustment.

Despite the ensuing chaos, in the early years of independence the Mauritian state, overseen by a relatively autonomous and increasingly capable central bureaucracy, was largely successful in administering key economic reforms. The first act of the government was to stabilize the economy through the imposition of a public sector wage freeze and cuts to transport subsidies, after which growth was to rely on the twin pillars of sugar exports and ISI. As Thomas Meisenhelder (1997: 283) suggests, the key to Mauritius's development strategy at this point was boosting sugar production to provide both private capital accumulation and public revenues as the basis for economic diversification and industrialization. Here two key policy instruments played a crucial role. The first was the levying of a progressive tax on sugar exports to fund increased welfare spending and economic diversification. Although the introduction of the tax was a response to the establishment of the 1975 Sugar Protocol – which, as we have already seen, granted sugar exporters a guaranteed annual quota of some 500,000 tons way in excess of world market prices – it was nonetheless very controversial among the Franco-Mauritian plantocracy, not least because Indo-Mauritian smallholders were exempt from paying it (Bräutigam 2008: 155). But the fact that the tax was introduced has been interpreted as an early indication of the bureaucratic autonomy of the Mauritian state: that is to say, although the Franco-Mauritian elite vehemently objected to the introduction of the tax (prompting the PMSD to quit the coalition), the government was successful in overriding the veto power of sectional interests, despite the obvious economic power of the sugar industry (Meisenhelder 1997: 284).

The second policy instrument designed to propel economic diversification was the creation of an EPZ in 1970. The concept of EPZ-led industrialization was reportedly introduced to Mauritius in 1969 by Professor Lim Fat of the School of Industrial Technology at the University of Mauritius, following a fact-finding mission to the Kaoshiung EPZ in Taiwan and Free Foreign Trade Zone of Managuez in Puerto Rico (Lamusse 1989: 4). Although Mauritius was not the only country to attempt to replicate this strategy – EPZs were widely introduced across the islands of the Caribbean more or less at the same time – a number of factors appear to explain why it was more successful here than elsewhere in the developing world. For one, the presence of a sizeable ethnic Chinese diaspora played a key role in the establishment of the EPZ sector and the formation of transnational business networks crucial to the success of export dynamism in Mauritius (Bräutigam 2003). Another distinctive feature of Mauritius's experimentation with EPZs was that land scarcity prohibited the construction of large, geographically concentrated industrial zones or districts; thus Mauritius largely avoided the inadvertent creation of economic enclaves that became such a distinctive feature of EPZ experiments elsewhere (Roberts 1992). Finally, in accordance with Meisenhelder's aforementioned characterization, the economic rents generated by sugar exports in the context of buoyant international commodity prices became the major source of investment in the EPZ sector – almost exclusively in the textiles and clothing industry – in the early 1970s. What is more, in stark contrast to the experience elsewhere, the fact that sugar was predominantly in the hands of indigenous firms, coupled with the presence of strict foreign-exchange controls, ensured that the growth of the EPZ sector was to a significant extent financed by domestic as opposed to foreign sources of capital (Hein 1989; Lamusse 1989; Rodrik 1999; Subramanian and Roy 2001).

The importance of sugar profits as a fillip to the nascent EPZ sector was especially pronounced in the early 1970s when a succession of bumper crops coincided with a major upturn in world sugar prices (Bowman 1991: 116). This meant that Mauritius not only maximized its ACP sugar quota but was able to cash in on exceptionally high world market prices – which for a brief period were four times the price guaranteed under the Sugar Protocol – for out-of-quota sugar. This in turn fuelled the boom in EPZ-related investment: between 1970 and 1976, the number of manufacturing firms in the sector increased from four to 84, by which time approximately 17,400 workers were employed in the sector with over 40 per cent of equity capital coming from domestic sources (Lamusse 1989: 6). However, the initial take off of the EPZ sector took place against the backdrop of a general worsening of the economic climate. By the mid-1970s, a massive increase in the cost of oil imports triggered by the first OPEC 'oil shock', coupled with a major cyclone in 1975 that disrupted sugar production to such an extent that Mauritius was unable to meet even its allocated ACP quota, contributed to a sharp deterioration in the country's balance of payments position. This occurred just as Mauritius had committed itself to costly increases in public sector wages, welfare programmes and investment in public infrastructure. The combination of an increasingly overvalued exchange rate and higher wages put an end, at least for the time being, to the expansion of the EPZ sector. By the end of the 1970s Mauritius was running persistent and acute balance of payment deficits, external debt had more than quadrupled and the country reportedly only had sufficient foreign reserves to pay for just two further weeks of imports (Bräutigam 2007: 50–1; Bowman 1991: 119).

What happened next in Mauritius had all the markings of a classic case of third world indebtedness followed by externally imposed austerity and structural adjustment. But whereas in other parts of the developing world structural adjustment became a byword for policy failure, economic stagnation and social immiserization, in the case of Mauritius – the island was subject to no less than five separate IMF standby agreements and two World Bank structural adjustment programmes between 1978 and 1986 – these policies were later deemed, in the judgement of two well-informed commentators, to have 'succeeded brilliantly in restoring the economy to a sound footing, and opening the doors for a period of even more rapid economic growth' (Carroll and Carroll 1999: 189). In the short term, however, the implementation of structural adjustment proved to be deeply unpopular and politically destabilizing. Even though the first standby agreement struck with the IMF in 1978 was thwarted by social unrest, structural adjustment policies in Mauritius gradually gained more traction. These included drastic cuts to wages, the introduction of consumption taxes, the slashing of food subsidies, the lifting of price controls and cuts to education and welfare payments. In October 1979, the Mauritian rupee was devalued by some 30 per cent (a further 20 per cent devaluation was implemented in 1981) leading the

MMM opposition to organize a brief general strike. Inflation and unemployment remained stubbornly high and budget and current account deficits persisted. However, the general macroeconomic climate began to improve steadily from late 1982 onwards, by which point the MMM had taken office in a new centrist coalition.

A notable feature of structural adjustment in Mauritius was the degree to which the state bureaucracy was able to retain a degree of control over the pace and scope of policy reform. In the area of wage policy, for example, even though nominal pay increases negotiated between government, business and labour unions were kept well below the rate of inflation for the entirety of the structural adjustment period, the lowest wage earners were given preferential treatment in a conscious attempt to maintain support for the reform process among poorer workers (Bowman 1991: 121). Another area where the Mauritian bureaucracy left its mark was trade policy. Although Mauritius has been cited as testimony of the merits of openness to trade and economic integration (Sachs and Warner 1995), a closer inspection reveals a more complex picture. As Subramanian and Roy (2001: 15) report, even though the recovery and subsequent expansion of exports was the key to Mauritius's remarkable economic performance in the 1980s and 1990s, this occurred in spite of – or, perhaps more accurately, because of – the maintenance of a relatively restrictive trade policy regime. Indeed, even as late as 1998, following a decade of gradual liberalization, Mauritius's trade policy was still classified by the IMF as among the most restrictive in the world.

The conundrum of how Mauritius was able increase exports so dramatically within this policy context is the subject of an important contribution from Dani Rodrik (1999, 2000, 2007; see also Hein 1989; Saw and Wellisz 1993; Subramanian and Roy 2001). Rodrik argues that Mauritius prospered where so many other developing countries failed because, in effect, it segmented the EPZ sector from the rest of the economy, thus ensuring that that scare resources were not diverted to the inefficient import-substituting sector. This was achieved in three ways. First, because the EPZ regime permitted duty-free access to imported raw materials and intermediate inputs, outward-oriented firms escaped the implicit tax on exports normally associated with restrictive trade policies. Second, firms operating in the EPZ benefited from a series of tax exemptions. These measures served as an additional export subsidy and provided further immunization from import restrictions applied to the economy at large. Third, and most importantly, the EPZ labour market was segmented from the rest of the economy by permitting firms much greater flexibility with respect to pay and conditions, overtime, hiring and firing, and so on. The fact that wages in the EPZ were allowed to fall below those in the rest of economy (primarily because the bulk of EPZ workers were women, for whom the statutory minimum wage was set at a lower level than for men) provided another form of export subsidy by making it more attractive for firms to produce for the overseas rather than the domestic market. Finally, the segmentation of the labour market, coupled with the fact that in the main the EPZ sector drew women workers from the household rather than male workers from the import-competing sector, ensured that export-led growth did not drive up wages in the rest of the economy and hence was not at the expense of domestically oriented firms.

In summary, then, the segmentation of the economy, added to other aspects of Mauritius's EPZ discussed earlier, provided the basis for the export-led boom of the 1980s and 1990s. But it is unlikely that this would have occurred had it not been for the presence of unilateral trade preferences. Subramanian and Roy (2001: 20–1) argue that, although Rodrik's interpretation is broadly correct, the insulation of the EPZ sector was not in itself sufficient to offset the anti-export bias implicit in Mauritius's import regime. The missing ingredient was preferential access to overseas markets. As we have seen, the economic rents generated by eligibility for the Sugar Protocol – which Subramanian and Roy estimate were worth an average of 5.4 per cent of GDP each year between 1977 and 2000 – played a crucial role in financing the investment boom in manufactures and ensured that the EPZ sector could rely on a substantial domestic savings pool. Meanwhile, trade preferences granted under the Lomé protocol benefited Mauritius in two other ways. On the one hand, Lomé granted DFQF access to the EU market for EPZ firms specializing in the assembly of textiles and clothing. On the other hand, the establishment of Lomé in 1975 more or less coincided with the creation of the MFA, which placed quantitative restrictions on larger and more competitive exporters. This not only provided a niche for Mauritius and other small suppliers that, at least at this point, were exempt from MFA quota restrictions; it also rendered such countries an attractive investment destination for overseas firms using outsourcing as a means to bypass trade restrictions (Heron 2012). In the case of Mauritius, the presence of a sizeable ethnic Chinese diaspora – it should to be recalled that East Asia was the main target of quotas – ensured that the island was a major beneficiary of trade diversion under the MFA. It is also worth noting that the Chinese diaspora in Mauritius proved to be an important pull factor for entrepreneurs fleeing Hong Kong after Great Britain began negotiations to return the colony to China in 1983 (Bräutigam 2003: 456).

Preference erosion and the politics of trade adjustment in Mauritius, 2000–2010

By the late 1990s, the economy of Mauritius had experienced more than a decade and half of continuous economic expansion at a remarkable rate of six per cent per annum. This, coupled with negligible population growth, meant that the island had witnessed a tripling of real income in less than thirty years (World Bank 2010). The twin pillars of agriculture (sugar) and manufacturing (garments) were still responsible for the bulk of economic activity, with the latter alone accounting for some 11 per cent of GDP and 54 per cent of exports in 1997 (Mistry 1999: 559). But the economic recovery of Mauritius after the early 1980s was also characterized by a reasonable amount of diversification (Sandbrook 2005). During the 1980s, luxury tourism – which like the EPZ sector is characterized by an unusually high degree of local ownership – emerged as a third dynamic source of economic growth. By the late 1990s, tourism in Mauritius accounted for around a fifth of export earnings and appeared to show reasonable growth prospects going forward (Mistry 1999: 561). Finally, the diversification of the Mauritian economy had by this stage begun to embrace information technology and financial services. In regard to the latter, the island has been the fortuitous beneficiary of a 'double taxation' agreement with India, whereby firms domiciled in Mauritius are permitted to trade on the Indian stock market while escaping local tax liabilities.[4] This somewhat dubious practice has enabled Mauritius to lay claims to being the world's 'largest' source of foreign direct investment in India! Meanwhile, the early 2000s witnessed the construction of a 'cyber city' in Ebene close to the island's main university, 15 kilometres from the capital of Port Louis. By the middle of the decade, approximately 65 per cent of Ebene's purpose built office space had reportedly been occupied by many of the world's leading corporations, with the government boasting that a 90 per cent occupancy rate in the 2000s, providing an estimated 2000 jobs (Sandbrook 2005: 569).

Textiles and clothing

Significantly, this date coincided with the formal ending of the MFA on 31 December 2004. This had been agreed to as part of the 1993 GATT Uruguay round, whereafter quantitative restrictions that had been in place since 1974 were phased out over a ten-year period in four progressive but unequal stages, culminating in the removal of the most sensitive import quotas on 1 January 2005. The timing of the MFA phase out was significant for another reason. Although not an original signatory to the Uruguay round, following important bilateral accession agreements with the US and the EU, China was admitted to the WTO in December 2001 – and was thereafter accorded, among other things, most-favoured nation treatment in the newly liberalized textiles and clothing sector. Even at this stage, China was already the world's most dynamic textiles and clothing exporter: by 2002, before the most significant stages of the MFA phase out, it accounted for 13.5 per cent of global textiles exports and 20.6 per cent for clothing (OECD 2003). Part of the reason for this performance was China's extremely low labour costs. But analysts were quick to point to its relatively high-skilled workforce, strong productive capacity in the manufacture of cotton and synthetic fibres, plus very close trade and investment links with South Korea, Taiwan and Japan (Nathan Associates 2002).

Yet the significance of China's accession to the WTO for Mauritius and other preference-dependent countries did not simply rest with its cost structure, production capacity or enmeshment in regional production networks. Its sheer size also heralded a wider, structural shift in the global division of labour. By the mid-1990s, China accounted for over one-fifth of the world's population and one-quarter of the global labour force. The implication of this for global manufacturing is that China now plays a decisive role in determining product availability and hence global prices – thus not only influencing its own terms of trade but of all developing countries competing in overseas markets. To illustrate the point, Raphael Kaplinsky (2005: 181–6) cites the link between China's increased participation in global trade and production after 1985 and the dramatic fall in the price of manufactures following two decades of sustained and rapid price *increases*. These price changes cannot be attributed solely to China – technological changes and greater macroeconomic stability in the 1990s also played a role – but Kaplinsky does point to an important correlation between the income group of the exporter and the tendency of prices to fall. Examining the price data for manufactured exports to the EU between 1988 and 2001, Kaplinsky reveals that low-income countries specializing in low-technology products such as textiles and clothing experienced a greater reduction in export prices than higher-income countries specializing in medium- or high-technology product categories – and the unit prices of manufacturers from China fell by more even than the lowest-income group of countries. In other words, China's increased participation in global trade and production is associated with falling unit prices (especially for low-technology products), leading to what Kaplinsky (2001: 52) refers to as 'immiserizing growth' for low- and medium-income countries: that is, 'an expansion of economic activity which coincides with a decline in real incomes'.

In summary, liberalization heralded the end of an era in which relatively high-waged developing countries could export textiles and clothing at competitive international prices; it also spelled the end of trade and investment diversion generated by the MFA of which Mauritius was a major beneficiary. However, the news was not all bad. Because Mauritius itself had been subject to quota restrictions under the MFA – that is, in the United States market – liberalization did offer the opportunity to make up for falling prices through greater export orders. Moreover, the 2000s witnessed the launching of the AGOA. The importance of this for sub-Saharan Africa as a whole is discussed at greater length in the next chapter, but insofar as it relates specifically to the issues discussed here the following points should be noted. First of all, AGOA was modelled on President Reagan's 1984 CBERA offering preferential market access to the United States for Caribbean Basin countries (Heron 2004, 2012) – at least to the extent it granted DFQF market access to beneficiary countries exporting textiles and clothing products to the US market. In addition, unlike the CBERA, AGOA is predicated on more liberal rules of origin: whereas the CBERA stipulates that yarn and fabric manufacture must take place in the beneficiary country (or in the US or another CBERA-eligible country) in order to qualify for duty-free entitlements, AGOA (under the social-called 'special fabric' provision) permits global sourcing provided that assembly and finishing take place locally.

Although somewhat technical, this distinction has had a crucial bearing on the significance of AGOA for Mauritius – both before and after liberalization. Under Lomé, clothing firms in Mauritius traded under rules of origin similar to the CBERA (the so-called 'double transformation' requirement); this fostered an export industry characterized by generally high levels of local ownership and vertical integration. In contrast, because AGOA is premised on global sourcing it has tended to favour an investment model benefiting lower-waged countries where local firms are tasked with basic assembling functions (for example, t-shirts, blouses, trousers and so on) from imported yarns and fabrics to the strict specification of the foreign investor (Gibbon 2003). Hence, while the textiles and clothing sector in Mauritius received an import fillip from AGOA the lion's share of the gains went to new entrants like Swaziland, Madagascar and Lesotho (the latter replacing Mauritius as Africa's largest garment exporter to the US in 2002 – see Chapter 6). By the same token, however, it now appears that the abolition of the MFA reversed a substantial proportion of the trade gains obtained by sub-Saharan Africa since 2000. It may also be the case that the general orientation of Mauritian industry towards the EU rather than the US market has, to a degree, immunized local firms from the worst effects of liberalization. The reason for this is that effective rates of protection under the MFA were higher in the US than in the EU, meaning that the adverse distributive effects of liberalization for preference-receiving countries were felt most keenly by firms most dependent on the US market (Heron 2012; Nordås 2004).

This does not mean that Mauritius escaped liberalization unscathed. Although it managed to maintain (and even consolidate) its position in the EU market in spite of the removal of quotas, in the US case sectoral exports plummeted from US$254 million in 2002 to just US$101 million in 2009 (see Chapter 6: esp. Table 6.1; Heron 2012). The decline of export orders manifested itself domestically with the closure of some 112 factories with the reported loss of some 25,000 jobs between 2001 and 2005, even as new enterprises were created in response to AGOA (Ancharaz 2008: 10). The bulk of factory closures have been attributed to the departure of foreign firms, a situation compounded by the expiry of the 'third fabric' provision of AGOA in September 2008.[5] But it is also true that the textiles and clothing industry was encountering difficulties linked to a tightening labour market and rising costs well before the ending of the MFA – something evidenced by the fact that the sector had become increasingly dependent on migrant labour by the late 1990s (Mistry 1999: 559–60). According to Peter Gibbon (2000), Mauritian clothing firms first attempted to deal with the loss of competitiveness associated with rising costs in the 1990s by experimenting with forward integration into original brand manufacturing. When this failed many leading firms in Mauritius returned to a 'back to basics' industrial strategy of producing large volumes of basic garments and – increasingly – by moving offshore to neighbouring Madagascar in the search of cheaper labour. Finally, it is also worth noting that since liberalization both government and industry have played increasingly prominent roles in organizations such as the African Cotton and Textile Industries Federation (ACTIF) and the Africa Group in the WTO to lobby against the extension of DFQF treatment to non-Africa LDCs in order to protect the last vestiges of Lomé/Cotonou and AGOA preferences (Heron 2012: esp. chapter 7).

Sugar

As if the problems encountered with the liberalization of textiles and clothing were not enough to contend with, the mid-2000s marked the beginnings of a process signalling the end of Mauritius's privileged access to the EU sugar market. The sources of preference erosion affecting sugar are both multilayered and complex – the understanding of which requires appreciation of how the Sugar Protocol was itself 'nested' within a wider system of market interventions administered under the auspices of the Common Agricultural Policy (CAP). In essence, the CAP (in the case of sugar, in the guise of the Common Market Organisation of Sugar, or CMO) benefited both domestic sugar producers in the EU and beneficiaries of the Sugar Protocol in three different ways: a *price-support system* offering guaranteed income for fixed quantities of sugar designed to insulate eligible producers from fluctuations in world market prices; *tariff protection* sufficiently prohibitive to ensure that the guaranteed price was not disrupted by cheaper imports; and *export subsidies* financed by a consumption levy (paid directly by both sugar processing companies and indirectly by consumers in the form of higher prices) and by the EU Development Budget (equivalent to the ACP annual sugar quota of approximately 1.5 million tons[6]) to ensure that the implicit structural surplus generated by the CMO could be profitably offloaded onto the world market. Finally, a further category existed for so-called 'C-quota' sugar, that is, the amount of sugar produced exceeding annual quotas. Although this was ineligible for export subsidies, the profits generated by in-quota sugar were nonetheless sufficient to serve as a cross-subsidy, even at (much lower) world market prices.

As Ben Richardson (2009: 94) notes, the sheer complexity of the EU's sugar regime resulted in the perception that the CMO was largely self-financing and hence politically sustainable. This helps to explain why sugar was excluded from the various changes to the CAP introduced by the 1992 MacSharry reforms, Agenda 2000 and the Fischler reforms of 2003 – all of which sought to shift the CAP away from 'market distorting' commodity price support to 'non-market distorting' direct income support for farmers (Gibb 2004: 568). As early as 1993 the European Commission proposed changes to the CMO in the form of a 25 per cent cut to the intervention price, only to be thwarted by the sugar lobby and recalcitrant member-states; similar proposals were again rejected in 2000 and 2003 before a package of reforms was finally agreed in 2005 – and only then after the Commission had put together a compensation fund worth an estimated €7 billion (the ACP, for its part, was offered €1.3 billion in compensation to offset anticipated losses in export earnings of some €2.5 billion – Richardson 2009: 103). By this point, however, the efficacy of the CMO had been challenged on two other fronts. In February 2001, Trade Commissioner Pascal Lamy launched his EBA initiative, promising LDCs DFQF access to the EU for all goods except arms and munitions, sugar included.[7] Although EBA was primarily conceived in WTO circles as an early component of what later became the DDA, industry insiders interpreted it as a deliberate act of economic sabotage against the CMO.[8] The reason for this is that by offering LDCs duty- and quota-free access the EBA violated a key principle of the EU sugar regime, that is, the necessity of high tariffs for ensuring that internal prices were not distorted by cheap imports. The EU's sugar regime then received a further blow in the form of an unfavourable ruling by a 2004 WTO dispute-settlement panel, in a case brought by Australia, Brazil and Thailand. Although the judgement did not challenge the legality of the sugar regime in entirety, it nevertheless decreed that the means by which the EU offloaded the structural surplus generated by the CMO onto world markets constituted an export subsidy in excess of the quantitative limit of 1.3 million tons agreed under the Uruguay round Agreement on Agriculture (AoA). In short, the annual export of some 4.0 million tons of sugar exported by the EU (including 1.5 million tons equivalent to the ACP quota which the EU had claimed was exempt from the AoA) was deemed to be directly or indirectly subsidised (South Centre 2007a: 12).

As with earlier WTO rulings against the EU banana protocol, the importance of the sugar case lay not just with the actual outcome of the dispute-settlement process, but also the way in which the judgement was internalized by EU policy makers and subsequently used to justify liberalization. In this case three separate imperatives were used to justify reform. First, the WTO ruling provided the pretext for the sugar reform package launched in February 2006, the centrepiece of which was a dramatic 36 per cent cut to the intervention price (to be implemented over a four year period), alongside the provision of a €7 billion compensation fund to encourage farmers to leave the industry. These reforms were primarily aimed at domestic farmers, but they nevertheless had an important knock-on effect for the ACP given the close link between the guaranteed price offered under the Sugar Protocol and the EU internal price. However, the EU sugar reforms posed an even more direct challenge to the ACP in September 2007 when the EU denounced the

Sugar Protocol entirely, leading to its termination in October 2009. Although the denunciation of the protocol was partially (and somewhat disingenuously given that the 2004 ruling had not challenged the right of the EU to import sugar from the ACP at preferential prices) justified in terms of the 2004 WTO ruling, it was also done with reference to a second imperative: namely, the need to bring ACP preferences into line with WTO rules following the earlier judgement against the EU's banana protocol and the impending expiry of the Cotonou waiver in December 2007. Although this interpretation is open to question – not least because the Sugar Protocol was a legally distinct commodity agreement separate from Lomé and Cotonou, supposedly for an 'indefinite duration'[9] – the important point is that the EU chose to interpret it to mean that the only way of safeguarding sugar preferences from further litigation was through inclusion in a 'WTO compatible' EPA. Finally, the aforementioned EBA provided a third imperative for reform. In this case the opening up of the EU sugar market to the LDCs not only underscored the EU's commitment to severing the link between the internal market price and the Sugar Protocol; it also provided the EU with an important source of bargaining leverage in the EPA negotiations, since by this stage the non-LDCs were confronting noticeable amounts of trade and investment diversion towards the LDCs now operating under a more liberal trade regime (Goodison 2007: 27–8).

For Mauritius, then, the EU sugar reforms of the 2000s represented something of a 'triple whammy' – a 36 per cent price reduction for sugar exports destined for the EU market with the expectation of a further drop in prices brought about by the EBA (and the prospect of further liberalization of third country exports), coupled with a less secure investment climate following the denunciation of the Sugar Protocol and the expiry of the Cotonou waiver on 31 December 2007. As the principal beneficiary of the Sugar Protocol with the highest cost structure Mauritius was thus expected to be the major casualty of liberalization (Gibb 2004: Milner, Morgan and Zyovu 2004; Chaplin and Matthews 2006). By the same token, it was arguably better placed than other beneficiaries of the Sugar Protocol on account of the structural reform and modernization that had already taken place. The modernization process in Mauritius began in earnest in the mid-1980s following the publication of the *Action Plan for the Sugar Industry 1985–1990* and then, later, the passage of the 1988 Sugar Industry Efficiency Act (Bowman 1991: 124–6). These initiatives focused on, among other things, enhancing smallholder productivity, the consolidation of the island's sugar mills, plans to build bagasse-fuelled power stations and greater investment in research and economic diversification. It is worth noting that by this point the overall significance of sugar in the Mauritian economy had declined markedly: by the end of the 1980s sugar employed a mere 14 per cent of the island's population while its share of national output had shrunk from 30 per cent in the 1960s to just 8 per cent. Similarly, even though sugar remained at this point the island's largest net export earner its share of exports declined from around 95 per cent at the time of independence to below 40 per cent.

Returning to the specific consequences of the EU sugar reforms, three factors appear to explain why Mauritius was relatively well placed vis-à-vis other beneficiaries of the Sugar Protocol, despite its high cost structure. First, the experience of the sugar adjustment strategies – and arguably the wider economic reforms of the early 1980s – instilled a strong sense of national purpose and elite unity on the necessity of economic reform, generally missing elsewhere in the ACP.[10] In other cases such as Belize, for example, the absence of this manifested itself in widespread worker resistance to the introduction of new technologies deemed essential to economic modernization;[11] elsewhere in the Caribbean the reform process came up against problems of weak state capacity, an antipathy to risk taking on the part of sugar elites and a disinclination of former plantation workers to engage in smallhold farming, preferring in many cases urban migration in order to eke out a precarious living in the informal sector (Richardson 2009: 110; see also Weis 2004). Second, despite its complex racial structure Mauritius largely avoided problems such as those encountered in Fiji – a country which inherited colonial structures not entirely dissimilar to Mauritius – due to tensions between the Indo-Fijian planter class and indigenous Fijian landowners. Third, Mauritius has evidently been more successful than other members of the ACP in tapping into the EU's 'accompanying measures' put in place to cushion the abolition of the Sugar Protocol. According to a report produced by the Swaziland Sugar Association (Matsebula 2009), Mauritius has shown by far the highest absorption rates in the ESA region – accounting for no less than €39.8 million or 84 per cent of the estimated €47.3 million that had been disbursed out of a total allocation of €143 million by February 2009. Outside of Mauritius, the study claims, something in the order of just 11 per cent of allocated funding had been disbursed to the ESA region four years after the launching of the programme; but whereas countries like Swaziland, Malawi and Zambia struggled to access the adjustment finance provided by the EU, accessing just 4.7 per cent, 10.1 per cent and 4.9 per cent of their allocations respectively, Mauritius reportedly spent 53 per cent of its allocation in the same period.

In Mauritius's case, the EU 'accompanying measures' took the form of direct budget support, constituting a relatively small component of a projected €675 million Multi-Annual Adaptation Strategy (MAAS) aimed at streamlining and improving the international competitiveness of the sugar sector. This is focused on much the same goals as previous adjustment strategies, that is, improving productivity through further mechanization and consolidation allied to an export strategy targeted at high value-added sugars.[12] Yet despite Mauritius's impressive absorption rates and an institutional environment conducive to successful reform, the challenges confronting the sugar industry remain formidable. In the case of the EU's 'accompanying measures', for example, the government's Voluntary Retirement Scheme (VRS) – accounting for some €94 million out a total allocation of €138 million – seems to have had a modest record in finding alternative employment or suitable retraining opportunities for the 8,000 or so plantation workers made redundant since the early 2000s (Sawkut et al. 2009). It also appears that the 36 per cent price cut introduced in 2009 that provided the pretext for the MAAS constitutes the opening gambit rather than the endpoint, as the EU now considers the abolition of production quotas as part of the next stage of CAP reform scheduled for 2013 (Richardson 2013). Finally, and more importantly for our purposes, the reform process in Mauritius remains clouded by the continuing impasse in ESA-EU EPA negotiations. As we discovered earlier, the termination of the Sugar Protocol was intended to be replaced by a WTO-compatible EPA; in the absence of such an agreement, however, ACP states have relied for market access on a temporary legal instrument provided unilaterally by the EU. The situation is complicated even further with respect to the former beneficiaries of the Sugar Protocol – including Mauritius – since the EU envisaged replacing bilateral quotas with a 'global' quota for each EPA region. But since the EBA provides the LDCs (in this case Djibouti, Eritrea, Ethiopia, Malawi and Sudan) with little incentive to sign a reciprocal EPA, the question remains how the quota will be divided in the absence of a regional agreement? In short, the reform process in Mauritius is inextricably tied to the fate of region-wide EPA negotiations.

The elusive quest for reciprocity: Mauritius and the ESA-EU Economic Partnership Agreement

The position of Mauritius in the EPA negotiations can be likened to that of the CARIFORUM countries examined in Chapter 3; indeed, one could argue that in respect of the characteristics said to be most relevant in that case – namely, a combination of negotiating capacity and underlying economic interests – the objective conditions are even more favourable. Mauritius's colonial inheritance of a strong, capable and relative autonomous bureaucracy has left it well equipped for the demands of reciprocal trade negotiations – one of the reasons why it is frequently cited as the embodiment of 'small state activism' in the WTO (Lee and Smith 2010). Furthermore, Mauritius's acute dependence on the EU market (which even by the late 2000s still absorbed close to 70 per cent of its exports – it may be recalled from Chapter 3 that the respective figure for CARIFORUM stood at just 11 per cent), coupled with ineligibility for DFQF preferences granted to LDCs under EBA, provides more compelling grounds for justifying a reciprocal agreement than is arguably the case with CARIFORUM. Finally, the economic reforms undertaken unilaterally by Mauritius since the 1980s onwards suggest the island is left with far fewer 'defensive interests' than is the case either with CARIFORUM or other countries and regions in the ACP. Although, as noted, structural adjustment left many features of Mauritius' development state model intact, subsequent reforms in the 1990s and 2000s led gradually to the fall of import protection to negligible levels (World Bank 2010, 2010a). The first tranche of reforms starting in the mid-1980s led to the elimination of quantitative restrictions, lifting of price controls and, most notably, the liberalization of the sugar import tax; subsequent reforms in the 1990s focused on the removal of import licensing for most goods and the easing of credit restrictions. The most dramatic reforms, however, came in the midst of the 'triple crises' of mid-2000s with the announcement of what the World Bank (2010: 4) described as a 'bold package of policies and institutional reforms' with the ultimate aim of establishing Mauritius as a 'duty-free island'.

Despite circumstances apparently favourable to the realization of a reciprocal EPA, Mauritius nonetheless suffers from comparison with the Caribbean countries in one crucial respect: namely, the general absence of regional interlocutors with which to conclude such an arrangement. As was argued in Chapter 4, the key problem with the trade arrangement envisaged by Cotonou was the lack of congruence between its two principle objectives – WTO consistency and the promotion of regional integration – meaning that LDCs have few incentives to sign an EPA because equivalent benefits are available on a non-reciprocal basis while non-LDCs may have a strong incentive to sign because of the threat of being downgraded to GSP. All this has meant that it has proved extremely difficult to establish a common negotiating position at the regional level. Although the Caribbean is not totally immune from this problem – we can recall that Haiti is an LDC although it is a full member of both CARICOM and CARIFORUM – it is by some measure the region least affected by heterogeneity. By contrast, the ESA group, to which Mauritius belongs, constitutes the largest and most heterogeneous bloc in the ACP, cutting across numerous existing regional institutions, which are in turn characterized by overlapping membership and, in many cases, mutually incompatible obligations (Stevens 2006).

This pattern has, not surprisingly, rendered the realization of a region-wide EPA problematic. The ESA region is split according to more or less equal numbers of LDCs and non-LDCs. And even among the latter category very few members have economic motives as strong as Mauritius for seeking to secure a reciprocal EPA. To make matters worse, in November 2007, Burundi, Kenya, Rwanda and Uganda decided to break away from the ESA, together with Tanzania (which originally belonged to the SADC negotiating region), to sign a separate interim agreement with the EU under the guise of the EAC (see, again, Chapter 4). Of the remaining membership of the ESA (at least at the time of writing – February 2013) less than half had signed an interim EPA, with officials on both sides citing the disparate nature of the group and associated difficulties in reaching common negotiating positions.[13] This has reportedly led to the suggestion of transforming the ESA group into a COMESA group or even through the smaller Indian Ocean Commission

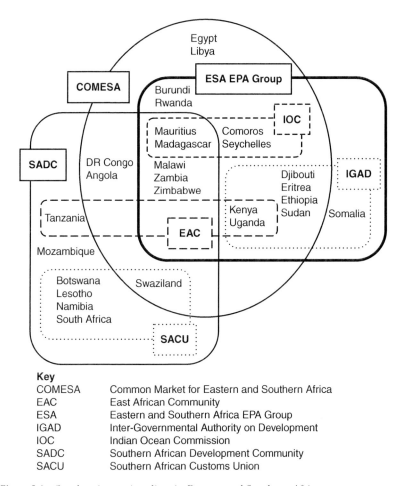

Figure 5.1 Overlapping regionalism in Eastern and Southern Africa

(IOC); officials in the European Commission have also indicated that a way out of the negotiating impasse maybe found by allowing for more 'variable geometry' in the search for a region-wide EPA.[14] None of these proposals are entirely straightforward, however. In Mauritius's case, the prospect of a full EPA concluded either on a bilateral or sub-regional basis is rendered problematic due to its existing obligations under COMESA and SADC. In the case of COMESA, for example, members are already committed to the establishment of a customs union with the adoption of a common external tariff. This raises the question of how such commitments could be squared with a reciprocal EPA premised on 'variable geometry'. Even in the (very unlikely) circumstances that such an agreement could be made to fit existing regional configurations, there is the additional problem that COMESA membership extends to countries like Egypt and Libya that are not party to the EPA negotiations (South Centre 2007b: 6).

And yet, while the contradictions of the EPA process reveal themselves the economic imperatives underpinning Mauritius's need to conclude an agreement as a means of salvaging what remains of its preferential access to the EU market remain compelling. Indeed, a number of recent developments have further underscored this need. First of all, in relation to sugar, the failure to conclude the regional EPA leaves the EU's post-Sugar Protocol vision incomplete. But more pertinently, it means that Mauritius's preferential access to the European sugar market now rests precariously on a temporary legal instrument provided unilaterally by the EU. The EU originally envisaged replacing the Sugar Protocol (albeit on the basis of a substantial cut in the intervention price) with a series of regional quotas, thus ensuring WTO compliance while squaring the circle between the different market access regimes offered to LDCs and non-LDCs provided by the EBA and the EPAs respectively. The difficulties with this, however, lay with the fact that, whereas the EBA granted unlimited access to the EU sugar market to the LDCs, the non-LDCs would be subject to an automatic safeguard clause alongside the overall quantitative limit defined by the regional quota (which could obviously only come at the expense of the non-LDCs). The successor to the Sugar Protocol envisaged by the EU thus entails potentially significant distributional consequences within each region while also tempering the ability of the non-LDCs previously benefiting from the Sugar Protocol to offset the effects of the price reduction by increasing the volume of exports (South Centre 2007a). In the case of the ESA, however, this scenario seems unlikely given the parlous state of negotiations which we have just discussed. In this case, the issue to be resolved for Mauritius is how the EU's current market access offer in sugar can be maintained in the event of the establishment of an agreement premised on 'variable geometry', or indeed in the circumstances of the failure to reach agreement at all.

As if the stakes for Mauritius were not sufficiently clear, further policy pronouncements by the European Commission in 2010 and 2011 have served to further underline the precarious nature of its preferential access to the EU market. First, in March 2010 Trade Commissioner Karel de Gucht announced a public consultation paper on the future of the EU's trade policy towards developing countries, including most notably reform of the GSP. The essence of the proposed reforms to the GSP centre on changes to 'income' and 'product' graduation thresholds, as a subsequent European Commission (2011: 2) report put it, in order to 'focus the GSP preferences on the countries most in need'. However, as Gabriel Siles-Brügge (2012: 210–11) has shown, the motive behind the reform can only be properly understood in the context of the EU's increasing bilateral activism: the proposed changes, in other words, are designed to enhance the EU's trade bargaining leverage by applying pressure to developing countries currently in receipt of GSP to sign reciprocal FTAs. Although Mauritius is not the most obvious of targets in this regard it is notable that what the EU is proposing under 'income graduation' is that high- and upper-middle-income countries as classified by the World Bank would no longer be eligible for the scheme. The potential implications of this for Mauritius – the country currently sits comfortably in the 'upper-middle income' category with an estimated GDP per capita in 2011 of some US\$7593 – has not been lost on it trade policy-making community, not least because the GSP scheme is widely regarded as the fallback option for ACP countries failing to sign a reciprocal EPA.[15]

Finally, in September 2011 the European Commission announced that countries that have not signed and taken steps to ratify and implement an EPA would no longer be eligible for the EU MAR – the temporary legal instrument that has underpinned preferential access to the EU market for the ACP since the expiry of the Cotonou Agreement on 31 December 2007 – as of 1 January 2014. Significantly, the timing of this coincides with the date when the aforementioned proposed changes to the GSP would come into effect. This suggests the Commission has finally lost patience with the ACP and is now seeking to draw a line under the EPA negotiations and thus bring an end to the entire tortuous process (Bilal and Ramdoo 2011). Yet how much effect this latest upping the ante will have remains to be seen. We have noted in the case of Mauritius – a country evidently not short of bureaucratic competence and negotiating capacity and seemingly with very few reasons to resist reciprocal liberalization with the EU – just how fraught with contradictions the EU's post-Cotonou trade vision is turning out to be. In this case, the continuing importance of sugar to the Mauritian economy, coupled with the additional leverage afforded to the EU by the proposed changes to the GSP, will probably be enough to ensure that some form of agreement will be concluded. Indeed, it now appears that the European Commission is satisfied that Mauritius itself along with three other members of the ESA group (Madagascar, Seychelles and Zimbabwe) has taken sufficient steps towards ratifying and implementing the interim EPA signed in 2009, thus avoiding the possibility of losing preferential access to the EU market in 2014 (ICTSD 2012). But just what shape the ultimate agreement will take and how it will affect Mauritius and the other members of the ESA group in terms of meeting the EU's stated objective of promoting economic growth and diversification though regional integration is, for the time being, anyone's guess.

Conclusion

In this chapter, we have offered an in-depth study of the political economy of trade preference erosion and economic adjustment with detailed reference to the case of Mauritius – perhaps the mostly widely celebrated 'success story' of the Lomé era. We began with a short detour via the development state literature to provide us with the theoretical vocabulary to understand how and under what circumstances the post-colonial Mauritian state was able to influence and ultimately recast its terms of trade. Specifically, the development state concept helped to pinpoint the institutional correlates that lay behind Mauritius's export dynamism – and, even more relevant for our purposes, enabled the island to make more effective use of trade preferences than was apparently the case elsewhere in the ACP.

We then turned our attention to two more specific questions of political economy that reoccur throughout this book – the first concerning the fallout from the loss of traditional, unilateral trade preferences and the second concerning the (unequal) bargaining dynamics associated with reciprocal free trade. In addressing the first question, we were able to show that the presence of a strong, capable and relatively autonomous bureaucracy, coupled with a degree of political consensus over national policy goals, has in many ways served to ameliorate the effects of liberalization, in spite of Mauritius's heavy dependence on trade preferences. Even so, the analysis also revealed the precariousness of Mauritius's development model and its ongoing vulnerability to external shocks, notwithstanding the amount of economic diversification which has taken place in recent decades. In the case of sugar, for example, even though Mauritius was evidently more successful than other members of the ACP in tapping into the EU's 'accompanying measures' put in place to cushion the abolition of the Sugar Protocol, it is worth recalling that this compensation represents a one-off payment whereas the losses in export earnings are expected to reoccur on an annual basis. In a similar way, in textiles and clothing, while Mauritius has done better than might have been expected in maintaining and even consolidating (at least in the case of the EU market) its export performance since the elimination of the MFA, the island appears to have little answer to the structural changes brought about by the increasing dominance of China and other low-waged countries in sectoral trade and production networks.

Turning to the second question, there appears to be little doubt that the objective conditions are relatively favourable towards the conclusion of a reciprocal free trade agreement between Mauritius and the EU, not least due to the unilateral trade reforms undertaken by the latter since the 1990s. And since the European Commission now appears satisfied that Mauritius has taken sufficient steps to render the interim EPA signed in 2009 a done deal, there appears to be little more to say on this topic. Yet, for reasons outlined here and in the previous two chapters, these favourable conditions are not, and in the near future are unlikely to be, sufficient to produce the kind of region-wide EPA originally envisioned by the Cotonou Agreement. It also worth reiterating that, as with CARIFORUM, the main sources of preference erosion affecting Mauritius (in this case relating to sugar and textiles and clothing) are more or less independent from the shift towards reciprocity signalled by the abandonment of Lomé. Hence, while the ratification of the interim EPA does at least allay the immediate fear that Mauritius was about to be downgraded to the GSP or even MFN rates of duty, it provides few clues to how the island might eventually overcome its long-standing dependence on unilateral trade preferences.

6
Southern Africa and the Global Politics of Trade Preference Erosion

In this final substantive chapter, we turn our attention to southern Africa and, more particularly, the cases of Lesotho and Swaziland – two tiny, landlocked countries almost entirely surrounded by South Africa (entirely so in the case of Lesotho), regularly cited as among those most highly exposed to preference erosion. Whereas Chapters 3 and 4 focused exclusively on EU trade preferences, the main point of reference here is the United States, specifically its AGOA trade programme. This has operated since 2000 and is often compared favourably to the EU's more elaborate system of trade preferences, especially with regard to AGOA's more flexible rules of origin affecting textiles and clothing exports. In this vein, Peter Gibbon (2003: 1809) has described AGOA as the 'most far reaching initiative both in the history of US-African relations, and more generally in relation to the claim that concessions in the area of trade provide better long-term prospects for developing countries' economic development than do ones in aid'. In the first two years of AGOA's existence, the five leading African exporters of textiles and clothing – Kenya, Lesotho, Madagascar, Mauritius and South Africa – increased their exports to the United States by a reported 85.3 per cent (Gibbon 2003). For Lesotho – in many ways, the 'poster boy' for AGOA's initial success – the introduction of these preferences had an especially dramatic effect: between 1999 and 2003, garment exports to the United States grew from US$111 million to US$393 million, yielding an annual increase of some 37.2 per cent, which was sufficient to sustain some 54,000 jobs, accounting for half the country's formal sector and virtually all manufacturing employment, approximately 75 per cent of its exports and 50 per cent of GDP (Gibbon 2003; Lall 2005). By the same token, the abolition of the MFA as part of the Uruguay round (see Chapter 5), coupled with China's accession to the WTO in 2001, reversed a substantial proportion of these trade gains as Lesotho witnessed the closure of 12 of its 47 garment factories with the loss of some 14,000 jobs within a year of the removal of quotas (Kaplinsky and Morris 2008). Although the situation stabilized somewhat after 2006, with China and other low-income countries like Cambodia and Vietnam continuing to make inroads into the

US import market – and with further trade reforms likely and the renewal of AGOA beyond 2015 uncertain – the longer-term prospects for garment assembly in Lesotho and the rest of sub-Saharan Africa appear, to say the least, uncertain.

The lessons of AGOA raise obvious and important questions about the appropriateness of unilateral trade preferences and low-skilled export-oriented manufacturing in the context of sub-Saharan Africa. But this case is also significant because it feeds more directly into a policy consensus in which preference erosion – the ostensible cause of AGOA's problems – is perceived to be not only unavoidable but also desirable. As we discovered in Chapter 2, preferential trade was traditionally synonymous with the concept of SDT, designed to gear the international trading system to the particular needs of developing countries (Hoekman and Özden 2005). In contrast, the dominant view now is that unilateral trade preferences rarely succeed in promoting either long-term economic growth or export diversification. The explanation provided for this is that preferences are, generally speaking, either characterized by low-utilization rates (because 'supply-side' constraints or bureaucratic obstacles such as complicated rules of origin discourage the take-up of preferences) or the bulk of the economic rents fall to importing firms rather than preference-receiving countries (Mattoo, Roy and Subramanian 2003; Brenton and Manchin 2003; Olarreaga and Özden 2005). In addition, preferential trade is said to inhibit the process of internal policy reform, distort trade and constitute an impediment to multilateral liberalization, since preference-receiving countries have a vested interest in defending the status quo in order to protect preference margins (Panagariya 2002; Francois, Hoekman and Manchin 2006; Hoekman 2006). Finally, because multilateral liberalization is seen here as a 'global public good', the best means of supporting preference-dependent countries is now argued to be through targeted financial assistance and compensatory schemes which serve to build 'supply-side' capacity in these countries but in ways that are 'non-trade distorting' for third parties. This, in essence, is the emergent consensus that now dominates the policy debate around preference erosion, including most notably in the diplomatic settings of the DDA and the EPAs.

In this chapter, then, we explore the impacts of multilateral liberalization on the efficacy of the Unites States' trade preferences for sub-Saharan Africa. We do this with reference to the wider global politics of preference erosion and the emergent development consensus that underpins it. For this purpose, the chapter is divided into three sections. In the first we introduce the AGOA trade programme before looking, in more specific detail, at the cases of Lesotho and Swaziland. Here, we provide a brief outline of their main economic characteristics and explore the role of AGOA in facilitating regional trade and investment flows – both 'before' and 'after' liberalization. In the second section of the chapter, we relate these effects to the wider context of the WTO's multilateral trade disciplines by describing, albeit rather briefly, the changing institutional and ideational parameters that now delineate the policy choices available to preference-granting countries. In addition, we also consider specific proposals that have been advanced as part of the DDA for ameliorating the effects of trade preference erosion. In the third and final substantive section of the chapter, we reflect on the evolving global and regional politics of preference erosion in southern Africa in the light of the probable failure of the Doha round, by exploring the options available to Lesotho and Swaziland with respect to regional integration through SADC and the possibility of an EPA with the EU.

The African Growth and Opportunity Act

Although AGOA offers DFQF market access to a range of exports from eligible African countries, by far the most significant provisions relate to textiles and clothing. In this respect, the programme has many similarities with President Reagan's 1984 CBERA, which offered preferential market access to the United States for beneficiary Caribbean Basin countries exporting textiles and clothing assembled with locally- or US-manufactured yarns and fabrics (see Heron 2004). In addition to this, AGOA grants duty-free treatment to garments made from 'third country' yarns and fabrics, subject to an annual cap of approximately 3.5 per cent of total apparel imported into the United States in the preceding 12 months, until 30 September 2015.[1] For these purposes, AGOA makes a distinction between 'Lesser Developed Beneficiary Countries' (LDBCs) – defined as countries whose per capita income did not exceed US$1500 in 1998 as measured by the World Bank – and other countries deemed ineligible for the 'third country' fabric provision. For the LDBCs, the relevant rules of origin stipulate only that the assembly and finishing must take place in the beneficiary country; whereas for non-LDBCs the rules require that yarn and fabric manufacture must also take place in the beneficiary country (or in the US or another AGOA-eligible country) in order to qualify for duty-free entitlements.[2] Finally, an overall quantitative limit of approximately 3 per cent of the volume of all US garment imports was placed on AGOA trade preferences, although this limit was increased to 7 per cent in 2002.

In the early 2000s, AGOA had a dramatic effect on garment production in sub-Saharan Africa, southern Africa especially. Prior to its implementation, sectoral imports from the region entered the United States at MFN rates of duty – which in 2003 amounted to an estimated 13 per cent of landed value for cotton goods and 25 per cent of landed value for synthetics (Gibbon 2003: 1881) – while imports from Mauritius and Kenya were also subject to MFA quotas. Table 6.1 provides a snapshot of the initial impact of AGOA on African garment exports to the United States, which was especially impressive between 1998 and 2004. As can be seen, total AGOA sectoral exports in

Table 6.1 US garment imports from selected AGOA countries in US$ million, 1998–2009

	1998	2000	2002	2004	Growth 1998–2004 (%)	2005	2007	2009	Growth 2005–2009 (%)
Kenya	34	44	125	277	727	271	248	195	−28
South Africa	79	142	181	141	80	67	24	11	−84
Lesotho	100	140	321	456	355	391	384	278	−29
Mauritius	233	245	254	227	−3	167	115	101	−40
Swaziland	16	32	89	179	996	161	135	94	−41
Madagascar	22	110	89	323	1369	277	289	212	−24
All other	29	18	30	150	411	129	98	31	−76
AGOA total	513	730	1090	1754	242	1462	1292	922	−37

Source: Adapted from Heron 2012.

this period grew by close to 242 per cent from US$513 million in 1998 to US$1.8 billion in 2004. Significantly, also, it is among the LDBCs – that is, excluding South Africa and, at least at this point, Mauritius – eligible for the 'third country' fabric provision that the most impressive performances were to be found. For example, Lesotho (arguably the major beneficiary of AGOA – to be discussed in more detail below) increased its exports by approximately 355 per cent from US$100 million in 1998 to US$456 million in 2004; meanwhile, albeit starting from a much lower base, Kenya, Madagascar and Swaziland (also discussed below) experienced comparable, if not even more rapid, growth rates in this period. A number of inferences can be drawn from these figures. First, the presence of relatively liberal rules or origin for the LDBCs was the key to the initial success of the AGOA programme. Second, since its implementation AGOA has generated export growth from a greater number of sources than might have been expected – certainly when compared with the EU. Here, Gibbon (2003: 1814) notes that traditionally EU garment imports from Africa have been dominated (in excess of 90 per cent of the total) by just three countries – South Africa, Mauritius and Madagascar – whereas in this case the two leading suppliers – Mauritius and Lesotho – only accounted for about one-half of the total in 2003. Third, the evidence indicates that AGOA led only to a very limited amount of trade diversion from the EU to the US. This implies that the major effect of AGOA was not, as some feared, to consolidate the dominant position of traditional suppliers like Mauritius, but rather to facilitate the establishment of new sources of export-oriented garment production within the region. Fourth and linked to this, the establishment of AGOA-related export platforms in sub-Saharan Africa appeared to be predicated on a model of industrial organization entirely different to that which typified traditional, export-oriented firms based in Mauritius or South Africa: whereas these firms typically targeted the EU market (or, in other cases, the South Africa domestic market) on the basis of semi-autonomous and domestically integrated manufacturing, new entrants came to be associated with a 'buyer-driven' (Gereffi 1999) business model characterized by tightly controlled, long runs of relatively undiversified products with local – but largely foreign-owned – firms engaged to assemble basic items (for example, t-shirts, blouses, trousers and so on) from imported yarns and fabrics to the strict specification of the buyer. These differences in industrial organization partially explain why AGOA did not lead straightforwardly to trade diversion from the EU to the US; it also pointed to the fact that Asian firms specializing in buyer-driven production were best placed to take advantage of AGOA – not least because the liberal rules of origin associated with the 'third fabric' provision suited this business model perfectly.

Lesotho

As a key beneficiary, Lesotho offers a neat illustration of the politico-economic dynamics behind the initial success of the AGOA programme and the problems it subsequently encountered. Although a close affinity exists between Lesotho's manufacturing success and the establishment and subsequent operation of AGOA, it is possible to trace the origins of the country's garment export boom to an earlier period: during the early 1980s a number of South African firms opened factories close to Maseru, the country's capital – in some cases to service the South African domestic market, in others to avoid political sanctions on overseas exports and to take advantage of the temporary derogation of the rules of origin requirements of the EU's Lomé convention. The attractiveness of Lesotho as an export platform was due to a combination of low wages, fiscal incentives and other economic inducements provided by the host government, alongside good communications and infrastructure (in this case close proximity and relatively easy road access to South Africa and the major port of Durban). It was for much the same reason that ethnic Chinese – predominantly Taiwanese – firms began to flock to Lesotho from the mid-1980s onwards as industrial employment continued to grow, reaching approximately 19,000 by the end of the 1990s, by which point – and even before the implementation of AGOA – the balance of exports had already shifted to the United States on the basis of the 'buyer-driven' business model outlined earlier (Gibbon 2003a).

Despite a number of common features between AGOA and the United States' earlier CBERA programme, the two generated almost completely different supply responses in terms of assembly-related investment. In the case of the CBERA, the dominant source of foreign investment in the Caribbean Basin came from import-competing firms seeking to remain price-competitive in their own domestic market by outsourcing basic assembly operations while continuing to source yarns and fabrics exclusively from US textile mills (see, again, Heron 2004). In contrast, AGOA's 'third fabric' provision granted extra-regional firms preferential access to the US market – albeit according to specified quantitative limits – without the need to satisfy prohibitive rules of origin requirements. It is this difference which explains why Asian firms specializing in buyer-driven production were attracted to, and hence best placed to take advantage of, production sharing in sub-Saharan Africa in the post-AGOA environment. In Lesotho's case, the number of export-oriented garment manufacturers operating out of the country's two main industrial districts (one close to the capital Maseru and another at Maputsoe – a third industrial district was subsequently opened in Thetsane), increased from approximately 21 in 1999 to 54 by 2004. This, according to one study (Bennett 2006), was sufficient to support an estimated 53,087 jobs, accounting for half the country's formal sector and virtually all manufacturing employment, approximately 75 per cent of its exports and 50 per cent of GDP. All told, AGOA had a remarkable and transformative effect on Lesotho's export profile: as Table 6.1 shows, exports to the United States under AGOA grew from $US100 million in 1998 to US$140 million in 2000 to US$321 million in

2002 to US$456 million in 2004. This, it hardly needs adding, was no small feat for a tiny, mountainous, landlocked country blighted by HIV/AIDS with a declining population, falling incomes, few natural resources or much in the way of arable land.

By the same token, the abolition of the MFA, coupled with China's accession to the WTO in 2001, reversed a substantial proportion of these trade gains by the middle of the decade. Even though AGOA brought undeniable economic benefits to Lesotho with respect to employment and foreign exchange earnings, one did not need to probe too deeply beneath the façade of the kingdom's much heralded 'manufacturing miracle' to see the reasons behind these losses – most of which were apparent even before MFA quotas were removed in 2004. First of all, despite the impressive nature of Lesotho's post-AGOA export performance, the kingdom's manufacturing success in the early 2000s – like that in other parts of sub-Saharan Africa – rested on no more than a handful of tariff lines. In 2004, approximately 63.7 per cent of Lesotho's exports were concentrated in just three tariff lines while approximately 87.1 per cent were covered by the top ten (Heron 2012: 161). This suggests that, not only was Lesotho completely dependent on AGOA preferences for its presence in the US market – which in the early 2000s absorbed an estimated 80 per cent of the country's entire exports of which approximately 98 per cent was reportedly made up of garments (Morris and Sedowski 2006) – but that this dependence rested precariously on only a handful of product categories. Even so, in the immediate aftermath of the removal quotas, the highly concentrated nature of Lesotho's garment exports turned out to be something of a 'blessing' since a number of these were covered under a textiles 'safeguards' agreement introduced by the US against China in late 2005. Although the introduction of these safeguards was designed principally to shield domestic producers rather than preference-dependent countries (even though this justification was disingenuously advanced at the time), in Lesotho's case it just so happened that its top ten tariff lines, accounting for the overwhelming majority of the kingdom's exports, were all either fully or partly covered by the agreement, which placed a ceiling cap on Chinese exports until the end of 2008 (US-China Memorandum of Understanding 2005). One can, therefore, speculate, had these safeguards not been in place, Lesotho may well have suffered a greater impact from the removal of quotas. It is also significant that the tariffs lines in which Lesotho's garment exports have been concentrated are ones in which above average MFN rates of duty – in the mid-2000s these ranged from 14.9 per cent to 32 per cent compared to just 3 per cent for US manufacturing imports as a whole – offered sizeable preference margins vis-à-vis other developing countries which did not qualify for duty-free concessions (Heron 2012: 162). As we shall see, this is an important point to take note of since these export categories are also where Lesotho's non-African competitors tend to be found – and it is these countries that would stand to benefit most from the implementation of the DDA or a separate DFQF agreement that has been proposed, even in the absence of a successful conclusion to the Doha round.

Swaziland

Unlike Lesotho, the textiles and clothing sector in Swaziland had a negligible role in the country's export profile prior to the implementation of AGOA – a fact that renders the subsequent growth of the sector in the early 2000s all the more remarkable. Up until this point, three characteristics defined the Swazi economy. First, as in the case of Lesotho, is the high degree of de facto integration with South Africa: although free circulation within the South African Customs Union (SACU), coupled with the size and significance of the informal sector in the Swazi economy, complicates the picture somewhat, a World Bank report from 2007 estimated that more than 60 per cent of the country's exports were at this point destined for South Africa while 80 per cent of its imports were calculated to originate from there. Second, unlike Lesotho, the Swazi economy has been historically, and remains, dominated by agriculture, with two-thirds of the country's population reliant on the sector for income and livelihood (Madonsela 2006). Swaziland's rural-based economy lies at the heart of the country's highly skewed pattern of income and land distribution. Even though Swaziland is currently classified as a 'lower middle-income' country by the UN with a per capital GDP in 2012 of some US$5300, this conceals the dualistic and highly unequal nature of the country's economy, characterized by a land tenure system whereby the most fertile land is set aside under a title deed system for commercially oriented, high productivity and capital intensive agriculture (especially in the sugar sector), while the remainder that makes up more than half the country's cultivatable land is based on insecure tenancies and small-scale, subsistence farming (WTO 2003: 309). The third – and not unrelated – characteristic of the Swazi economy is the country's historically acute reliance on Lomé preferences, the Sugar Protocol specifically. As we discovered in the previous chapter, between 1975 and 1999 the Sugar Protocol offered guaranteed prices for fixed quantities of sugar for eligible ACP producers but has since given way to a more liberal regime. In other words, the importance of AGOA to Swaziland needs to be understood within the wider context of trade liberalization and the political responses that this has given rise to – not least in this case because of its prior dependence on other models of preferential trade.

Turning to AGOA specifically, despite the negligible role of manufacturing in the Swazi economy prior to 2000, preferential access to the United States textiles and clothing market had a transformative effect comparable to neighbouring Lesotho. In this case, sectoral exports started from a low base of some $US22 million in 1998 to reach US$32 million in 2000, to US$89 million in 2002 before peaking at US$179 million in 2004 (see Table 6.1). Expressed in terms of the number of enterprises and employment, these trade gains were manifest in the creation of some 30 assembly plants mainly based in an industrial district on the outskirts of Matsapha, employing close to 30,000 workers by 2004 (Madonsela 2006: 251). As in our other case, the main supply response to AGOA in Swaziland came predominantly from Taiwanese investors specializing in 'buyer-driven' production of basic garments such as cotton jeans and women's synthetic underwear, again assembled with imported yarns and fabrics (Kaplinsky and Morris 2008). This, once more, pointed to the crucial importance of AGOA's 'third county fabric' provision; indeed, one can infer that this was even more significant in Swaziland's case because of the more or less complete absence of export-oriented manufacturing prior to 2000. Still, the attractiveness of Swaziland as an export platform does appear to have been partly influenced by factors independent of AGOA. For one, although Swaziland does not possess transport infrastructure comparable to Lesotho, its landlocked status was nonetheless mitigated to a degree during the 1990s following the ending of civil war in neighbouring Mozambique, which opened up access to the Indian Ocean port of Maputo (WTO 2003). Swaziland's post-AGOA boom was – like Lesotho's – also associated with the provision of a range of government incentives designed to lure foreign investors to its assembly sites. In Swaziland's case, textiles and clothing firms were offered, among other things, tax exemptions, the provision of factory shells and subsidised utility bills (de Han and Stichele 2007). The overall significance of these measures is, however, a matter of some dispute with some local sources suggesting that this may in some circumstances have even encouraged capital flight by lessening the sunk costs required of foreign firms investing in Swaziland.[3]

All in all, these sketches provide us with a brief snapshot of the growing importance AGOA for southern Africa during the early 2000s. They also provide us with a context in which to understand the significance of the changes brought about by the phasing out of the MFA in 2004. In Lesotho's case, as Table 6.1 reveals, garment exports under AGOA fell by approximately 29 per cent from US$446 million in 2004 to US$278 million in 2009. Most of the decline occurred immediately following the removal of quotas between 2004 and 2005 when Lesotho witnessed the closure of 12 of its 47 garment factories with the loss of some 14,000 jobs (Kaplinsky and Morris 2008). For Swaziland, the picture was a similar one: in 2004 garment exports stood at US$179 million but had fallen back to US$94 million in 2009, a decline of more than 40 per cent. In 2005 alone, the fallout from the liberalization of the textiles and clothing trade regime was sufficient to cause the loss of close to one-half of all the approximately 28,000 jobs created since 1998 (Kaplinsky and Morris 2008: 264). Meanwhile, the other major beneficiaries of AGOA – Kenya, Mauritius and Madagascar – all experienced trade losses comparable with Lesotho and Swaziland, while AGOA garment exports as a whole shrank by 37 per cent from US$1462 million in 2005 to US$922 million in 2009. Interesting, though, the largest casualty of the removal of quotas was South Africa itself. As Table 6.1 shows, despite its ineligibility for AGOA's 'third fabric' provision South Africa's exports to the United States still reached a respectable US$141 million by 2004; yet by the end of the decade this trade had been decimated to the point that it was actually worth less than before AGOA was introduced. Further, unlike other AGOA beneficiaries, liberalization did not just affect South Africa's exports but domestic production also (Roberts and Thoburn 2004). The key summative point is that the problems that AGOA has encountered since the mid-2000s stem not just from the specific economic characteristics of export-oriented garment assembly in sub-Saharan Africa or the AGOA programme. They also hinge on a more general tension that has reoccurred throughout this book: namely, that between the shift towards wider and deeper forms of multilateral trade liberalization and the special and differential needs of developing countries.

The global politics of trade preference erosion

In situating the present case within the broader political context of the WTO's multilateral trade disciplines it is worth reminding ourselves of the changing institutional and ideational parameters that have come to delineate the policy choices available to preference-granting as well as preference-receiving countries. As was shown in Chapter 2, the principle of SDT became synonymous with unilateral trade preferences, designed to gear the international trading system to the particular needs of developing countries. In contrast, such measures are now often thought of as neither practical nor desirable. The starting point for this perspective is the belief that, as a development tool, unilateral trade preferences have rarely – if ever – succeeded in promoting either long-term economic growth or export diversification. Although the reasons for this are many and varied, critics of traditional preferences generally focus on the low-utilization rates of these schemes (because 'supply-side' constraints or bureaucratic obstacles such as complicated rules of origin discourage the take-up of preferences) and on the tendency of the economic rents to fall predominantly to importing firms rather than preference-receiving countries. In the case of the EU's version of the GSP, for instance, Brenton and Manchin (2003) claim that, even though 99 per cent of imports from developing countries of products subject to duty in the EU were eligible for free trade in 1999, the actual utilization rate of these preferences (that is, the ratio of imports receiving preferences to eligible imports) was a mere 31 per cent. Meanwhile the assumption that once preferences are taken up all rents will accrue automatically to the exporting firm is questioned on the grounds that it ignores the way in which market imperfections allow the importing firm to capture the lion's share of the preference margin (Mattoo, Roy and Subramanian 2003; Olarreaga and Özden 2005). In the case of AGOA – which as we have just shall seen is characterized by relatively liberal rules of origin and therefore high rates of utilization – Olarreaga and Özden (2005) claim that the export price brought about by duty-free access increased by an average of 6 per cent even though the preference margin for eligible products was some 20 per cent. Olarreaga and Özden also observed a tendency for the rate of export price increase to shrink in accordance with the level of development of the exporting country: in the case of Malawi a mere 13 per cent of the preferences margin went to the exporting firm while in Mauritius the respective figure stood at some 53 per cent.

The emphasis placed by critics on the technical deficiencies and perverse effects of trade preferences are buttressed by an additional set of arguments concerning the wider impact of these schemes on the collective action dynamics of the multilateral trading system. In other words, because unilateral trade preferences are by definition *non*-reciprocal it is alleged that they serve to inhibit the process of internal policy reform, distort trade and constitute an impediment to multilateral liberalization. The reason for this is that preference-receiving countries have a vested interest in defending the status quo in order to protect preference margins (Panagariya 2002; Francois, Hoekman and Manchin 2006; Hoekman 2006). This type of behaviour, so it is argued, is rarely warranted on the basis of straightforward economic rationality because it ignores the general equilibrium effects of multilateral liberalization wherein the losses attributed to preference erosion are usually expected to be offset by the liberalization of third markets, increasing import demand and hence world prices for affected commodities (Francois, Hoekman and Manchin 2006). Finally, because further multilateral liberalization is deemed to a 'global public good', even in the case of the most preference-dependent countries where the gains for freer trade do not fully make up for the losses incurred through preference erosion, it is argued that that the best means of support is targeted financial assistance and compensatory schemes which served to build 'supply-side' capacity in these countries but only to the extent that such measures are 'non-trade distorting' for third parties (Alexandraki and Lankes 2004; Hoekman and Prowse 2005).

The WTO's 'development' agenda and the politics of preference erosion in the Doha round

As we discovered in Chapter 2, arguments questioning the efficacy of traditional preferences are not just of theoretical significance. They also provide the intellectual underpinnings of the recasting of SDT under the WTO, away from unilateral trade preferences towards more targeted forms of development cooperation, such as technical assistance, trade-related capacity building and other measures deemed to be less trade distorting for third parties. In this section of the chapter, we consider the relevance of this recasting for our particular case. By relating the example of AGOA to the WTO's development agenda, we aim to gauge how far specific proposals advanced within the DDA might, in theory at least, serve to ameliorate the worst effects of preference erosion in southern Africa and, for that matter, other regions and countries similarly exposed to the indirect effects of multilateral trade liberalization. In order to do so, we must first reacquaint ourselves with the wider political backdrop to the DDA, since this provides important clues to why – as we aim to show – the Doha negotiations have been unable to produce a 'development' package capable of satisfying those very countries in whose interests the round has supposedly been designed.

According to James Scott and Rorden Wilkinson (2011: 617), the story of the Doha negotiations, at least insofar as its 'development' agenda is concerned, is one in which 'the development content of the round has been whittled away from a concern with issues of implementation, less than full reciprocity and enhanced special and differential treatment, among other things, to one that concentrates primarily on agriculture'. In understanding why this might be the case, it is necessary to briefly re-examine the origins of the round – and, more particularly, the North-South political dynamics behind the previous Uruguay settlement and its contested legacy. Although the DDA was launched in the immediate aftermath of the terrorists attacks of 11 September 2001, the real backdrop to the round was the acrimonious failure of the 1999 Seattle ministerial, when mass civic mobilization and violence demonstrations on the streets mirrored deep divisions between developed and developing countries inside the meeting regarding the content and indeed the overall desirability of a further round of trade negotiations. As we saw in Chapter 2, the key to understanding this impasse was the belief among the majority of developing county delegations that the developed countries had failed to live up to their side of the 'grand bargain' of the Uruguay round – the 'implementation issues' – but were now seeking to open up negotiations in new trade areas such as competition policy, investment, trade facilitation and government procurement – the 'Singapore issues' – without first addressing these grievances. Following the collapse of the Cancún ministerial in September 2003 – after which the three most controversial 'Singapore issues' were dropped from the agenda but so, for that matter, was mention of the 'implementation' issues – there was a considerable lowering of expectations for what could be achieved by the round. It was within this setting that the Hong Kong ministerial meeting took place in November 2005, at which point the WTO introduced the aforementioned initiatives of DFQF and AfT that, though arguably less globally significant than the prospect of agricultural liberalization, were deemed especially relevant to developing countries blighted by preferences erosion and hence least likely to support further multilateral liberalization. It is important to note, in this regard, that the twin initiatives of DFQF and AfT were directly informed by the policy debate concerning the alleged deficiencies of unilateral preferences and presumed advantages of 'supply-side' solutions to the problems associated with them.

First, then, the backdrop to the Hong Kong proposal to grant DFQF to LDCs was the inadequate way that unilateral preferences, as the principal form of SDT, were previously enshrined in the GATT through the GSP. Although the GSP – and the 1979 Enabling Clause more particularly – empowered the contracting parties for the first time to grant non-reciprocal trade preferences to developing countries (provided that they were offered to all developing countries and did not discriminate between them), there was nothing requiring them to do so. As a consequence, the GSP under the GATT was defined by its 'permissive' rather than 'mandatory' character (Hudec 1987: 60), meaning that all decisions regarding the duration of preferences, country eligibility, graduation, product coverage and preference margins were left entirely to the discretion of the preference-granting country (Hoekman and Özden 2005). The upshot of this was that, in practice, the GSP regime either played second fiddle to non-GATT sanctioned schemes such as Lomé, as in the EU case, or else became marred by prescriptive forms of policy conditionality, which made a mockery of the principle of non-reciprocity, as in the US case.

Placed in this context, the DFQF initiative could thus be interpreted as an attempt to bring the GSP squarely into line with the WTO rules-based system, by placing preferences on a more stable and legally secure footing. Yet, a closer inspection of the precise character of the DFQF initiative hints that it is perhaps less of a significant departure from past GATT practice than some have claimed. We have seen in the case of the EBA, for example, that the EU has largely retained the GSP's complex and often prohibitive rules of origins, suggesting that the discretion to shape the character of preferences still largely rests with the preference-granting country or countries. Similarly, the decision by Japan, Canada and the United States to stop short of agreeing to extend market access to 100 per cent of tariff lines underscores the permissive rather than mandatory character of the DFQF initiative. But arguably the most important continuity between the GSP and DFQF is the maintenance of the principle established de jure (if not de facto) under the GATT, whereby preferential trade is only technically permissible in the case of those developing countries formally classified as LDCs. This demarcation, to recall, stems not from a purely legal or ethical principle but from the highly idiosyncratic way in which special and differential treatment for the developing countries evolved under the GATT, according to which eligibility for such treatment in the case of non-LDCs came to rest on the principle of self-declaration. To put the point another way, even though the DFQF initiative – *if* implemented multilaterally – might at least place preferences for LDCs on a more permanent basis, it does little to clear up the legal ambiguities concerning preferences for non-LDCs, or cases where preferential market access is offered to both LDCs *and* non-LDCs. In our specific case, this ambiguity is of some relevance since our two examples – Lesotho and Swaziland – fall on different sides of the LDC/non-LDC demarcation, despite their similar structural characteristics and economic vulnerabilities. In the case of Swaziland, even though its tiny land-locked economy is characterized by structural dualism, subsistence agriculture and widespread and endemic poverty – the country currently has the highest HIV/AIDS infection rate in the world – its 'lower middle-income' status nonetheless means that formally it is no more entitled to special and differential treatment than China or the two-thirds of the WTO's members that have declared themselves as non-LDC 'developing' countries.

Turning more specifically to AGOA, the potential threat posed by DFQF comes not primarily because it challenges the legal standing of AGOA in the WTO (although in theory this could be one of its long-term effects), but rather because it promises to extend preferential market access to non-African LDCs like Bangladesh and Cambodia. This is a crucial point, since these are precisely the countries that specialize in the tariff lines that have been utilized most by Lesotho, Swaziland and other AGOA-eligible countries (Heron 2012). It thus comes as no surprise to find that Africa's support for DFQF in the Doha round has, to say the least, been equivocal.[4] Although the Africa Group in the WTO initially approved the Hong Kong Ministerial Declaration on DFQF (with the exception of Mauritius and Uganda which spoke out against it), AGOA beneficiaries have used every opportunity since then to lobby for the exclusion of 'all textile and apparel products from the DFQF initiative in order to nurture the textile and apparel industry in Africa to become a sustainable and competitive global industry' (ACTIF 2008). Most of this lobbying has been targeted at the United States, for obvious reasons;[5] and, to the extent that the US's DFQF proposal sought to exclude something in the order of 300 tariff lines, one can say that it has been receptive to AGOA's concerns. Indeed, AGOA's privileged access to the US market appears to be relatively secure, at least for now, because of the reluctance of the latter even to offer its relatively modest DFQF proposal unilaterally as part of a so-called 'early harvest' before the rest of the DDA is completed.

Unlike DFQF, it is easier to trace a direct link between AfT and the problems that AGOA has encountered since the abolition of the MFA in 2004 (in addition to the numerous other cases of preference erosion explored elsewhere in the book). The reasons for this are that AfT, more than any other aspect of the DDA, has been informed by the emergent policy consensus questioning the utility of traditional trade preferences while, at the same time, making the case for 'supply-side' solutions. Although, in many ways, AfT chimed with the intellectual zeitgeist of the late 1990s and 2000s associated with the 'post-Washington Consensus' (PWC) and the shift from 'first generation' market liberalization to 'second generation' institutional reform (see, especially, Stiglitz and Charlton 2005), it is more important for our purposes to draw attention to its political dimension: that is, with respect to the collective action dynamics of the WTO. In other words, although an obvious intellectual affinity exists between the PWC and the policy agenda underpinning AfT, an arguably more important driver of the latter, at least initially, was the need to secure the support of preference-dependent countries for further and deeper MFN liberalization. Indeed, the advocacy for AfT was initially couched in specific terms of a 'compensation' clause (Page 2005) rather than the longer-term goal of integrating developing and least-developed countries into the world trading system. This distinction is an important one because those developed countries most exposed by preference erosion were not necessarily the poorest or most marginal (Alexandraki and Lankes 2004). To the extent that the DDA was driven by the need to secure the support of preference-dependent countries for liberalization, then, AfT was designed to mobilize resources to compensate for the losses incurred as a result of a successful outcome to the DDA – and to do so *explicitly*.

Turning to the specific concerns of this chapter, there are two aspects of the AfT initiative that merit closer critical scrutiny. The first concerns the financial implications of assisting preference-dependent countries through AfT: crudely put, how much money is needed and how much is available? Here a number of econometric simulations have calculated the likely impact of further liberalization on preference-dependent economies. These studies generally offer both 'optimistic' and 'pessimistic' scenarios, depending of the particular methods used and modelling assumptions made. In a study conducted for the Commonwealth Secretariat, for instance, Grynberg and Silva (2004) estimated the annual losses to preference-dependent countries from the Doha round, coupled with the abolition of MFA quotas, would amount to approximately US$1.7 billion, and that affected producers would require up to 20 years to come to terms with the changes. In another, widely-cited study the IMF (2003) concluded that a 40 per cent MFN tariff cut on the part of Canada, the EU, Japan and the United States would create an annual income loss for preference-dependent countries of some US$530 million. In contrast, Francois, Hoekman and Manchin (2006) concluded that, in the EU case at least, liberalization by non-EU OECD countries would offset EU liberalization: assuming complete preference erosion – that is, a MFN rate of zero – they concluded that liberalization would impose a welfare loss of approximately US$460 million on African LDCs. Interestingly, though, they concluded that the potential for preference erosion under the Doha round, even assuming a highly implausible zero per cent MFN rate of duty, would be only one-tenth of that caused by the abolition of the MFA.

As we discovered in Chapter 2, the Hong Kong pledge did not mandate the WTO Task Force to deal in detail with either the quantity or the nature of financing, leaving this to the WTO Director General. The Task Force nevertheless did reiterate the principle of 'additionality', that is, increased funding for AfT should be *in addition* to planned increases in general aid budgets. According to the OECD, total multilateral and bilateral AfT disbursements amounted to US$28.4 billion in 2009, but there still appears to be no agreed definition of what constitutes AfT.[6] Developing countries claim that, since the reporting of AfT spending is primarily the responsibility of aid donors, there is nothing to prevent the relabelling of existing funds – suspicions fuelled by the difficulties aid recipients have reportedly had in obtaining independent scrutiny of the OECD's Creditors Reporting System used to collate aid statistics.[7] Similarly, critics point to the fact that the trade needs of countries in receipt of AfT appears to be a poor indicator of resource allocation, with the lion's share of disbursements going to war-torn states like Afghanistan and Iraq alongside emerging economies including China, India, Turkey and Vietnam (Calì 2008; Langan and Scott 2011).

The second issue concerns the modalities for AfT or, to put it straightforwardly, assuming development finance is available how is it accessed and, more pertinently, is it 'complementary' or 'integral' to the DDA? The simple answer to this question is that, in the form of the so-called Enhanced Integrated Framework (EIF), there appears to be a direct relationship between AfT and the WTO but *not* the DDA. The EIF is a multi-donor AfT scheme for LDCs, set up to replace the Integrated Framework – the previous AfT scheme for LDCs set up in 1996, whose results were judged to be modest – on the basis of recommendations of a Task Force Report on an Enhanced Integrated Framework (2006). Although the EIF is invariably flagged up in WTO communiqués, it is best understood as part of the new global aid architecture designed to 'mainstream' trade in national development plans and to coordinate multilateral and bilateral trade assistance (Hoekman and Prowse 2005), rather than as a response to specific issues raised in the WTO. In any case, given the EIF's relatively modest funding target of US$250 million is not expected to have much of an impact on trade-related assistance, regardless of whether or not it is considered formally as part of the DDA.

In addition to DFQF and AfT, a further aspect of the Doha negotiations relevant to our discussion is the so called 'non-agricultural market access', or NAMA, agenda. In 2011, the WTO Director-General Pascal Lamy described NAMA as the single biggest obstacle in the way of a successful conclusion to the DDA, at the heart of which was the unwillingness of large developing countries like Brazil, China and India to accede to US and EU demands to eliminate or cut deeply tariffs across entire industrial sectors (ICTSD 2011a). The current impasse notwithstanding, the Chairman of the WTO Negotiating Group on NAMA's revised text, which was published in February 2008, does at least provide us with some scope for evaluating the extent to which an eventual NAMA deal, however unlikely, might affect AGOA and other unilateral preferences schemes. The basic objective of the NAMA agenda is to effect further liberalization of non-agricultural products – including the most relevant sector for us, textiles and clothing – and ultimately 'to reduce, or as appropriate eliminate tariffs, including the reduction or elimination of tariff peaks, high tariffs, and tariff escalation, as well as non-tariff barriers, in particular on products of export interest to developing countries' (WTO

2001). The draft modalities for achieving these tariff reductions, as set out in the Chairmen revised text, are based largely on the so-called 'Swiss formula', designed to narrow the gap between high and low tariffs with an in-built maximum for final bound rates,[8] while containing a number of exemptions and flexibilities for different categories of developing countries.

The sections of the draft text most relevant to our discussion centre on the Swiss Formula coefficient for the developed countries – which would determine the actual reductions to US tariffs and hence AGOA preference margins – and safeguards for mitigating the effects of preference erosion. According to a report by the South Centre (2008a) on the revised NAMA text, the application of the Swiss Formula (based on the developed countries' interpretation of this) would imply an average NAMA tariff cut to US tariffs of approximately 28.5 per cent and 85.7 per cent for peak tariffs. The implementation of NAMA could thus be potentially more significant even than a DFQF agreement, since it would level the playing field not just with non-African LDCs but *all* developing countries which do not currently qualify for duty-free trade. It is for this reason that the draft text contains a number of flexibilities designed specifically to mitigate the effects of preference erosion – all of which have been shaped by the wider politics of the DDA. The first set of flexibilities built into the NAMA text offer a ten-year transition period (otherwise tariff reductions for the developed countries are to be implemented in four equally-weighted annual stages) designed to provide preference-dependent countries with the necessary breathing space to adjust to freer trade. The specific tariff lines eligible for these longer transition periods are set out in Annexes 2 and 3 of the draft text, and in AGOA's case all of its major clothing export categories are included. But the story does not end there. In order to accommodate the export interests of others deemed to be 'disproportionately affected' by discriminatory preferences, nominated developing and least-developing countries will benefit from shorter transition periods. However, the precise list of nominated countries has not been entirely straightforward, entailing a number of acute distributional squabbles among the developing countries about who should and should not be considered 'disproportionately affected'.[9] Indeed, some members of the LDC Group in the WTO group have even questioned the need for a list at all, on the grounds that the implementation of a comprehensive DFQF agreement would make it unnecessary. Meanwhile, some of the larger developed countries such as Argentina have reportedly attacked the whole idea of a 'preference erosion' list as a cynical ploy to enable preference-granting countries to delay the liberalization of protected markets.[10]

Whatever the rights and wrongs of these debates, the key summative point from our perspective is that the first set of flexibilities contained in the draft NAMA text may postpone but will not ultimately prevent a drastic reduction in, if not the complete elimination of, the margins of preference that have enable schemes like AGOA to function. This point is significant, since few if any AGOA-eligible states were able to take advantage of the window of opportunity for restructuring and diversification afforded by the ten-year backloading of the MFA phase out – indeed, most beneficiaries continue to rely on the same handful of tariff lines that they have done since AGOA first came into effect in 2000. The logical inference to draw here would therefore be that longer transitions periods *alone* are unlikely to do much to prevent the collapse of the Africa garment sector in the event of the successful conclusion of the Doha round. This brings us to the second set of flexibilities built into the NAMA text. Alongside the adoption of longer transition periods, the draft text also makes reference to 'non-trade' measures designed to combat preference erosion through additional financial assistance and non-financial capacity building measures. However, even though the language on these 'non-trade' measures has been strengthened under the revised draft text modalities, the document appears to stop short of binding language linking NAMA to trade adjustment and capacity building finance. Instead, it simply states that 'preference granting Members, and *other Members in a position to do so*, are urged to increase their assistance to these Members through mechanisms including the Enhanced Integrated Framework for Least Developed Countries and other Aid-for-Trade initiatives' (WTO 2008: 11, emphasis added). In other words, the draft text implies that the 'non-trade' component of NAMA flexibilities designed to cushion the effect of MFN tariff reductions is primarily the responsibility and therefore presumably at the discretion of the preference-granting country. As such, NAMA reaffirms AfT as a 'best endeavour' commitment that is complementary rather than integral to the DDA.

All told, by July 2011 the WTO Director General Pascal Lamy had declared that, 'what we are seeing today is the paralysis in the negotiating function of the WTO, whether it is on market access or on the rule-making. What we are facing is the inability of the WTO to adapt and adjust to emerging global trade priorities' (ICTSD 2011). What this suggested was that, after a decade of often fraught negotiations, missed deadlines and persistent deadlock in successive ministerial meetings, even the WTO Secretariat was now close to throwing in the towel on the Doha round. This prospect clearly puts a different perspective on the issues explored here. Although there had been a good deal of support for the idea an 'early harvest' (the irony of this concept has not been lost on the developing country delegations to the WTO), whereby the 'development' dimension of the DDA might be implemented in advance, perhaps even independent, of the rest of the Doha round, the prospect of this now appears unlikely. In any case, given that much of the development package under discussion rests on initiatives that are, for the most part, based on 'best endeavour' commitments, or pledges designed to be complementary rather than integral to the DDA, the true economic value of an 'early harvest' is questionable. What this leaves us with, then, at least in respect of the countries dealt with specifically in this chapter (and elsewhere in the book), is something of a double-edged outcome: on the one hand, the probable failure of the DDA – NAMA in particular – provides a temporary reprieve for the beneficiaries of AGOA; on the other, this outcome serves to underscore the illusory nature of AfT and other 'supply-side' measures that have been used to buttress the case for abandoning traditional, unilateral preferences. Finally, it hardly needs to be added that, despite the failure of the Doha round and notwithstanding the impact of the 2008 global financial crisis and subsequent politics of austerity in dampening the global appetitive for free trade, regional and bilateral liberalization continues to gradually but inexorably eat away at what remains of the tariff margins that have sustained preferential trade up to this point – eventually leading to the further marginalization of preference-dependent countries in the world trade system.

The inter- and intra-regional regional politics of preference erosion in southern Africa: Lesotho, Swaziland and the SADC-EU EPA

In this, the penultimate section of the chapter, we consider the above predicament in relation to our two case studies by exploring, albeit briefly, the alternative options available to Lesotho and Swaziland – specifically through regional integration via SADC and the proposed EPA with the EU. Although SACU (Botswana, Lesotho, Namibia, South Africa and Swaziland) has, for some considerable time, been actively engaged in free trade talks with the United States,[11] negotiations with the EU have reached a more advanced stage and thus have more immediate relevance for the issues explored here. The first point of discussion regarding the proposed EPA concerns the precise make up of the regional configuration conceived for the purpose of the negotiations. As was argued in Chapter 4, the plethora of regional institutions throughout sub-Saharan Africa with overlapping membership and conflicting mandates is often seen as an indicative sign of the dysfunctional nature of African regionalism – and is regularly cited as the main impediment to successful economic integration across the continent (see, for example, Draper et al. 2007). Yet as Peg Murray-Evans (2013) argues, such a perspective is not always properly sensitive to the historical genesis of these various regional-building projects, which – in the past – were characterized by a far greater degree of functional differentiation. It was only in the 1990s and 2000s with a convergence around market-oriented integration, especially through the creation of customs unions, that the overlapping character of these regional institutions became an issue (Qualmann 2006).

It was within this setting that the EPA negotiations began in 2002, with the stated objective of creating a series of WTO compatible agreements by 31 December 2007, according to the regional configurations indentified for this purpose. The EU's ambition, as we have seen, was not simply to satisfy multilateral trade rules but create a series of comprehensive, region-wide free trade agreements that, among other things, would solve the issue of overlapping membership, which had by now been identified by the European Commission as an especially acute problem in southern Africa (Buzdugan 2013). To recall from Chapter 4, the means by which this was to be achieved was through the insistence that, while the precise make-up of the regional configurations was a matter for the ACP countries to decide, each must be actively engaged in an economic integration process leading to a single agreement and, more crucially, participating countries could not belong to more than one subregion (European Commission 2001; see also Chapter 4). For southern Africa, the latter stipulation immediately raised the problem of deciding which configuration to align with, given that members straddled five – SADC, SACU, COMESA, EAC and ECOWAS – separate economic blocs (Murray-Evans 2013).

In the specific case of SADC, this dilemma led to fragmentation almost as soon as the negotiations got underway in 2004 with almost half (DR Congo, Mauritius, Madagascar, Malawi, Seychelles, Zambia and Zimbabwe) of its 15 members deciding to negotiate as part of other configurations, together with Tanzania which joined the breakaway EAC in 2007. For SACU members, this option was of course negated by the obligations of the customs union, meaning that member states could not unilaterally negotiate free trade agreements with third countries without violating the terms of the common external tariff. Even so, this is precisely what South Africa did when it concluded a separate free trade agreement – the TDCA – with the EU in 2004, without first consulting the other members of SACU. To complicate matters further, South Africa was initially omitted from the EPA negotiations, by which point SACU had declared that further free trade deals with third countries would in future require the explicit consent of *all* member states (Stevens 2008: 220). This anomaly helps to explain why South Africa was formally invited to join the EPA process in 2006, despite the fact that this immeasurably altered the political dynamics of the negotiations – a point not lost on EU officials, given the former's economically dominantly position in the region and its (not entirely unrelated) well known lack of enthusiasm for the Singapore agenda, especially the liberalization of services and investment.[12]

For its part, South Africa's ostensible motive for joining the EPA process – which came at the behest of the existing members of the SADC-minus configuration – was supposedly to prevent the further fragmentation of SADC (Hurt 2012: 503). Yet it is also clear that South Africa had other interests at stake – not least of which was the belief that the EPA offered an opportunity to address the perceived lopsidedness of the TDCA through obtaining greater access to the EU market, while simultaneously guarding against the threat that the remaining SADC-minus states might strike a deal on the aforementioned Singapore issues without its involvement.[13] Either way, the formal presence of South Africa served to add a further complication to what was already proving to be among the most problematic of all the EPA configurations.

Turning to Lesotho and Swaziland, the former's main interests still lay in protecting the last vestiges of its AGOA preferences, which were deemed to be best served by deploying its scarce diplomatic resources by working with the Africa Group and other like-minded coalitions to persuade WTO members – the Unites States especially – to exclude textiles and clothing products for any extension of DFQF treatment to non-African LDCs. The EPA negotiations, by necessity, were considered of less importance. Nonetheless, interviews with trade officials in Maseru conducted in 2010 revealed a number of distinctive, and somewhat counterintuitive, negotiating priorities for Lesotho.[14] First, it was noted that the prospect of a free trade agreement with the EU presented few economic anxieties for Lesotho – especially since one had existed de facto since 2004 in the form of the TDCA, because of the free circulation of goods in SACU and the fact that virtually all the kingdom's imports arrive via South Africa. Second, trade officials pointed to the importance of garment exports to the EU (and to the superior rules of origin offered by the EPA vis-à-vis the EBA) as a strong incentive to sign a comprehensive agreement. This, as we discovered in Chapter 4, explains why Lesotho was willing to sign an interim EPA (the only African LDC to do so apart from the four belonging to the EAC) despite the fact that equivalent benefits were available on a non-reciprocal basis through EBA. Third, trade officials signaled, contrary to the widely-held view among critical scholars (see, for example, Hurt 2013) that ACP countries were, by and large, uniformly opposed to the Singapore issues, a strong desire to conclude a comprehensive agreement as a means of stimulating foreign direct investment and lessening the kingdom's acute dependence on South Africa for the supply of goods and services.

In Swaziland's case, although analogous to Lesotho with respect to the level of economic dependency on South Africa, the main issues centred on the abolition of the Sugar Protocol and the subsequent liberalization of the EU sugar market. As was shown in the previous chapter, the liberalization of the EU's regime presented not one, but three separate challenges – a 36 per cent price cut, increased competition from LDCs and a less secure investment climate – with the principal form of adjustment assistance coming in the guise of the EU 'accompanying measures'. In this case, Swaziland's poor absorptive capacity meant it was far less successful than Mauritius in tapping into the trade adjustment facility – to the extent that five years into the seven-year programme it reportedly had only spent 10 per cent of its total funding allocation (Richardson 2013). Unlike Mauritius, the government of Swaziland was unable to persuade the EU delegation that it possessed the necessary bureaucratic transparency to use the 'accompanying measures' for direct budget support.[15] Instead, the principal means of support came in the more cumbersome form of large-scale infrastructural investment, especially roads and irrigation projects. While this was not unwelcome, it meant money did not go directly to existing smallholders – the Swazi sugar industry's preferred target[16] – or do much to help those caneworkers made redundant through restructuring, who not only lost income and livelihood but also access to municipal services, including health and education, provided in the past by the sugar companies (Richardson 2013).

Technically speaking, the denunciation of the Sugar Protocol and the subsequent (partial) liberalization of the EU sugar market were both independent of the demise of Lomé and the shift towards reciprocity. This meant that liberalization would, in all likelihood, continue to eat away at Swaziland's tariff margins irrespective of whether or not the country signed a reciprocal EPA. But even in this environment Swaziland's acute dependence on sugar meant that – like Mauritius and Fiji – it was still among those ACP countries deemed likely to be 'most affected' by a downgrade to GSP rates of duty in the event of the failure to reach a reciprocal agreement with the EU (see ODI 2007). As such, Swazi's tiny trade unit, alongside the country's powerful sugar lobby, evidently saw the conclusion of such an agreement as a necessary step to at least draw a line under the sugar reforms and lessen the economic insecurity caused by the expiry of the Cotonou waiver and the subsequent declaration by the European Commission that the temporary Market Access Regulation would cease to be available on 1 January 2014.[17]

Unlike Lesotho, however, Swaziland is also a member of COMESA (although the former was also member until 1997) and, in the past, has expressed interest in negotiating as part of the ESA group, despite being a full member of both SADC and SACU. Indeed, during interviews government officials in Mbabane hinted that the attractiveness of the ESA as an alternative basis for an EPA was precisely because South Africa was not a member. Finally, as with Lesotho, officials also cited the prior existence of the TDCA and South Africa's dominant economic position in the region as reasons why they were not unduly worried about the prospect of reciprocal free trade with the EU.

All told, the dilemma's facing Lesotho and Swaziland in respect of the EPA provide us with a brief snapshot of the intra- and interregional politics of preference erosion, all of which points to the diminishing policy space available for unilateral trade preferences and the illusory nature of alternatives to this. At the time of writing, the SADC-EU EPA negotiations appeared to be deadlocked with no resolution in sight. Even the already fractured SADC-minus grouping – which now boils down to SACU plus Angola and Mozambique – is threatening to splinter further between those member states (Botswana, Lesotho, Mozambique and Swaziland), on the one hand, willing to entertain the prospect of a comprehensive agreement, and those (Angola, Namibia and South Africa) that have so far steadfastly refused to sign even a limited goods only agreement, on the other. Of course, an important part of the explanation for this impasse does lie with the overlapping and, in some cases, mutually incompatible nature of regional organization and institutional affiliation that characterizes regionalism in southern Africa. But an arguably more important factor is the presence of South Africa (Murray-Evans 2013), whose initial omission and subsequent inclusion in the SADC configuration has done much to expose the latent contradictions in the EU's attempt to use an interregional approach to secure what are, in effect, a series of bilateral free trade agreements (see Chapter 4). Either way, it is important to underscore the point that the conclusion of a region-wide EPA – to borrow a phrase from an earlier chapter – is neither a necessary nor sufficient condition for safeguarding preferences, given that the issue of WTO compatibility is no longer necessarily the dominant concern for those vulnerable economies on the receiving end of third-country liberalization.

Conclusion

The key purpose of this chapter has been to analyse the global political economy of trade liberalization in southern Africa. This has been done mainly with reference to AGOA, both before and after the elimination of the MFA. In doing so, we have focused not just on the immediate economic impacts of the removal of quotas but, in addition, on the wider politics of preference erosion leading up to, and including the WTO's Doha 'development' agenda. The case of AGOA – and the more specific examples of Lesotho and Swaziland – illustrates the diminishing space for unilateral trade preferences in the face of the changing institutional and ideational parameters that have come to delineate the policy choices available to preference-granting as well as preference-receiving countries. The introduction of AGOA had an early and dramatic effect on southern Africa's export profile, but by the same token the abolition of the MFA, coupled with China's accession to the WTO in 2001, revealed the shaky foundations on which these trade gains rested.

It was on this basis that the chapter looked at the evolving politics of the DDA. The intention here was to tease out some of internal tensions, ambiguities and contradictions that lie within the emergent policy consensus underpinning AfT and other aspects of the DDA; and, more practically, to consider how far, if at all, concrete measures might potentially ameliorate the effects of preference erosion in southern Africa and other preference-dependent regions and countries. The failure of the Doha round notwithstanding, there is evidence that the influence of the 'supply-side' discourse associated with the PWC has not been insignificant, at least at a rhetorical level. But in more substantive terms, it is far from clear that the DDA – in terms offering effective forms of SDT or, in our specific case, credible commitments on AfT or other compensatory mechanisms for dealing with the fallout from preference erosion – is anymore 'development friendly' than previous GATT rounds.

Lastly, we turned briefly to the specific regional context of southern African – SADC in particular – to examine how and in what ways Lesotho and Swaziland's encounter with preference erosion at the multilateral level has fed into the EPA negotiations at the regional level. In both cases, we can see how the very limited choice available to these two countries points to just how few policy options exist for those heavily preference-dependent countries exposed by third party liberalization. In the specific case of the EPAs, both states have expressed a desire to sign a comprehensive agreement in the hope of attracting much-needed foreign investment and perhaps lessening their economic dependency on South Africa. But this desire arguably says more about the lack of realistic alternatives than any genuine sense that an EPA is capable of matching or exceeded the economic gains hitherto offered by unilateral preferences. In any case, the ambivalent position of South Africa (among other things) in the SADC-minus configuration suggests that such an outcome is far from likely. Although this might be cited as further evidence of the dysfunctionality of regional and economic organization in southern African, parallels with other regions – including those examined elsewhere in this book – suggests a more generic set of problems with the way in which the EPAs were conceived in the first place. The blame does not, however, lay solely, or even perhaps predominantly, with those EU policy makers responsible for conflating the legal necessity of reciprocal free trade with its political desirability. It also must be traced to the broader institutional pathologies outlined at the very beginning of this book to do with the successive failures to properly enshrine principles of SDT for developing countries in the multilateral trading order.

7
Conclusion

This book began by quoting opening declarations launching the DDA and the EPAs respectively – two separate initiatives offering an ambitious prospectus for redefining trade and development cooperation between rich and poor countries that have since foundered, or at least fallen well short of expectations. While duly acknowledging the different policy agendas, participants and political dynamics behind these two initiatives the aim of the book has been to trace a common institutional pathology they share with respect to the recasting of SDT. In exploring pathways from preferential trade, then, our aim has not been in the first instance to focus on the economic consequences of liberalization for countries in receipt of preferences or to make the case for their maintenance and the abandonment of trade reforms. Instead, our primary task has been to analyse the wider political implications signalled by these reforms, away from asymmetrical reciprocity and unilateral trade preferences to reciprocal free trade accompanied by 'supply-side' forms of development assistance. In other words, we are interested in how these reforms have played out *in practice*.

The initial point of departure for the book was the intellectual consensus that has come to dominate the policy debate over preference erosion – a process that is now viewed as both inevitable *and* desirable. The book departed from this viewpoint not so much on the basis of its diagnosis of the technical deficiencies of trade preferences (although this too is open to question) but for overlooking the logically prior question of how preferences actually worked under the GATT. This, we argued, holds the key to understanding why the reforms advocated by critics of unilateral trade references have not panned out in exactly the way envisaged. Our point of departure allowed us to shed light on the peculiar way that SDT was operationalized under the GATT, that is, on the basis of a series of ad hoc concessions rather than legally definable principles. Hence preferences fell foul of the WTO not due to an intrinsic mismatch with the MFN principle, but because special and differential treatment for the developing countries was never placed on a properly secure legal footing. Furthermore, even though the establishment of the DSU under the WTO can be argued to have at least heralded the shift to a more rule-oriented system, this neither ended the informal institutional practices that typified decision making under the GATT nor did it provide guidance for how SDT might be re-operationalized in accordance with new multilateral trade disciplines.

These insights duly provided the backdrop to our thematic case studies tackling the various different aspects of what we might call the new policy consensus for preference-receiving developing countries. The first of these, addressed in Chapter 3, concerned the political implications of the shift towards reciprocal trade bargaining, characterized by power asymmetry and skewed patterns of North-South trade diplomacy. We can recall from Chapter 2 that the abandonment of unilateral preferences – in this case those associated with Lomé – was justified on the basis of the twin logic of complying with multilateral trade rules while simultaneously exposing preference-dependent countries to global market pressures in the expectation that this would help to underscore policy reforms now deemed essential for economic development. But what this did not take into account is how the marked power asymmetries between preference-granting and preference-receiving countries might skew the outcome of reciprocal trade bargaining – especially since precedents for crafting reciprocal free trade arrangements in accordance with (redefined) principles of SDT were so few and far between.

In Chapter 3, then, it was necessary to consider questions of political agency – that is, why CARIFORUM was willing to break ranks with the rest of the ACP to sign a comprehensive EPA – alongside questions of institutional context and economic structure – that is, how power asymmetries and uneven bargaining dynamics shaped the ultimate outcome of the negotiations. On the one hand, although the bureaucratic autonomy and technical competence of the CRNM, coupled with the regional coherence and collective economic interests of the CARIFORUM negotiating bloc, provided part of the explanation it was necessary to consider how the power asymmetries associated with the EU's market and financial power, combined with the very limited choice-set available to CARIFORUM, shaped the latter's strategic calculation regarding the necessity and desirability of concluding a comprehensive agreement. On the other hand, these very same power asymmetries helped to explain the skewed outcome of the negations wherein, to the extent that the CRNM was able to extract concessions from the EU, it was only able to achieve this at the cost of surrendering significant amounts of policy space in exchange for trade benefits generally lacking in discernable SDT commitments, which in any case may turn out to be illusory.

The second of our thematic case studies focused on what is – after reciprocity – undoubtedly the most prominent element of the new policy consensus on trade preferences: namely, the promotion of regional integration. In contrast to Chapter 3, the task was to explain not 'success' but failure – at least insofar as the EU's vision for recasting its trade and development role in the ACP on the basis of interregionalism has fallen way short of initial expectations. Although the promotion of regional integration has figured in the policies of most preference-granting countries to some extent, the EU case is arguably the most intriguing because of the observed link between its distinct institutional form and the attempt to legitimize itself as a global actor and promote regionalism as a model for global governance. This helps to account for why EU policy makers continued to insist on regional integration as an integral component of the EPAs – including in our case of the Pacific where ulterior political or economic motives were difficult to discern – long after it became clear that this prerequisite made the task of securing reciprocal free trade with the ACP more difficult rather than easier to achieve.

What makes this case even more intriguing is that the limited success in promoting regional integration came in spite of the fact that the EU possessed an obvious source of policy leverage in the form of preferential access to its huge internal market – *and* that the ACP appeared to share the goal of closer regional economic integration. However, on close inspection, the model of regional economic governance being promoted was revealed to be beset by a number of internal tensions, ambiguities and contradictions that, when taken together, explain the suboptimal outcome rather well. The key point is that conflating the *necessity* of reciprocity for the purpose of satisfying multilateral trade rules with its *desirability* as a means of fostering neoliberal policy reform only served to expose the incongruence of the EU's norm-based advocacy of the EPAs. This could be seen, for example, in the extent to which reference to the 'imperative' of WTO compliance ended up limiting the timeframe and negotiating options for both EU and ACP policy actors, which in turn shed a light on the limited and uneven nature of the aforementioned political leverage. But the most crucial dimension of this episode was revealed to be the entanglement of the EU's development and commercial trade objectives. On the surface, the presence of the Singapore issues in the negotiations lends credence to those accounts that interpret the EPAs through the prism of the EU's independent, political and commercial interests. What we have shown, however, is that the presence of these issues are understood best as part of a norm-based policy agenda associated with the internalization and subsequent promotion of neoliberal conceptions of development. In fact, it precisely because EU policy makers informed by this doctrine sought to collapse the distinction between 'development' and 'competitiveness' (and hence the distinction between the EU's economic interests and its normative preferences for dealing with the ACP) that actors opposed to the EPAs were able to contest and, in no small measure, successfully block the EU's attempt to promote reciprocal free trade with the ACP on the basis of regional integration.

Turning to Chapter 5, the theme here was the individual experiences of preference-dependent countries with the politics and political economy of trade adjustment following the loss of traditional preferences. In an important sense the question to be explored here was the economic consequences of liberalization; however, our aim was to highlight the political and not just the economic significance of these reforms. Taking the case of Mauritius – perhaps the most celebrated success story of the Lomé era – the objective was to locate the institutional correlates that lay behind its export dynamism that enabled the island to make effective use of trade preferences and, by implication, to cope with their removal. Through this case, we were able to probe two key questions of political economy that reoccur throughout this book – the first concerning the fallout from the loss of traditional, unilateral preferences and the second concerning the (unequal) bargaining dynamics associated with reciprocal free trade. In addressing the first question, we were able to show that the presence of a strong, capable and relatively autonomous bureaucracy, coupled with a degree of political consensus over national policy goals, in many ways served to ameliorate the effects of liberalization, in spite of Mauritius's heavy dependence on trade preferences. Even so, the analysis also revealed the precariousness of Mauritius's development model and its ongoing vulnerability to external shocks, notwithstanding the amount of economic diversification which has taken place in recent decades. Turning to the second question, there appears to be little doubt that the objective conditions are relatively favourable towards the conclusion of a reciprocal free trade agreement between Mauritius and the EU, not least due to the unilateral trade reforms undertaken by the latter since the 1990s. Yet these favourable conditions seem unlikely to be enough to produce the kind of region-wide EPA originally envisioned by the Cotonou Agreement. It also significant that – as with CARIFORUM – the main sources of preference erosion affecting Mauritius need to be viewed as more or less independent from the demise of Lomé. Hence, while the ratification of the interim EPA does at least allay the immediate fear that Mauritius might be downgraded to the GSP or even MFN rates of duty, it provides few clues to how the island might eventually overcome its long-standing dependence on unilateral trade preferences.

Finally, in Chapter 6, the book returned to surveying the overall results of the attempt to recast SDT in the context of the WTO and DDA more specifically. Whereas much of the rest of the book has concentrated on EU trade preferences, the primary focus in this chapter was the United States and its AGOA programme. The objective here was to probe a little deeper into global trade and development politics, with respect to multilateral sources of preference erosion and policy responses to it. In many ways, the MFA provided the ideal test case for evaluating policy responses to multilateral liberalization since its abolition is usually cited as among the most relevant trade reforms vis-à-vis the diminishing space for preferential trade. This is certainly true in the case of AGOA, as we were able to amply demonstrate. But, as elsewhere in the book, the aim was not simply to highlight the adverse economic and distributive effects of freer trade (although this is obviously an important part of the story), but to test the plausibility of the political responses that these changes have prompted in the form of specific measures designed to ameliorate the effects of preference erosion. In this case, institutional legacies were found to weigh heavily on the attempt to combat preference erosion through the insertion of reformulated versions of SDT in the negotiating texts of the DDA. For one, the ambiguous link between the concrete measures to emanate from the Hong Kong declaration – AfT and DFQF – and the core issues of the Doha round has distinct echoes of institutional practices under the GATT where the contracting parties repeatedly struggled to establish SDT commitments on the basis of legally enforceable principles. In a similar way, the long-standing ambiguity regarding eligibility for preferential treatment arguably lies behind the failure of WTO members to agree on appropriate modalities for providing breathing space to countries disproportionately affected by preference erosion in relation to the NAMA agenda. The failure to embed 'non-trade' forms of financial or technical support in the NAMA draft texts on anything other than 'best endeavour' pledges likewise shows the difficulties of escaping the path dependencies associated with past institutional practices.

And yet, while the blockages persist they need to be measured against the fact that preference erosion is an ongoing, if uneven, process. It is true that the Doha round is now almost certain to end in failure and that the impact of the 2008 global financial crisis and subsequent politics of austerity has tempered somewhat the global appetitive for ambitious free trade plans. But elsewhere liberalization has continued even in the midst of economic crisis (see Siles-Brügge 2011) and, if anything, now appears to be gaining fresh momentum. The difficulty with this is that, because these initiatives are now increasingly seen as delinked from the WTO, they are unlikely to coalesce around the regions, countries and policy agendas analysed in this book. The upshot of this is that those most exposed to the effects of preference erosion will find themselves even further marginalized in the world trade system.

Notes

1 Introduction

1. Article XXIV of GATT 1947 provides an exemption from the MFN clause for customs unions and free trade areas, provided that such arrangements cover 'substantially all trade' and are implemented within a 'reasonable length time'. In practice, however, the contracting parties have never been able to agree on what in strict legal terms these two stipulations actually mean. Thus despite the fact that Article XXIV still constitutes the only permanent form of derogation from MFN available under the WTO, the Committee on Regional Trade Agreements has been unable to reach agreement on the legality or otherwise of any of the 400 or so free trade agreements (FTAs) that have been reported to it since 1995 or, indeed, those concluded before then.

2 The Rise and Fall of Preferential Trade

1. Technically speaking, the first official sanction of non-reciprocal preferences came five years earlier in 1966 when Australia was granted a temporary waiver by the contracting parties, permitting it to accord preferential treatment to developing countries on a non-reciprocal basis. See Table 2.1 below.
2. The original UN list from November 1971 rested on three criteria: (1) GDP income of US$100 or less; (2) manufacturing as a proportion of GDP of 10 per cent or less; and (3) an adult literacy rate of 20 per cent or less. Nowadays, a more sophisticated methodology is deployed based on composite measures drawn from gross national income (GNI), human assets and economic vulnerability indices. Tellingly, since the original list was published it has grown from 25 to 48 LDCs, while only three countries – Botswana in 1994, Cape Verde in 2008 and Maldives in 2011 – have ever graduated from the category.

3 Understanding the EU-ACP Economic Partnership Agreements: The case of CARIFORUM

1. CARIFORUM was established in 1992 to facilitate cooperation between the English-speaking Caribbean Community (CARICOM) and the Dominican Republic and Haiti, following the accession of the latter to the Lomé convention. Although 13 of the 15 members of CARIFORUM – Antigua & Barbuda, Bahamas, Barbados, Belize, Dominica, Dominican Republic, Grenada, Jamaica, St. Kitts & Nevis, St. Lucia, St. Vincent & the Grenadines, Suriname and Trinidad & Tobago – signed the EPA on 15 October 2008, Guyana initially refused to sign, only to do so five days later on 20 October. Haiti, which qualifies for EU unilateral trade preferences as an LDC, signed on 11 December 2009.
2. The rest of the chapter draws extensively on interviews and background briefings with CRNM staff, government officials, representatives of private sector and other relevant non-governmental organizations conducted in the Caribbean in

January-February 2009. It also draws on a series of follow-up interviews conducted by Matt Bishop with EU and Caribbean officials in Brussels and Geneva in February 2009. I would like to thank Matt for very kindly giving me access to the transcripts from these interviews. At the request of interviewees, all subsequent references made to the interviews have been anonymized.

3. World Trade Organization (WTO), 'Regional trade agreements', see http://wto.org/English/tratop_e/region_e/region_e.htm [retrieved 16 June 2009].

4. Many of these coalitions are cross-cutting in membership and policy objectives. In terms of the issues explored in this chapter, it is notable that through membership in these coalitions Chile, Colombia, Costa Rica, El Salvador, Guatemala, Mexico and Peru have all fought against the Singapore Issues while simultaneously agreeing to such measures in FTAs with the USA. Likewise, members of CARICOM at various points in the run up to the Cancun Ministerial actively resisted the inclusion of many of the same issues within the Doha round that subsequently ended up in the final text of the CARIFORUM-EU EPA.

5. This happened, for example, in December 2001 when a deal struck between the G. W. Bush administration and Congressional leaders regarding the reinstatement of 'fast track' or Trade Promotion Authority (TPA) led to the removal of important flexibilities in the 'rules of origin' provisions contained in the CBTPA. The CBTPA had originally stipulated that the 'cutting and dyeing' of garments produced in the Caribbean would be eligible for duty-free treatment; after intensive lobby by the domestically oriented textile caucus in Congress, however, these provisions were removed from the revised version of the programme. Some estimates suggest that these activities would have been responsible for as much as 75 per cent of the value added in the Caribbean, hence political intervention had denied the region a key development opportunity. See Heron 2004, pp. 125–6.

6. In November 2007, the five countries of the East African Community (EAC) – Burundi, Kenya, Rwanda, Tanzania and Uganda – broke away from the East and Southern Africa 'region' and signed a separate interim agreement with the EU, thus creating a seventh ACP group. For more on this, see Chapter 4.

7. Interestingly, the origins of the EBA lay in the Doha negotiations rather than the Cotonou Agreement, which partly explains the imperfect fit between the former and the trade component of the latter. Although the EBA is 'Lomé-equivalent' in the sense that it offers eligible countries DFQF market access to all goods except arms and munitions, it actually shares more in common with the GSP than with Cotonou. For instance, the EBA adopts the GSP 'rules of origin' rather than the more flexible provisions of Cotonou (the GSP allows for 'diagonal cumulation' but stipulates the highest value added must occur in the final stage of production, whereas Cotonou allows 'full cumulation' to occur anywhere in the ACP). Although this difference may seem like a narrow, technical point, rules of origin rather than tariffs or quotas are often pointed to as the main trade barrier facing LDCs (see, for example, Brenton 2003). Against this, the EBA does not require reciprocity and there are no provisions for WTO-plus coverage comparable to those set out in Articles 41–52 of the Cotonou Agreement.

8. During the 30th Annual Conference of CARICOM Heads of Government, held in Guyana 2–4 July 2009, the decision was taken to rename the CRNM as the Office of Trade Negotiations (OTN) and to redefine its operational remit. Among other things, the OTN has now been re-incorporated into the CARICOM Secretariat. These changes are seen as a direct result of the fallout from the EPA negotiations where the quasi-autonomous status of the CRNM was widely criticized in the

region. The controversy surrounding the CRNM provides an interesting commentary on the EPA process as a whole, which is premised on using collective regional institutions to negotiate what are in effect a series of bilateral FTAs

9. Although the Cotonou Agreement also required preference-receiving countries to grant to the EU any more favourable treatment offered to other developed countries, the CARIFORUM text extends this to advanced developing countries and regions which account for more than 1 per cent and 1.5 per cent of world trade respectively. ECLAC (2008: 32) estimates that, on the basis of 2005 trade data, this provision would be sufficient to preclude CARIFORUM from signing an FTA with China, Brazil, Hong Kong, Singapore, Mexico, Taiwan, the Association of South East Asian Nations (ASEAN) and the Southern Common Market (MERCOSUR) without offering MFN treatment to the EU.

10. Confidential interviews, Jamaica, 29 January 2009.

11. Along with the justifications dealt with here, the CRNM (2008: 2) policy briefing also mentions the importance of EPA as a 'forceful signal – to both investors and development partners – of the earnestness of a Caribbean's programme of economic reform'.

12. In 2006, the EU moved to a 'tariff only' banana regime based on an MFN rate of €176 per tonne; in December 2009, however, EU came to a new agreement with the Latin American banana producers which saw the MFN rate cut immediately to €148 per tonne and thereafter further annual cuts will be made until a final MFN rate of €116 per tonne is reached in 2017. This agreement brought to end one of the longest, most controversial of WTO disputes and all but ended the prospects of future commercial banana production in the Caribbean (the Dominican Republic and, possibly, Belize being the exceptions). The sugar reforms have followed an analogous pattern after the EU took the decision in February 2006 to denounce unilaterally the ACP Sugar Protocol (SP) and to impose a 36 per cent cut to the domestically-administered price – and therefore the export price received by beneficiaries of the SP – to be implemented over a four-year period. Although Caribbean beneficiaries of the SP (Belize, Jamaica, Trinidad & Tobago and St. Kitts & Nevis), along with the Dominican Republic, were granted an additional quota of approximately 60,000 tonnes on a transitional basis until September 2009, the ability to offset the effects of the price reduction by increasing the volume of exports is tempered by the presence of an 'anti-surge' safeguard mechanism within the CARIFORUM agreement. Furthermore, Caribbean sugar producers have faced significant price competition since September 2009 when beneficiaries of the EBA became eligible for DFQF treatment, while the EPA does little to assuage the probability of further EU price reductions as part of the ongoing reform of the CAP. See Chapter 5 for more details.

13. Confidential telephone interview with a senior CRNM official, Kingston, Jamaica, 8 January 2009.

14. Confidential interviews, Geneva, Switzerland, 3 February 2009.

15. Confidential interviews, Geneva, Switzerland, February 2009; Kingston, Jamaica, January 2009.

16. Although Article XXIV of GATT 1947 stipulates that FTAs must cover 'substantially all trade' (hence the need for reciprocity), in practice WTO members have been unable to agree on what in strict legal terms this actually means – to the extent that the Committee on Regional Trade Agreements has been unable to reach agreement on the legality or otherwise of any of the current crop of FTAs. In its previous FTAs the EU has adopted a quantitative interpretation of

90 per cent of all trade – thus enabling it to exempt agriculture from market opening commitments – and this seems to be the template that has informed the CARIFORUM agreement. Since the EU has liberalized 100 per cent of its goods sector, CARIFORUM would arguably need only to liberalize around 80 per cent of imports, rather than the 87 per cent actually agreed to, in order to meet the this quantitative interpretation. Furthermore, taking into account the dynamic effects of trade liberalization, which presumably means that the volume of bilateral trade covered by the FTA is expected to grow over time, CARIFORUM would have been entitled to claim even more flexibility than the 20 per cent exclusion cited above. However, given that Article XXIV has yet to be tested under the WTO DSU, the extent to which CARIFORUM did or did not exploit the full range of available flexibilities remains, to say the least, moot.

17. Confidential interviews, Ministry of Trade, Belmopan, Belize, 3–6 February 2009.

18. During the Hong Kong ministerial in 2005, the EU pledged to contribute €2 billion a year to the WTO's Aid for Trade fund by 2010 – half coming the Commission and half from member states. This commitment is, however, far from assured: A 2008 European Commission report (cited in South Centre 2008a: 22) acknowledged that while the Commission itself was close to reaching its annual €1 billion contribution, members states would need to increase their collective spending by approximately 56 per cent in order to match the Commission's contribution. It hardly needs to be added that the onset of the global financial crisis makes the likelihood of this happening even less likely.

4   European Policy Diffusion and the Politics of Regional Integration in the Pacific

1. Indeed, as we shall see below, the central thrust of the *Green Paper* was that the EPAs necessitated a region-based approach because of the practical difficulties associated with the principle of uniform reciprocity. It was only later that the insistence on free circulation became a policy objective in and of itself.

2. Personal correspondence, Brussels-based trade consultant, 13 April 2010.

3. Confidential interviews, Pacific Islands Forum Secretariat, Suva, Fiji, October 2010.

4. Another motive for signing in the case of Fiji and PNG was that they became the first two Pacific states to benefit from a new 'global sourcing' rules of origin regime for fisheries, meaning that fish processed and canned locally, regardless of origin, would now be deemed to originate in the region and thus qualify for DFQF preferences.

5. Confidential interviews, Pacific Islands Forum Secretariat, Suva, Fiji, October 2010.

6. Interestingly, Australian trade officials in Canberra – like their counterparts in the EU – have described PACER-plus in terms of promoting 'development through greater regional trade and economic integration'. Confidential Interviews, Department of Foreign Affairs and Trade, Canberra, Australia, September 2010.

7. The background to this ultimatum is a long and complicated story, that goes well beyond the remit of this chapter, suffice to say that Fiji's tumultuous political situation (the island has experienced no less than four separate coups since 1987) has proven to be an ongoing bone of contention among ANZ and the Pacific island members of the PIF. Fiji was also suspended from the Commonwealth of Nations in 2009.

8. Although investment and competition policy were also mentioned in the Cotonou Agreement, this was in the context of regional and national economic development rather than as trade negotiation issues. Government procurement was not mentioned at all.

9. The latter is of some significance, since we can recall that the transfer of competence for the ACP from DG Development to DG Trade is often cited as a key factor in the hardening of the European Commission's attitude towards non-reciprocal preferences.

10. Confidential interviews, Pacific Islands Forum Secretariat, Suva, Fiji, October 2010.

11. Confidential interviews, European Commission, Brussels, December 2009.

5 Developmentalism and the Political Economy of Trade Adjustment in Mauritius

1. Confidential interviews, Mauritius Chamber of Agriculture, Port Louis, Mauritius, 28 September 2011.

2. Confidential interviews, Department of Foreign Affairs, Regional Integration and International Trade, Port Louis, Mauritius, 27 September 2011. Interestingly, the one 'defensive interest' actually mentioned by trade officials in the context of the EU's controversial 'behind the border' trade agenda was transparency in government procurement. Even in this case, trade officials indicated it was because of its effects on regional solidarity rather than any problems such a clause might pose for Mauritius itself.

3. The most obvious exception to this general pattern is Botswana.

4. Confidential interview, retired academic and local businessmen, Port Louis, Mauritius, October 2011.

5. Confidential interviews, Mauritius Exporters Association, Port Louis, Mauritius, September 2011. Although AGOA originally restricted the 'special fabric' provision (global sourcing) to 'lesser developed beneficiary countries' – that is, countries whose per capita income did not exceed US$1500 in 1998 as measured by the World Bank – Mauritius was granted temporary eligibility between October 2004 and September 2005. The importance of the expiry of this provision should not, however, be overstated: Mauritius was actually exporting more in 1995 than in 2005 and even by this later date less than half (compared to over 95 per cent for sub-Saharan Africa as a whole) of its sectoral exports entered the US under AGOA. In any case, Mauritius's temporary eligibility for the 'special fabric' provision was reinstated in November 2008 for a further four years.

6. The 18 members of the Sugar Protocol, plus India, benefited from a further source of duty-free access under the so-called Special Preferential Sugar (SPS) arrangement. This arrangement provided a quota of some 300,000 tons, generated by the additional requirements of EU sugar processing companies following the enlargement of the EU in 1986 (when Spain and Portugal were admitted), once all other sources of supply had been exhausted. Since 2001, however, SPS has had to accommodate the progressively larger quotas bestowed on LDCs courtesy of the EBA initiative, while the entire arrangement expired in June 2006.

7. Sugar was one of only three commodities (the other two being bananas and rice) for which the benefits of DFQF access were not offered immediately to LDCs through EBA: in this case, liberalization was backloaded until 2006 before tariff reductions were introduced in four incremental stages, leading to full duty-free access in 2009. At the same time, the LDCs were granted progressively larger

quotas from 2001 onwards, from an initial quota of some 74,185 tons in 2001–02 to 197,335 tons in 2008–09, and quota-free access thereafter.

8. Personal correspondence, sugar industry consultant, 13 September 2011.

9. Although the Sugar Protocol was for an 'indefinite duration', the EU invoked Article 10 of the agreement, which stipulated that 'the Protocol may be denounced by the Community with respect to each ACP State and by each ACP State with respect to the Community, subject to two years' notice'.

10. Confidential interviews, World Bank, Port Louis, Mauritius, 22 September 2011.

11. In February 2009, I was to gain firsthand experience of this during fieldwork in Belize when a demonstration by cañeros (sugar cane workers) in the so-called 'sugar city' of Orange Walk turned to violence, leading to the shooting dead of at least one cañero by the police. The demonstration centred on the introduction of core sampling technology designed to measure the sugar content of the cane and hence improve productivity though a quality-based payment system. The cañeros, however, demanded the withdrawal of the core sampling technology leading to the standoff with the owners of the country's only sugar mill and the police. For more on this episode, see A. Hughes, 'Sugar and Blood', *Amandala* online <http://www.amandala.com.bz/index.php?id=8094> (retrieved 5 February 2009).

12. Confidential interviews, Mauritius Chamber of Agriculture, Port Louis, Mauritius, 28 September 2011.

13. Confidential interviews, European Commission, Brussels, March 2010; Department of Foreign Affairs, Regional Integration and International Trade, Port Louis, Mauritius, 27 September 2011.

14. Confidential interviews, Department of Foreign Affairs, Regional Integration and International Trade, Port Louis, Mauritius, 27 September 2011.

15. Confidential interviews, Department of Foreign Affairs, Regional Integration and International Trade, Port Louis, Mauritius, 27 September 2011.

6   Southern Africa and the Politics of Trade Preference Erosion

1. The original expiry date of the 'third country' provision was set at 30 September 2004 but this was extended under 'AGOA III' to 2007, then under 'AGOA IV' to 2012 and, most recently, to 2015.

2. AGOA was signed into law on 18 May 2000 as Title 1 of the Trade and Development Act, and has since been renewed on three separate occasions (in 2002, 2004, 2006). Under 'AGOA II' (signed into law by President Bush on 6 August 2002), the 'third country' provision was extended to Namibia and Botswana, and under 'AGOA IV' it was extended to Mauritius also. Presently only Gabon, South Africa and the Seychelles are ineligible for the 'third country' provision.

3. Confidential interviews, Industry informants, Mbabane, Swaziland, April 2010.

4. Confidential interviews, various informants, WTO, Geneva, January 2011.

5. Confidential interview, informant, UNCTAD, Geneva 19 January 2011.

6. Confidential interview, developing country delegation, WTO Geneva, 20 January 2011.

7. Confidential interview, developing country delegation, WTO Geneva, 21 January 2011.

8. This is in contrast to the Uruguay round which was based on average percentage reductions which granted members the flexibility to cut rates on sensitive products by a bare minimum – the key reason why tariffs (and hence preference

margins) in textiles and clothing, among other sensitive sectors, escaped largely unscathed.

9. Confidential interviews, developing country delegations, WTO, Geneva, 19 and 21 January 2011; informant, UNCTAD, Geneva 19 January 2011.

10. Confidential interview, developing country delegation, WTO, Geneva, 19 January 2011.

11. Negotiations leading to a SACU-US FTA began in June 2003 but were later suspended in 2006, due to a lack of progress. However, in 2011 the two parties signed a 'Trade and Investment Development Cooperation Agreement' (TIDCA), which may eventually lead to a fully-fledged free trade deal in the future.

12. Confidential interviews (via telephone), officials at the EU Delegation to South Africa and Department of Trade and Industry of South Africa respectively, Pretoria, March 2010.

13. Confidential interview (via Skype), former senior official, Department of Trade and Industry of South Africa, Pretoria, March 2010.

14. This paragraph is based on a series of interviews and background briefings with government and non-government staff, conducted in the Maseru, Lesotho in March 2010.

15. Confidential interviews, officials at EU Delegation to Swaziland and Swaziland Sugar Association respectively, Mbabane, Swaziland, April 2010.

16. Confidential interviews, Swaziland Sugar Association, Mbabane, Swaziland, April 2010.

17. Confidential interviews, Ministry of Commerce, Industry and Trade, Mbabane, Swaziland, April 2010.

Bibliography

ACTIF (2008) 'Duty-Free, Quota-Free access for Least Developed Countries: Textiles and Apparel', Submission to the Office of the USTR, Trade Policy Staff Committee, Nairobi: ACTIF.

Action Aid (2005) *The Trade Escape: WTO Rules and Alternatives to Free Trade Economic Partnership Agreements* (Johannesburg: Action Aid).

Aggarwal, V. K. and Fogarty, E. A. (eds) (2004) *EU Trade Strategies: Between Regionalism and Globalism* (London: Palgrave Macmillan).

Alexandraki, K. and Lankes, H. P. (2004) 'The Impact of Preference Erosion on Middle-Income Countries', IMF Working Papers, September, WP/04/169, <http://www.imf.org/external/pubs/ft/wp/2004/wp04169.pdf> retrieved 29 September 2009.

Alter, K. J. And Meunier, S. (2006) 'Nested and Overlapping Regimes in the Transatlantic Banana Trade Dispute', *Journal of European Public Policy*, 13: 3, 362–82.

Amsden, A. (1989) *Asia's Next Giant: South Korea and Late Industrialisation* (Oxford: Oxford University Press).

Amsden, A. H. and Hikino, T. (2000) 'The Bark is Worse than the Bite: New WTO Law and Late Industrialisation', *Annals of the American Academy of Political and Social Sciences*, 570: 1, 104–14.

Ancharaz, V. D. (2008) 'David v. Goliath: Mauritius Facing up to China', paper prepared for the African Research Consortium, <http://www.aercafrica.org> retrieved 28 September 2011.

Armstrong, H. W. and Read, R. (1998) 'Trade and Growth in Small States: The Impact of Global Trade Liberalisation', *The World Economy*, 21: 4, 563–85.

Bajo, C. S. (1999) 'The European Union and Mercosur: A Case of Inter-Regionalism', *Third World Quarterly*, 20: 5, 927–41.

Barfield, S. (2003) 'Development, the World Trade Organisation and the "Banana Trade War"', unpublished PhD. dissertation, University of Sheffield.

Bennett, M. (2006) 'Lesotho's Export Textiles and Garment Industry', in H. Jauch and R. Traub-Merz (eds) *The Future of the Textile and Clothing Industry in Sub-Saharan Africa* (Bonn: Friedrich-Ebert-Stiftung).

Berger, M. T. (ed.) (2004) 'Special Issue: After the Third World?', *Third World Quarterly*, 25: 1.

Bernal, R. L. (2008) 'Globalisation: Everything but Alms – the EPA and Economic Development', The GraceKennedy Foundation Lecture, Kingston, Jamaica.

Bilal, S. (2006) 'EPAs Process: Key Issues and Development Perspective: With Specific References to East and Southern Africa', Paper prepared for Consumer Unity & Trust Society (CUTS) International, February 2006, available at <http://www.ecdpm.org/> retrieved 11 December 2012.

Bilal, S. and Ramdoo, I. (2010) *Which Way Forward in EPA Negotiations*, ECDPM Discussion Paper 100 (Maastricht: ECDPM).

Bilal, S. and Ramdoo, I. (2011) 'The Honeymoon is Over', *Trade Negotiations Insights*, 10: 7.

Bilal, S. and Stevens, C. (eds) (2009) *The Interim Economic Partnership Agreements between the EU and African States: Concepts, Challenges and Prospects*, ECDPM and ODI

Policy Management Report 17, available at: <www.ecdpm.org/pmr17> retrieved 11 December 2012.

Bishop, M. L. (2012) 'The Political Economy of Small States: Overcoming Vulnerability', *Review of International Political Economy*, 19: 5, 942–60.

Bishop, M. L., Heron, T. and Payne, T. (2013) 'Caribbean Development Alternatives and the European Union-CARIFORUM Economic Partnership Agreement', *Journal of International Relations and Development*, 16, 82–110.

Börzel, T. A. and Risse, T. (2009) 'Diffusing (Inter-) Regionalism: The EU as a Model of Regional Integration', KFG: The Transformative Power of Europe, working paper No. 7 (Berlin: Freie Universität).

Bowman, L. (1991) *Mauritius: Democracy and Development in the Indian Ocean* (Boulder, CO: Westview Press).

Bräutigam, D. (1997) 'Institutions, Economic Reform, and Democratic Consolidation in Mauritius', *Comparative Politics*, 30: 1, 45–62.

—— (2003) 'Close Encounters: Chinese Business Networks as Industrial Catalysts in Sub-Saharan Africa', *African Affairs*, 102, 447–67.

—— (2008) 'Contingent Capacity: Export Taxation and State-building in Mauritius', in D. Bräutigam, O.H. Fjeldstad and M. Moore (eds) *Taxation and State Building in Developing Countries: Capacity and Consent* (Cambridge: Cambridge University Press).

Brenton, P. and Manchin. M. (2003) 'Making EU Trade Agreements Work: The Role of Rules of Origin', *The World Economy*, 26, 755–69.

Brenton, P. (2003) 'Integrating Least Developed Countries into the World Trading System: The Current Impact of EU Preferences under Everything but Arms', *World Bank Policy Research Paper*, 3018, 1–31.

Breslin. S. and Higgott, R. (2000) 'Studying Regions: Learning From the Old, Constructing the New', *New Political Economy*, 5: 3, 333–52.

Brewster, H., Girvan, N. and Lewis, V. (2008) 'Renegotiate the Cariforum EPA', *Trade Negotiations Insights*, 7: 3, 8–10 .

Briguglio, L. (1995) 'Small Island Developing States and their Economic Vulnerabilities', *World Development*, 23: 9, 1615–32.

Brown, W. (2000) 'Restructuring North-South Relations: ACP-EU Development Cooperation in a Liberal International Order', *Review of African Political Economy*, 85, 376–83.

Buzdugan, S. R. (2013) 'Regionalism from Without: External Involvement of the EU in Regionalism in Southern Africa', *Review of International Political Economy*, early online: DOI:10.1080/09692290.2012747102.

Calì, M. (2008). 'Scale and Types of Funds for Aid for Trade', in D. Njinkeu and H. Cameron (eds) *Aid for Trade and Development* (New York: Cambridge University Press).

Carbone, M. (2007) 'EBA, EU Trade Policy and the ACP: A Tale of Two North-South Divides', in G. Faber and J. Orbie (eds) *European Union Trade Politics and Development: 'Everything But Arms' Unravelled* (London: Routledge).

Caribbean Regional Negotiation Machinery (CRNM) (2008) CRNM Note on CARIFORUM Economic Partnership Agreement: What Europe is Offering Africa, Barbados: CRNM. <http://www.thecommonwealth.org/files/177256/FileName/RNM%20COMSEC%200408.pdf> retrieved 5 June 2009.

Carroll, C. W. and Carroll, T. (1999) 'The Consolidation of Democracy in Mauritius', *Democratization*, 6: 1, 179–97.

Chang, H. J. (2002) *Kicking Away the Ladder: Development Strategy in Historical Perspective* (London: Anthem Press).

Chaplin, H. and Matthews, A. (2006) 'Coping with the Fallout for Preference-receiving Countries from EU Sugar Reform', *The Estey Centre Journal of International Law and Trade Policy*, 7: 1, 15–31.

Clark, D. P. and Zarrilli, S. (1992) 'Non-Tariff Measures and Industrial Nation Imports of GSP-Covered Products', *Southern Economic Journal*, 59: 2, 284–93.

Clarke, C. and A. J. Payne (eds) (1987) *Politics, Security and Development in Small States,* (London: Allen & Unwin).

Commonwealth Secretariat (1997) *A Future for Small States: Overcoming Vulnerability* (London: Commonwealth Secretariat).

Cooper, A. F. and T. M. Shaw (eds) (2009). *The Diplomacies of Small States: Between Vulnerability and Resilience* (London: Palgrave MacMillan).

Dam, K. W. (1970) *The GATT: Law and International Economic Organization* (Chicago: University of Chicago Press).

Dawar, K. (2008) 'Policy Space vs Policy Lock-in; Public Procurement in the CARIFORUM EPA', *Trade Negotiations Insights*, 7: 7, 8–19.

de Han, E. and Stichele, M. (2007) *Footloose Investors: Investing in Africa* (Amsterdam: SOMO).

Devault, J. (1996) 'Competitive Need Limits and the US Generalized System of Preferences', *Contemporary Economic Policy'*, 14: 4, 58–65.

Doidge, M. (2011) *The European Union and Interregionalism: Patterns of Engagement* (Aldershot: Ashgate).

Draper, P. et al. (2007) SACU, *Regional Integration and the Overlap Issue in Southern Africa: From Spaghetti to Cannelloni?*, Trade Policy Report No. 15, South African Institute of International Affairs.

European Commission (1996) *Green Paper on Relations between the European Union and ACP Countries on the Eve of the 21st Century,* Luxemburg: Office for Official Publications of the European Communities.

—— (2001) *Orientations on the Qualification of ACP Regions for the Negotiation of Economic Partnership Agreements* (Brussels: European Commission). <http://www.epawatch. net/general/text.php?itemID=24&menuID=5> retrieved 11 December 2012.

—— (2004) *A World Player: The European Union's External Relations* (Brussels: European Commission).

—— (2006) EU-CARFORUM Economic Partnership Agreement: An Overview (Brussels: European Commission Trade). <http://trade.ec.europa.eu/doclib/docs/2008/april/ tradoc_138569.pdf> retrieved 4 July 2009.

—— (2008) *Six Common Misconceptions about Economic Partnership Agreements (EPAs).* <http://trade.ec.europa.eu/doclib/html/137484.htm> retrieved 11 December 2012.

—— (2011) 'Proposal for a Regulation of the European Parliament and of the Council Applying a Scheme of Generalised Tariff Preferences', COM (2011) 241 final (Brussels: European Commission).

European Union (2000/2006) Cotonou Partnership Agreement Act (Luxemburg: Office for Official Publications of the European Communities).

Faber, G. and Orbie, J. (2009) 'The EU's Insistence on Reciprocal Trade with the ACP Group: Economic Interests in the Driving Seat?', in Gerrit Faber and Jan Orbie (eds) *Beyond Market Access for Development: EU-Africa Relations in Transition* (London: Routledge).

Farrell, M. (2005) 'A Triumph of Realism over Idealism? Cooperation Between the European Union and Africa', *Journal of European integration*, 27: 3, 263–83.

—— (2009) 'EU Policy Towards Other Regions: Policy Learning in the External Promotion of Regional Integration', *Journal of European Public Policy*, 16: 8, 1165–84.

Fialho, D. (2012) 'Altruism but not Quite: The Genesis of the Least Developed Country (LDC) Category', *Third World Quarterly*, 33: 5, 751–68.

Finger, M. and Schuler, P. (2000) 'Implementation of the Uruguay Round Commitments: The Development Challenge', *The World Economy*, 23: 4, 511–25.

Francois, J., Hoekman, B. and Manchin, M. (2006) 'Preference Erosion and Multilateral Trade liberalization', *The World Bank Economic Review*, 20, 197–216.

Gallagher, K. P. (2008) 'Trading Away the Ladder? Trade Politics and Economic Development in the Americas', *New Political Economy*, 13: 1, 37–59.

—— (2008a) 'Understanding Developing Country Resistance to the Doha Round', *Review of International Political Economy*, 15: 5, 62–85.

Gamble, A. (1995) 'New Political Economy', *Political Studies*, 43: 3, 516–30.

GATT (1961) *Committee III on Expansion of Trade*, L/1557 (Geneva: GATT).

—— (1984) *Textiles and Clothing in the World Economy* (Geneva: GATT).

George, C., Iwanow, T. and Kirkpatrick, C. (2009) 'EU Trade Strategy and Regionalism: Assessing the Impact on Europe's Developing Country Partners', in De Lombaerde, P. and Schultz, M. (eds) *The EU and World Regionalism* (Aldershot: Ashgate).

Gereffi, G. (1999) 'International Trade and Industrial Upgrading in the Apparel Commodity Chain', *Journal of International Economics*, 48, 37–70.

Gibb, R. (2000) 'Post-Lomé: The European Union and the South', *Third World Quarterly*, 21: 4, 457–81.

—— (2004) 'Developing Countries and Market Access: The Bitter-sweet Taste of the European Union's Sugar Policy in Southern Africa', *Journal of Modern African Studies*, 42: 2, 563–88.

Gibbon, P. (2000) '"Back to Basics" through Delocalisation: The Mauritian Garment Industry at the End of the Twentieth Century', *CDR Working Paper No 7* (Copenhagen: Centre for Development Research).

—— (2003) 'The African Growth and Opportunity Act and the Global Commodity Chain for Clothing', *World Development*, 31, 1809–27.

—— (2003a) 'AGOA, Lesotho's "Clothing Miracle" and the Politics of Sweatshops', *Review of African Political Economy*, 96, 315–20.

Girvan, N. (2008) 'Caribbean Integration and Global Europe: Implications of the EPA for the CSME'. <http://www.normangirvan.info/wp-content/uploads/2008/08/caribbean-integration-and-global-europe-18aug08.pdf > retrieved 6 January 2009.

Goldsmith, A. (1999) 'Africa's Overgrown State Reconsidered: Bureaucracy and Economic Growth', *World Politics*, 51, 520–46.

Goodison, P. (2007) 'What is the Future for EU-Africa Agricultural Trade after CAP Reform?', *Review of African Political Economy*, 112, 279–95.

—— (2007) 'EU Trade Policy and the Future of Africa's Trade Relationship with the EU', *Review of African Political Economy*, 112, 247–66.

Grant, C. (2000) 'An Experiment in Supra-national Governance: The Caribbean Regional Negotiation Machinery', in Kenneth Hall and Denis Benn (eds) *Contending with Destiny: The Caribbean in the 21st Century* (Kingston, Jamaica: Ian Randle Publishers).

Gruber, L. (2001) 'Power Politics and the Free Trade Bandwagon', *Comparative Political Studies*, 34: 7, 703–41.

Grugel, J. (2004) 'New Regionalism and Modes of Governance – Comparing US and EU Strategies in Latin America', *European Journal of International Relations*, 10: 4, 603–26.

Grynberg, R. and Silva, S. (2004) *Preference-Dependent Economies and Multilateral Liberalization: Impacts and Options* (London: Commonwealth Secretariat).

Grynberg, R. and Clarke, A. (2006) 'The European Development Fund and Economic Partnership Agreements', *Commonwealth Secretariat Economic Paper,* 75.

Hamilton, C. (1986) *Capitalist Industrialisation in Korea* (Boulder, CO: Westview).

Hardacre, A. and Smith, A. (2009) 'The EU and the Diplomacy of Complex Interregionalism', *The Hague Journal of Diplomacy,* 4: 2, 167–88.

Hay, C. (2007) 'What Doesn't Kill You Can Only Make You Stronger: The Doha Development Round, the Services Directive and the EU's Conception of Competitiveness', *Journal of Common Market Studies,* 45: annual review, 25–43.

Hein, P. (1989) 'Structural Transformation in an Island Economy: The Mauritius Export Processing Zones', *UNCTAD Review,* 1: 2, 41–58.

Heron, T. (2004) *The New Political Economy of United States-Caribbean Relations: The Apparel Industry and the Politics of NAFTA Parity* (Aldershot: Ashgate).

—— (2008) 'Small States and the Politics of Multilateral Trade Liberalisation', *The Round Table,* 97: 395.

—— (2011) 'Asymmetrical Bargaining and Development Trade-offs in the CARIFORUM-European Union Economic Partnership Agreement', *Review of International Political Economy,* 18: 3, 328–57.

—— (2012) *The Global Political Economy of Trade Protectionism and Liberalisation: Trade Reform and Economic Adjustment in Textiles and Clothing* (London: Routledge).

Heron, T. and and Richardson, B. J. (2008) 'Path Dependency and the Politics of Liberalization in Textiles and Clothing', *New Political Economy,* 13: 1, 1–18.

Heron, T. and Siles-Brügge, G. (2012) 'Competitive Liberalisation and the "Global Europe" Services and Investment Agenda: Locating the Commercial Drivers of the EU-ACP Economic Partnership Agreements', *Journal of Common Market Studies,* 50: 2, 250–66.

Hettne, B. (2005) 'Regionalism and World Order', in Farrell, M., Hettne, B. and Van Langenhove, L. (eds) *Global Politics of Regionalism* (London: Pluto Press).

Hettne, B., Payne, A. and Söderbaum, F. (eds) (1999) 'Special Issue: Rethinking Development Theory', *Journal of International Relations and Development,* 2: 4.

Hoekman, B. (2006) 'The Doha Round and Preference Erosion: A Symposium', *The World Bank Economic Review,* 20, 165–8.

Hoekman, B. and Manchin, M. (2006) 'Preference Erosion and Multilateral Trade Liberalization', *The World Bank Economic Review,* 20, 197–216.

Hoekman, B. and Özden, C. (2005) 'Trade Preferences and Differential Treatment of Developing Countries: A Selective Survey', World Bank Policy Research Paper No. 3566.

Hoekman, B. and Prowse, S. (2005) 'Economic Policy Responses to Preference Erosion: From Trade as Aid to Aid for Trade', World Bank Policy Research Paper, 3721.

Holland, M. (2002) *The European Union and the Third World* (London: Palgrave Macmillan).

Hudec, R. (1987) *The Developing Countries in the GATT Legal System* (London: Trade Policy Research Centre).

Hughes, A. 'Sugar and Blood', *Amandala* <http://www.amandala.com.bz/index.php?id=8094> retrieved 5 February 2009.

Hughes, S. and Wilkinson, R. (eds) (2002) *Global Governance: Critical Perspectives* (London: Routledge).

Hurrell, A. (1995) 'Explaining the Resurgence of Regionalism in World Politics', *Review of International Studies,* 21: 4, 331–58.

Hurt, S. R. (2003) 'Co-operation or Coercion? The Cotonou Agreement between the European Union and ACP States', *Third World Quarterly*, 24: 1, 161–76.
—— (2010) 'Understanding EU Development Policy: History, Global Context and Self-Interest?' *Third World Quarterly*, 31: 1, 159–68.
—— (2012) 'The EU-SADC Economic Partnership Agreement Negotiations: "Locking In" the Neoliberal Development Model in Southern Africa?', *Third World Quarterly*, 33: 3, 495–510.
ICTSD (2011) 'As Elsewhere in the Doha Talks, NAMA Negotiators Searching for a Way Forward', *Bridges Weekly Trade News Digest*, 18 May.
—— (2011a) '"Troubled State of Doha Talks Causing 'Paralysis'", says Lamy', *Bridges Weekly Trade News Digest*, 28 July.
—— (2012) 'First EU EPA with African Region Takes Effect', *Bridges Weekly Trade New Digest*, 16: 20 .
IMF (2003) *Financing Losses from Preference Erosion: Notes on Issues Raised by Developing Countries in the Doha Round* (Washington, DC: IMF).
Johnston, C. (1982) *MITI and the Japanese Miracle: The Growth of Industrial Policy* (Stanford, CA: Stanford University Press).
Julian, M., Dalleau, M. and de Roquefeuil, Q. (2011) 'EPA Update', 10: 2.
Kaplinsky, R. (1993) 'Export Processing Zones in the Dominican Republic: Transforming Manufactures into Commodities', *World Development*, 21, 1851–65.
—— (2001) 'Is Globalization all It's Cracked up to Be?', *Review of International Political Economy*, 8: 1, 45–65.
—— (2005) *Globalization, Poverty and Inequality: Between a Rock and a Hard Place* (Cambridge: Cambridge University Press).
Kaplinsky, R. and Morris, M. (2008) 'Do the Asian Drivers Undermine Export-Oriented Industrialization in SSA?', *World Development*, 36, 254–73.
Kearney, R. C. (1990) 'Mauritius and the NIC Model Redux: Or, How Many Cases Make a Model?', *Journal of Developing Areas*, 24 (January), 195–216.
Kelsey, J. (2005) *A People's Guide to the Pacific's Economic Partnership Agreement: Negotiations between the Pacific Islands and the European Union Pursuant to the Cotonou Agreement 2000* (Suva, Fiji: World Council of Churches).
Kothari, U. and Wilkinson, R. (2013) 'Global Change, Small Island State Response: Restructuring and Perpetuation of Uncertainty in Mauritius and Seychelles', *Journal of International Development*, 27: 1, 92–107.
Kowalczyk, C. and Wonnacott, R. J. (2002) 'Hubs and Spokes and Free Trade in the Americas', National Bureau of Economic Reseach (NBER) Working Paper, 4198, as cited in Kevin P. Gallagher. (2008) 'Trading Away the Ladder? Trade Politics and Economic Development in the Americas', *New Political Economy*, 13: 1, 42.
Kühnhardt, L. (2003) *Contrasting Transatlantic Interpretations. The EU and the US Towards a Common Global Role* (Stockholm: Swedish Institute for European Policy Studies).
Lall, S. (2005) 'FDI, AGOA and Manufactured Exports by a Landlocked, Least Developed African Economy: Lesotho', *Journal of Development Studies*, 41, 998–1022.
Lamusse, R. (1989) 'Adjustment to Structural Change in Manufacturing in a North-South Perspective – the Case of the Export Sector in Mauritius, International labour Organisation, *World Employment Programme Working Paper*, 27.
Lande, S. (2008) 'CARICOM's Trade Relations with the European Union Undermining Its Relations with the United States', Manchester Trade Update. <http://www.acp-eu-trade.org/library/files/Lande_EN_060608_Manchester-Trade-Ltd_CARICOM-s-relations-with-the-EU.pdf> retrieved 17 November 2008.

Langan, M. and Scott, J. (2011) 'The False Promise of Aid for Trade', Brooks World Poverty Institute Working Paper, 160, University of Manchester, <http://www.bwpi. manchester.ac.uk> retrieved 21 November 2012.

Lange, M. (2003) 'Embedding the Colonial State: A Comparative-Historical Analysis of State Building and Broad-Based Development in Mauritius', *Social Science History,* 27: 3, 397–423.

Lee, D. and Smith, N. (2010) 'Small State Discourse in International Political Economy', *Third World Quarterly,* 31: 7, 1091–105.

Leftwich, A. (2000) *State of Development: On the Primacy of Politics in Development* (Cambridge: Polity).

Lincon, D. (2006) 'Beyond the Plantation: Mauritius in the Global Division of Labour', Journal *of Modern African Studies,* 41: 1, 59–78.

Lombaerde, P. D. and Shultz, M. (eds) (2009) *The EU and World Regionalism* (Aldershot: Ashgate).

Madonsela, W. S. (2006) 'The Textile and Clothing Industry in Swaziland', in H. Jauch and R. Traub-Merz (eds) *The Future of the Textile and Clothing Industry in Sub-Saharan Africa* (Bonn: Friedrich-Ebert-Stiftung).

Manners, I. J. (2002) 'Normative Power Europe: A Contradiction in Terms?', *Journal of Common Market Studies,* 40: 2, 235–58.

Matsebula, M. (2009), 'EC Accompanying Measures: Experience and Lessons from the Swazi Sugar Industry', Paper presented at 'Aid for Trade Strategies and Agriculture: Towards a SADC Agenda', Windhoek, Namibia, 9–11 November 2009.

Mattoo, A., Roy, D. and Subramanian, A. (2003) 'The Africa Growth and Opportunity Act and its Rules of Origin: Generosity Undermined?', *World Economy,* 26, 829–52.

McQueen, M. (1998) 'Lomé Versus Free Trade Agreements: The Dilemma Facing the ACP Countries', *The World Economy,* 21: 4, 421–43.

Meisenhelder, T. (1997) 'The Development State in Mauritius', Journal *of Modern African Studies,* 35: 2, 279–97.

Meyn, M. (2008) 'Economic Partnership Agreements: A Historic Step Towards a Partnership of Equals?', *Development Policy Review,* 26: 5, 515–28.

Milner, C. (2005) *An Assessment of the Overall Implementation Costs for the ACP Countries of Economic Partnership Agreements with the EU* (London: Commonwealth Secretariat).

Milner, C., Morgan, W. and Zyovu, E. (2004) 'Would all ACP Sugar Protocol Exporters Lose from Sugar Liberalisation?', *The European Journal of Development Research,* 16: 4, 790–808.

Mistry, P. M. (1999) 'Commentary: Mauritius – Quo Vadis?', *African Affairs,* 98: 393, 551–69.

Morris, M. and Sedowski, L. (2006) *Report on Government Responses to New Post-MFA Realities in Lesotho,* Durban, South Africa: School of Development Studies, University of KwaZulu-Natal.

Murphy, C. N. (2000) 'Global Governance: Poorly Done and Poorly Understood', *International Affairs,* 76: 4, 789–803.

Murray-Evans, P. (2012) 'The European Union's Economic Partnership Agreements and Regional (Dis-) Integration', Paper presented at the BISA-ISA Conference, Edinburgh, 20–22 June 2012.

—— (2013) 'Agency in the Tightest of Corners: Southern African Responses to the Economic Partnership Agreements', unpublished manuscript, University of York.

Narlikar, A. (2003) *International Trade and Developing Countries: Bargaining Coalitions in the GATT and the WTO* (London: Routledge).

—— (2005) *The World Trade Organization: A Very Short Introduction* (Oxford: Oxford).

Narlikar, A. and Tussie, D. (2004) 'The G20 at the Cancun Ministerial: Developing Countries and their Evolving Coalitions in the WTO', *The World Economy*, 27: 7, 947–66.

Nathan Associates (2002) *Changes in the Global Trade Rules for Textiles and Apparel: Implications for Developing Countries* (Arlington, VA: Nathan Associates Inc.).

—— (2007) *Pacific Regional Trade and Economic Cooperation: Joint Baseline and GAP Analysis*, Report Submitted to the Pacific Islands Forum Secretariat (Suva, Fiji: PIF Secretariat).

Njinkeu, D. and Cameron, H. (eds) (2008) *Aid for Trade and Development* (New York: Cambridge University Press).

Nordås, H. K. (2004) 'The Global Textile and Clothing Industry post the Agreement on Textiles and Clothing', *WTO Discussion Paper No. 5*, Geneva, Switzerland: WTO.

OECD (2005) *Paris Declaration on Aid Effectiveness*. <www.oecd.org/dataoecd/15/3/46874580.pdf> retrieved 13 March 2006.

Olarreaga, M. and C. Özden (2005) 'AGOA and Apparel: Who Captures the Tariff Rent in the Presence of Preferential Market Access', *World Economy*, 28, 63–77.

Orbie, J. (ed.) (2008) *Europe's Global Role: External Policies of the European Union* (Aldershot: Ashgate).

Organization for Economic Cooperation and Development (OECD) (2004) *A New World Map in Textiles and Clothing: Adjusting to Change* (Paris: OECD).

Ostry, S. (2000) 'The Uruguay Round North-South Grand Bargain: Implications for Future Negotiations', <http://www.utoronto.ca/cis/minnesota.pdf> retrieved 25 June 2007.

Overseas Development Institute (ODI) (2007) 'The Costs to the ACP of Exporting to the EU under the GSP' (London: ODI).

Oxfam (2008) 'Partnership or Powerplay?', Oxfam Briefing Paper. <http://www.oxfam.org.uk/resources/policy/trade/bp110_epas.html> retrieved 14 January 2009.

Özden, C. and Reinhardt, E. (2005) 'The Perversity of Preferences: GSP and Developing Country Trade Policies, 1976–2000', *Journal of Development Economics*, 78, 1–21.

Pacific Institute of Public Policy (2008) *Pacific Lessons from the Economic Partnership Agreement* (Port Vila, Vanuatu: PIPP).

—— (2009) 'Putting Substance into PACER Plus', *Trade Negotiations Insights*, 8: 5.

Page, S. (2005) *A Preference Erosion Compensation Clause* (London: Overseas Development Institute).

—— (2007) 'Policy Space: Are WTO Rules Preventing Development?', *ODI Briefing Paper* (London: Overseas Development Institute).

Panagariya, A. (2002) 'EU Preferential Trade Arrangements and Developing Countries', *The World Economy*, 25, 1415–32.

Payne, A. J. (2004) 'Small States in the Global Politics of Development', *The Round Table*, 93: 376, 623–35.

—— (2005) *The Global Politics of Unequal Development* (London: Palgrave Macmillan).

Payne, T. and Phillips, N. (2010) *Development* (Cambridge: Polity).

Phillips, N. (2005) 'U.S. Power and the Politics of Economic Governance in the Americas', *Latin American Politics and Society*, 47: 4, 1–25.

—— (ed.) (2005) *Globalizing International Political Economy* (London: Palgrave Macmillan).

Primack, D. (2007) 'EPA Fails to Draw the Pacific Closer to the International Trading System', *Trade Negotiation Insights*, 6: 8, 4–5.

Prowse, S. (2002) 'The Role of International and National Agencies in Trade-Related Capacity Building', *The World Economy*, 25: 9, 1235–61.

Qualmann, R. (2006) 'Political, Legal and Economic Perspective', in Bertelsmann-Scott, T. and Draper, P. (eds) *Regional Integration and Economic Partnership Agreements: Southern Africa at the Crossroads* (Johannesburg: South African Institute of International Affairs).

Ravenhill, J. (1985) *Collective Clientelism: The Lomé Conventions and North-South Relations* (New York: Columbia University Press).

—— (2003) 'The New Bilateralism in Asia Pacific', *Third World Quarterly*, 24: 2, 299–317.

—— (2004) 'Back to the Nest? Europe's Relations with the African, Caribbean and Pacific Group of Countries', in V. K. Aggarwal and E. A. Fogarty (eds) *EU Trade Strategies: Between Regionalism and Globalism* (London: Palgrave Macmillan).

Richardson, B. J. (2009) *Sugar: Refined Power in a Global Regime* (London: Palgrave Macmillan).

—— (2013) 'Aid for Trade and African Agriculture: the Bittersweet Swazi Sugar', *Review of African Political Economy*, forthcoming.

Roberts, M. W. (1992) Export Processing Zones in Jamaica and Mauritius: Evolution of an Export-Oriented Strategy (San Francisco, CA: Mellen Research University).

Roberts, S. and Thoburn, J. (2004) 'Globalization and the South African Textiles Industry: Impacts on Firms and Workers', *Journal of International Development*, 16, 125–39.

Robinson, E. A. G. (ed.) (1960) *The Economic Consequence of the Size of Nations* (London: Macmillan).

Robles, A. (2008) 'EU FTA with SADC and MERCOSUR: Intergration into the Market Economy or Market Access for EU Firms', *Third World Quarterly*, 29:1, 181–97.

Rodrik, D. (1999) *The New Global Economy and Developing Countries: Making Openness Work* (Washington, DC: Overseas Development Council).

—— (2000) 'Institutions for High-Quality Growth: What They Are and How to Acquire Them', *Studies in Comparative International Development*, 35: 3, 3–31.

—— (2007) *One Economics, Many Recipes: Globalization, Institutions, and Economic Growth* (Princeton, NJ: Princeton University Press).

Roloff, R. (2006) 'Interregionalism in Theoretical Perspective: State of the Art', in Hänggi, H., Roloff, R. and Rüland, J. (eds) *Interregionalism and International Relations* (London: Routledge).

Rosamond, B. (2002) 'Imagining the European Economy: "Competitiveness" and the Social Construction of "Europe" as an Economic Space', *New Political Economy*, 7: 2, 157–77.

Rüland, J. (2010) 'Balancers, Multilateral Utilities or Regional Identity Builders? International Relations and the Study of Interregionalism', *Journal of European Public Policy*, 17: 8, 1271–83.

Ruggie, J. G. (1982) 'International Regimes, Transactions and Change: Embedded Liberalism in the Postwar Economic Order', *International Organization*, 36: 2, 379–415.

Sachs, J. D. and A. M. Warner (1995) 'Economic Reform and the Process of Global Integration', *Brookings Papers on Economic Activity*, 1.

Sandbrook, R. (2005) 'Origins of the Democratic State: Interrogating Mauritius', *Canadian Journal of African Affairs*, 39: 3, 549–81.

Sapir, A. And Lundberg, L. (1984) 'The US Generalized System of Preferences and its Impacts', in A. O. Kruger and R. E. Baldwin (eds) *The Structure and Evolution of Recent US Trade Policy* (Chicago: University of Chicago Press).

Saw, P. L. S and Wellisz, S. (1993) 'Mauritius', in R. Findlay and S. Wellisz (eds) *The Political Economy of Poverty, Equity, and Growth: Five Open Economies* (Oxford University Press).

Sawkut, R. et al. (2009) *Trade and Poverty in Mauritius: Impact of EU Sugar Reforms on the Livelihood of Sugar Cane Workers* (Pretoria, South Africa: TIPS).

Schimmelfennig, F. (2001) 'The Community Trap: Liberal Norms, Rhetorical Action, and the Eastern Enlargement of the European Union', *International Organization*, 55: 1, 47–80.

Scott, J. and Wilkinson, R. (2011) 'The Poverty of the Doha Round and the Least Developed Countries', *Third World Quarterly*, 32: 4, 611–27.

Shadlen, K. (2005) 'Exchanging Development for Market Access? Deep Integration and Industrial Policy under Multilateral and Regional-Bilateral Trade Agreements', *Review of International Political Economy*, 12: 5, 750–75.

—— (2008) 'Globalisation, Power and Integration: The Political Economy of Regional and Bilateral Trade Agreements in the Americas', *Journal of Development Studies*, 44: 1, 1–20.

Siles-Brügge, G. (2011) 'Resisting Free Trade after the Crisis: Strategic Economic Discourse and the EU-Korea Free Trade Agreement', *New Political Economy*, 16: 5, 627–53.

—— (2012) 'The Rise of "Global Europe": Interests and Ideas in the Making of EU Trade Policy', unpublished PhD thesis, University of Sheffield.

Sjursen, H. (2006) 'The EU as a "Normative Power": How Can This Be?', *Journal of European Public Policy*, 13: 2, 235–51.

Söderbaum, F. and Van Langenhove, L. (2005) 'Introduction: The EU as a Global Actor and the role of Interregionalism', *Journal of European Integration*, 27: 3, 249–62.

—— (eds) (2006) *The EU as a Global Player: The Politics of Interregionalism* (London: Routledge).

Söderbaum, F., Stålgren, P. and Van Langenhove, L. (2005) 'The EU as a Global Actor and the Dynamics of Interregionalism: A Comparative Analysis', *Journal of European Integration*, 27: 3, 365–80.

South Centre (2007) *EPA Negotiations in the Pacific Region: Some Issues of Concern* (Geneva: South Centre).

—— (2007a) *The Reform of the EU Sugar Sector: Implications for ACP Countries and EPA Negotiations* (Geneva: South Centre).

—— (2007b) *Trade Negotiations in the Eastern and Southern Africa Region: Issues for Consideration* (Geneva: South Centre).

—— (2008) 'Market Access for Trade in Goods in the Economic Partnership Agreements (EPAs)', *Fact Sheet 17* (Geneva: South Centre).

—— (2008a) 'Comments to the Chairman's revised draft modalities for WTO NAMA negotiations' (Geneva: South Centre).

Srinivasan, T. N. (1998) *Developing Countries in the Multilateral Trading System* (London: Westview Press).

Stevens, C. (2006) 'The EU, Africa and Economic Partnership Agreements: Unintended Consequences of Policy Leverage', *Journal of Modern African Studies*, 44: 3, 441–58.

—— (2008) 'Economic Partnership Agreements: What Can We Learn?', *New Political Economy*, 13: 2, 211–23.

Stevens, C., Kennan, J. and Meyn, M. (2008) *Analysis of Contents of the CARIFORUM and Pacific ACP Economic Partnership Agreements and Challenges Ahead* (London: Commonwealth Secretariat).

Stiglitz, J.E. and Charlton, A. (2005) *Fair Trade For All: How Trade Can Promote Development* (Oxford: Oxford University Press).

Stoneman, C. and Thompson, C. (2007) 'Trading Partners or Trading Deals? The EU and US in Southern Africa', *Review of African Political Economy*, 112, 227–45.

Streeten, P. (1993) 'The Special Problems of Small Countries', *World Development*, 21: 2, 197–202.

Subramanian, A. and Roy, D. (2001) 'Who can Explain the Mauritian Miracle: Meade, Romer, Sachs, or Rodrik?', IMF Working Paper, December.

Telò, M. (ed.) (2007) *European Union and New Regionalism: Regional Actors and Global Governance in a Post-Hegemonic Era* (Aldershot: Ashgate).

Thérien, J. P. (1999) 'Beyond the North-South Divide: Two Tales of World Poverty', *Third World Quarterly*, 20: 4, 723–42.

Tidiane Dièye, C. and Hanson, V. (2008) 'MFN Provisions in EPAs: A Threat to South-South Trade?', *Trade Negotiations Insights*, 7: 2, 1–3.

Traidcraft (2003) *Economic Partnership Agreements: The EU's New Trade Battleground* (London: Traidcraft).

Tsoukalis, L. (1997) *The New European Economy Revisited* (Oxford: Oxford University Press).

United Nations Conference on Trade and Development (UNCTAD) (2004) 'Draft São Paulo Consensus'. <http://www.unctad.org/en/docs/tdl380_en.pdf> retrieved 20 January 2009.

United Nations Economic Commission for Latin American and the Caribbean (ECLAC) (2008) *Review of CARIFORUM-EU EPA in Development Cooperation and WTO Compatibility* (Port of Spain, Trinidad and Tobago: ECLAC).

US-China Memorandum of Understanding (2005), 'Memorandum of Understanding between the governments of the United States of America and the People's Republic of China concerning Trade in Textiles and Apparel'. <http://otexa.ita.doc.gov/PDFs/US-China_Textile_MOU.pdf> retrieved 29 July 2011.

van den Hoven, A. (2007) 'Bureaucratic Competition in EU Trade Policy: EBA as a Case of Competing Two-Level Games?', in G. Faber and J. Orbie (eds) *European Union Trade Politics and Development: 'Everything But Arms' Unravelled* (Abingdon: Routledge).

VanGrasstek, C. (1998) 'What is the FTAA's Role in the USA's Global Strategy?', *Capítulos del SELA,* Vol. 54, pp. 163–73, as cited in Nicola Phillips (2005) 'U.S. Power and the Politics of Economic Governance in the Americas', *Latin American Politics and Society*, 47: 4, 9.

Wade, R. (1990) *Governing the Market: Economic Theory and the Role of Government in East Asian Industrialisation* (Princeton, NJ: Princeton university Press).

—— (2003) 'What Strategies are Viable for Developing Countries Today? The World Trade Organisation and the Shrinking of "Development Space"', *Review of International Political Economy*, 10: 4, 627–44.

Weis, T. (2004) 'Restructuring and Redundancy: The Impacts and Illogic of Neoliberal Agricultural Reforms in Jamaica', *Journal of Agrarian Change*, 4: 4, 461–91.

Weiss, L. (2005) 'Global Governance, National Strategies: How Industrialized States Make Room to Move Under the WTO', *Review of International Political Economy*, 12: 5, 723–49.

Westcott, T. S. J. (2008) 'Investment Provisions and Commitments in the CARIFORUM-EU EPA', *Trade Negotiations Insights*, 7: 9, 6–7.

Whalley, J. (1990) 'Non-Discriminatory Discrimination: Special and Differential Treatment Under the GATT for Developing Countries', *The Economic Journal*, 100: 3, 1318–28.

White, G. (1987) *Developmental States in East Asia* (New York, NY: St. Martin's Press).
—— (1998) 'Constructing a Democratic Developmental State', in M. Robinson and
   G. White (eds) *The Democratic Developmental State: Politics and Institutional Design*
   (Oxford: Oxford University Press).
Wilkinson, R. (2006) *The WTO: Crisis and the Governance of Global Trade* (London:
   Routledge).
—— (ed.) (2005) *The Global Governance Reader* (London: Routledge).
World Bank (2005) *A Time to Choose: Caribbean Development in the 21st Century*
   (Washington, DC: World Bank Group).
—— (2007) *Swaziland: An Assessment of the Investment Climate*, Report No. 43637-SZ
   (Washington, DC: World Bank).
—— (2010) *Mauritius: Enhancing and Sustaining Competitiveness*, Report No. 53322-MU
   (Washington, DC: World Bank).
—— (2010a) 'Mauritius Trade Brief', *World Trade Indicators 2009/10: Country Trade
   Briefs* (Washington, DC: World Bank).
WTO (1999) 'Annex 1: Chronology of Principal Provisions, Measures and Other
   Initiaitives in Favour of Developing and Least Developed Countries in the GATT
   and the WTO', <www.wto.org/english/tratop_e/devel_e/anexI_e.doc> retrieved
   27 July 2012.
—— (2001), *Doha Ministerial Declaration*, WT/MIN (01)/DEC/1 (Geneva: WTO).
—— (2003) *Trade Policy Review: Southern African Customs Union*, WT/TPR/s114.
—— (2006) *Recommendations of the Task Force on Aid for Trade*, WT/AFT/1 (Geneva:
   WTO).
—— (2008) *Fourth Revision of Draft Modalities for Non-Agricultural Market Access*, TN/
   MA/W/103/Rev.3 (Geneva: WTO).
WTO and OECD (2005) *Report on Trade-Related Technical Assistance and Capacity
   Building* (Geneva: WTO).
—— (2009) *Aid for Trade at a Glance 2009: Maintaining Momentum* (Geneva: WTO).
Young, A. R. (2007) 'Negotiating with Diminished Expectations: The EU and the Doha
   Development Round', in D. Lee and R. Wilkinson (eds) *The WTO after Hong Kong:
   Progress in, and Prospects for, the Doha Development Agenda* (London: Routledge).
Zoellick, R. B. (2002) 'Unleashing the Trade Winds', *The Economist*, 5 December.

Index